Housing the Urban Poor

A Publication of the
Joint Center for Urban Studies
of the Massachusetts Institute of Technology
and Harvard University

Housing the Urban Poor
A Critical Evaluation of Federal Housing Policy

Arthur P. Solomon

The MIT Press
Cambridge, Massachusetts, and London, England

This book was set in Linotype Baskerville
by Arrow Composition, Inc.,
printed on P & S Offset,
and bound in G.S.B. S/535/13 "Copper Tone"
by The Colonial Press Inc.
in the United States of America.

Library of Congress Cataloging in Publication Data

Solomon, Arthur P.
  Housing the urban poor.

  (A publication of the Joint Center for Urban Studies of the Massachusetts Institute of
Technology and Harvard University)
  Includes bibliographical references.
  1. Housing—United States. 2. Cities and towns—United States. 3. Poor—United
States. I. Title. II. Series: Joint Center for Urban Studies. Publications.
HD7293.S63   301.5′4   73–22360
ISBN 0–262–19120–2

To Marilyn, Jimmy, Jennifer, and Joshua

Contents

Tables and Figures

Figures

Preface

For the first time since the passage of the Housing Act of 1934, the federal government is reassessing the direction of national housing policy. The coincidence of three separate historical events has intensified this review. First of all, reports of widespread mortgage defaults and housing abandonment have crystallized public dissatisfaction with the cost, inequities, and ineffectiveness of existing federal housing programs. Second, a parallel reevaluation of the social welfare system and its proposed replacement by some form of income maintenance or earmarked allowances has raised questions about the future role of housing subsidies. If a reasonable floor is placed under all incomes, will there still be a need for a specific housing program? Third, with the recent proposal of special revenue sharing for community development and housing assistance, state and local officials suddenly confront the prospect of greater discretion, as well as responsibility, in the expenditure of housing funds.

Whether the locus of decision making remains at the national level or is shifted to the states and municipalities, a classic policy dilemma remains: with limited resources, a serious problem of housing deprivation, and a variety of strategy options, choices have to be made. Should the government subsidize new construction, rehabilitation, or housing allowances? How much additional money should be invested in housing production? How much should be allocated to preserving the existing housing stock? Who should benefit from public expenditures for housing? What are the likely effects, both direct and indirect, of alternative housing approaches on the urban housing market?

While political considerations will always influence, if not dominate, such choices, a more systematic evaluation of policy alternatives can clarify the options and reduce our singular reliance upon ideological assertions, political horse-trading, and undocumented rhetoric.

It is the purpose of this book to develop a more open and explicit method for making these choices. First of all, the government's housing objectives (economic, social, and environmental) are specified. These comprise not only the normative objectives included in traditional public expenditure analysis (efficiency and equity) but the more positivistic objectives embodied in federal legislation as well (racial and economic integration, neighborhood stability, etc.). Then the alternative strategies for attaining these objectives are enumerated. The consequences, both benefits and costs, for each alternative are estimated. Finally, a criterion for comparing and ranking these alternatives is set forth. Once developed, the methodology is used to compare the alternative strategies for housing the urban poor.

The empirical findings indicate an excessive reliance on the subsidization of new construction as opposed to the improved utilization of the existing housing stock through private leasing arrangements, rehabilitation, and direct consumer subsidies. The disturbing preoccupation of federal housing subsidies with new housing starts leaves the far more elusive but critical problems of neighborhood decline and excessive financial housing burdens largely unaffected. In low- and moderate-income neighborhoods, where the real estate market remains active, the additional purchasing power provided by government-assisted leasing arrangements (housing allowances or income maintenance) promises to counteract existing physical and environmental deterioration by helping to stabilize demand and thereby create an investment climate in which owners will be more disposed to conserve, or even enlarge, the supply of decent housing at moderate prices. This is *central* to any policy that is to avoid the same disappointments encountered by community development reforms of the 1950s and 1960s.

This book documents the overriding need to redirect national housing policy if we are to improve the living conditions of the poor, restore the confidence of private investors and lenders in aging neighborhoods, and eliminate, or at least reduce, the serious dichotomy between suburb and central city. There are at least three central components of any such policy:
—a national program of direct consumer subsidies;
—the elimination of existing housing and capital market barriers;
—the integration of direct housing subsidies into a broader program of community development.

My task in writing this book has been aided by the cooperation and assistance of many persons, to whom I am obligated and grateful. My earliest debt is to John T. Dunlop and John F. Kain, whose encouragement to undertake a comparative analysis of housing policies formed the basis of this book. Their continuous advice and comments were extremely helpful. Also, I have greatly benefited from discussions with many other colleagues—H. James Brown, Langley C. Keyes, George E. Peterson, John Pynoos, and Robert Schafer. Finally, I owe a special debt to my friend and colleague Bernard J. Frieden for reading and criticizing each version of the manuscript.

In addition, I wish to acknowledge, with appreciation, the assistance of two associates who helped in the preparation and editing of the final manuscript—Peter Epstein and Katherine Gardner. My secretary at the MIT-Harvard Joint Center, Barbara Stevens, was her usual competent and gracious self throughout. For their unqualified assistance in providing access to unpublished data I also wish to thank the many public officials at the Boston Housing Authority and City Office of the Assessor as well as the Regional Office of the U.S. Department of Housing and Urban Development. Finally, my thanks, love, and appreciation go to my wife and children, who endured all this.

Arthur P. Solomon

December 1973
Cambridge, Massachusetts

CHAPTER 1
Poverty, Housing, and Public Policy

Housing was a latecomer to the federal trough. The federal government historically made war, killed Indians, gave away land, tried cases,
raised taxes, regulated business, and appropriated money. It hardly ever
built houses, except for itself, its soldiers, and its prisoners. But in the
last generation or so the federal government has begun to make up for
lost time. . . . The federal effort now has a cabinet department of its own
—the new status is evidence of a new emphasis—or at least of a nagging
feeling in society that something is wrong and that something must
be done.
Lawrence M. Friedman,
"Government and Slum Housing,"
Law and Contemporary Problems

A history of federal policies for housing the urban poor would chronicle a
succession of programs, each, in its turn, oversold to the public only to
become sadly mired down in its operation, leaving the central dilemma—
millions of families trapped in squalid living conditions—as unresolved as
ever. The causes of disappointment have varied with circumstances: in
most cases, a host of unanticipated costs, red tape, and local political conflicts (over building codes, tenant selection, lending practices, and site location) have combined to frustrate congressional intent; in a few dramatic
cases, exposés of windfall profits, shoddy construction practices, and other
more or less familiar forms of human venality have culminated in outright
congressional hostility. It is symptomatic of our political system's indul-
gence that these programs have long outlived their fall from favor and have
been quietly pensioned off on a token annual appropriation rather than
administered a surgical and final coup de grace.

Confusion over Policy Goals
The variety of strategies employed by federal housing policy over the years
—mortgage insurance, land write-downs, favorable tax concessions, accelerated depreciation provisions, private turnkey contracts[1]—is a testimonial

1. The public housing Turnkey program is an approach used by local housing author-
ities to stimulate private enterprise to build and manage low-income housing. President
Johnson approved the so-called turnkey approach in a memorandum to the former
Secretary of the U.S. Department of Housing and Urban Development, Robert C.
Weaver. See the memorandum from President Johnson, August 17, 1967, in *Weekly
Compilation of Presidential Documents*, Vol. 3 (August 1967), p. 1166.

to legislative and bureaucratic ingenuity. However, despite this aptitude for social invention, our major housing programs reflect a disturbing single-mindedness in their basic approach: an excessive reliance on the subsidization of new construction, as opposed to the improved utilization of the existing housing stock through conservation, rehabilitation, or direct consumer subsidies.

The bias in favor of new construction persists despite the fact that building new low- and moderate-income housing has proved not only inefficient and inequitable but also politically explosive. If one is inclined to tolerance, this production bias can be attributed to an honest confusion among policy objectives and misconceptions about the realities of the urban housing market; for the cynical, the explanation may be found in deliberate efforts to subordinate the needs of the housing consumer to the interests of the housing producer.

In effect, we have pursued this *one* basic approach—the stimulation of new construction starts—to solve *two* distinct problems: what Henry Aaron calls the "too little housing" problem and the "bad housing" problem.[2] Federal objectives with respect to the first of these problems center on maintaining an equilibrium between supply and demand in the major urban housing markets as well as overall vigor in the residential construction sector of the national economy. Here the concern is for aggregate production and economic performance rather than for the welfare of specific target populations. With regard to the second problem—the "bad housing" issue—the government's objectives involve improving the living environment of persons unable to obtain a decent home through their own resources under existing market conditions. The objective here is one of social welfare, not production per se, of redistribution rather than economic growth. A departure point for improving the efficacy of housing services for the poor is to disentangle the present confusion between these two sets of objectives, along with their concomitant strategies and programs.

Foundations of National Policy: Economic Growth and Stability
The government's responsibility to encourage a high annual volume of residential construction has long been accepted as a relatively uncontro-

2. See Henry J. Aaron, *Shelter and Subsidies* (Washington, D.C.: Brookings Institution, 1972), p. 2.

versial aspect of public policy. This has been particularly evident since the conclusion of World War II when the Federal Housing Administration and Veterans Administration mortgage programs were created to relieve the pent-up housing demand accumulated during the war years. Our national culture assigns a high value to homeownership, so much so that it has virtually come to be considered as a God-given right for any family of moderate means. Moreover, the building materials and construction industries account for over 14–15 percent of the gross national product, while the construction industry alone employs almost 5 percent of the labor force.[3] Thus considerable political pressure exists both for bringing the price of a new home within reach of the average wage earner and for sustaining a volume of housing starts sufficient to keep the resources of the home-building industries fully employed. Trade unions, mortgage bankers, and home builders lobby actively in support of these ends, receiving at least tacit support from most other urban interest groups as well as the great mass of aspiring homeowners scattered throughout the body politic.[4]

Economic and political pressures have combined in recent years to support an aggregate housing production goal varying between 2 and 2.5 million units annually—volume enough to keep pace with the demand for new housing and to preserve a stock of vacant units that allows households to move without excessive friction. Demand, in any given urban housing market, is essentially a function of population increases, new household formations, and changing household preferences. Achieving production goals (that is, maintaining the equilibrium between housing supply and demand) eliminates involuntary overcrowding, precludes housing shortages, and relieves inflationary pressures on rentals and for-sale units.

This aspect of federal housing policy has, on the whole, been pursued with conspicuous success. Government mortgage insurance and loan guarantees, for example, have funneled previously unavailable credit to prospective homeowners, particularly those of middle and moderate incomes.

3. U.S. Department of Commerce, *Survey of Current Business,* March 1973, Tables S-1 and S-13. Construction as a proportion of GNP was 14.1 percent in 1971 and 15.1 percent in 1972. The employment calculation is based on the annual average percentage of employees on payrolls of nonagricultural establishments.
4. The National Association of Home Builders, the Mortgage Bankers Association, the National Association of Real Estate Boards, together with the National Savings and Loan League, comprise the core of the "housing lobby," although only the home builders specifically lobby for subsidized new production.

The secondary mortgage activities of FNMA and GNMA,[5] along with the advances of the Federal Home Loan Bank Board, have also significantly affected the cost and accessibility of mortgage funds. Income tax exemptions for the imputed rent of homeowners,[6] allowable deductions for property taxes, and interest payments on mortgages and other favorable income tax provisions have helped bring the cost of homeownership within reach of many moderate-income households. And the tax savings accruing from accelerated depreciation on rental housing have proved a real impetus to private multifamily construction. In addition, the federal categorical grant programs for highways, water and sewers, and other public facilities have helped provide the requisite services and infrastructure for residential land development. The sale of timber from our national forests also is adjusted to alleviate lumber shortages and their inflationary pressures on housing costs.

At the national level, housing production has often been viewed as a critical instrument in the arsenal of economic stabilization policies, since residential and other construction activities are particularly sensitive to changes in the cost of borrowing. As national economic conditions vary, policy makers try to stimulate or depress housing starts either to dampen inflationary pressures or to pump-prime a slack economy. At times, of course, the pursuit of stabilization may work against the goal of high-volume construction, but, in general, the two concerns have proved mutually reinforcing.

A Decent Home and Residential Environment: The Redistributive Objective
The second of the nation's broad housing objectives—the one to which this study is addressed—aims at improving the shelter and environmental conditions of the poor. Despite America's overall prosperity and continued rise in

---

5. FNMA is the acronym for the Federal National Mortgage Association, or "Fannie Mae" as it is more affectionately known; GNMA is an abbreviation for the Government National Mortgage Association, or "Ginnie Mae."

6. Despite the fact that homeowners hold a substantial amount of their assets as equity in their homes, they do not have to pay taxes on either the amount that could have been earned if the home were rented or on other investments that could have been made. Since the same person acts as both landlord and tenant, no cash for using the home changes hands, and thus there is no "imputed" rental income for tax purposes.

median per capita income, the fact remains that approximately 7.8 million American households—one in every eight—still cannot afford housing that meets minimum health and safety standards.[7]

Most Americans are able to satisfy their housing preferences through the workings of the private marketplace. ("Housing preference," as used here, denotes not only the nature of the dwelling unit itself—size, style, physical condition, and form of tenure—but also factors such as neighborhood character, quality of schools and other public services, as well as accessibility to jobs.) The low-income household, however, can obtain a decent shelter and environment only by devoting an excessive portion (30 to 35 percent) of its income to rent and, as a consequence, sacrificing much of its budget for food, clothing, and other necessities. Therefore many of the poor must resign themselves to living in deteriorated, dilapidated, or overcrowded dwellings, located, as often as not, in neighborhoods characterized by physical decay, inadequate public safety, and poor schools.[8]

From the perspective of the real estate investor, the rent-paying ability of poor families simply does not promise a rate of return sufficient to justify large expenditures on upkeep and services, not to mention major renovations and improvements. Rent defaults, vandalism, and other debilitating social factors compound the economic uncertainties inherent in the low-income housing market. Confronted with marginal profits or, in some instances, actual deficits, landlords respond by cutting back on maintenance and building services, thereby hastening the all too familiar process of housing deterioration and eventual abandonment. Unfortunately, when forced to maintain their dwellings at code standards, many landlords choose

7. Anthony Downs, "Moving Toward Realistic Housing Goals," in Kermit Gordon, ed., *Agenda for the Nation* (Washington, D.C.: Brookings Institution, 1968).
8. At least 11 million households paid more than 25 percent of their incomes for shelter—the figure that most housing experts (including the U.S. Bureau of Labor Statistics) consider a maximum if other necessities are not to be sacrificed. Of these households, it is not known how many also inhabit substandard or overcrowded units. Roughly 6.9 million households lived in physically dilapidated or deteriorated housing in 1970. Some 6 million families had less than one room per person, the U.S. Census criterion for overcrowding, with about one-third of them in substandard housing. For references to these estimates see David M. Gordon, ed., *Problems in Political Economy: An Urban Perspective* (Lexington, Mass.: D.C. Heath, 1970), pp. 355–356. For a more recent estimate of housing deprivation in the United States, see David Birch et al., *America's Housing Needs: 1970 to 1980* (Cambridge, Mass.: MIT-Harvard Joint Center for Urban Studies, 1973).

to liquidate their holdings, shifting their capital to more competitive investment opportunities.

The abandonment phenomenon—with property owners simply walking away from buildings in some cases still structurally sound—provides the most dramatic illustration of the breakdown of the housing market in many low-income neighborhoods.[9] The following quotation, taken from a journalistic account of housing problems in the South Bronx, conveys a street-level view of this phenomenon:[10]

The fire hydrants are open, even in this biting cold weather—town pumps that provide the sole water supply for drinking, washing and sanitation for thousands of tenants in 20 percent of the housing in the area. When one hydrant freezes over, the residents pry open another. . . . Packs of wild dogs pick through the rubble and roam the streets, sometimes attacking residents.

In this environment, piecemeal efforts at rehabilitation prove futile:

Within nine months, seven [of the newly renovated] buildings were vacated after being invaded by drug addicts, and shortly after that they were burned out. The plumbing and electrical fixtures were stolen, presumably by the junkies, who could sell the materials; windows were smashed, doors were removed, floorboards were taken.

Such extreme disorder in the functioning of a community tends to reinforce the bulldozer mentality—far simpler to sweep the rubble clear than to grapple with the bewildering array of economic, social, and psychological forces that have depopulated entire blocks of our inner cities. A few neighborhoods may indeed be terminal cases, already neglected beyond our best-intentioned (and well-funded) efforts to restore them to a viable life. However, most of the poorly housed live in communities whose condition is far from hopeless; decline may be incipient, or even well advanced, but, given a reasonable and timely expenditure of energy and money (the proverbial ounce of prevention), residents can be spared the fate of the

9. For a discussion of the abandonment phenomenon, see, for example, Ron Linton, Hugh Mields, Jr., and Dean Costen, *A Study of the Problems of Abandoned Housing*, report prepared for the U.S. Department of Housing and Urban Development (Washington, D.C., November 1971), and National Urban League and the Center for Community Change, *The National Survey of Housing Abandonment* (Washington, D.C., April 1971).
10. This quotation and the following are taken from the first of a four-part series on the South Bronx by Martin Tolchin in the *New York Times*, January 15, 1973.

Brownsvilles (New York), North Lawndales (Chicago), Montgomerys (St. Louis), and other crisis ghettos.

Instead of trying to reverse the process of housing and neighborhood disinvestment within the inner cities, however, national policy has attempted to solve the "bad housing" problem by subsidizing the construction of new units. In the case of conventional or turnkey public housing, for example, the federal government adds units directly to the low-rent housing stock by assuming the full capital cost of housing construction. The federal government also stimulates the private development of multifamily rentals (National Housing and Urban Redevelopment Act of 1968, Section 236) and single-family homes (Section 235) by subsidizing the interest rates on mortgages. In addition, the FHA guarantees banks, insurance companies, and other conventional mortgage lenders against losses or risks of default on mortgages provided for federally subsidized new construction or substantial rehabilitation programs. Unfortunately, even tragically, the isolated construction of individual housing projects has absolutely no impact on the wholesale deterioration of entire neighborhoods. Far too often these programs have been designed to stimulate the construction industry, despite the rhetoric of legislative preambles couched in terms of eradicating blight, providing improved low- and moderate-income housing, and revitalizing older neighborhoods.

The obsession with new construction has considerable historic precedent. Some observers, in fact, would argue that as far back as the New Deal, programs enacted for the alleged purpose of housing the poor (our redistributive goal) were really intended primarily to bolster the national economy. The following quotation describes this view:

Earliest federal legislation directly associated with housing—the Home Owners' Loan Act of 1933—was enacted to protect both mortgagors and mortgagees from losing their interest in real property because of the Depression. The National Housing Act of 1934, while ostensibly designed to promote homeownership through the establishment of the FHA, in reality was developed because of the general collapse of economic activity in the 1930's and the assumption that stimulation of the residential construction industry would stimulate the entire economy. The same reasons underlay the U.S. Housing Act of 1937. While all the legislation of the 1930's bowed in the direction of improving housing conditions for low-income groups, removing slums and improving housing in general, without the Depression, none of the legislation would ever have been enacted. The motivation was not to evolve a cohesive housing policy for the nation but to use housing as a means of aiding in the elimination of the Depression.[11]

Over the years the housing production orientation has prevailed. For example, in the landmark Housing Act of 1949, which spawned the urban renewal program, the underlying strategy was to bulldoze and rebuild rather than preserve and upgrade the existing housing stock. Since the mid-sixties, when it became embarrassingly apparent that the program had somehow contrived to destroy more housing than it replaced, emphasis has shifted toward housing rehabilitation and neighborhood conservation with selective rather than wholesale clearance. Some government grant and loan programs, in fact, have been effective in bringing old stock back into use for low- and moderate-income families. However, as often as not, such rehabilitation has been aimed at the upper- and middle-income markets, with poorer residents being priced out of their apartments in the process of seeing their communities renewed.

The debate over subsidizing the rents of poor families in private dwellings—what came to be known as the rent supplement program—once again revealed the fundamental schism over the use of subsidy programs: Should they be oriented toward the builder or the consumer? Some contend that former President Johnson, in his message to Congress, leaned toward the latter view, stressing the rent supplement's potential flexibility compared to previous policy instruments.[12] Placing the full subsidy directly in the hands of low- and moderate-income families would allow them to translate their needs into effective demand, whatever the conditions of the local housing market. Given a reasonable vacancy and turnover rate in the local housing market, the recipient family could shop around for an available unit in the location of its choice. The majority report of the House Committee on

---

11. This perception of the primary function of federal housing subsidies is expressed in many official as well as unofficial documents. See, for example, the Report of the President's Committee on Urban Housing, *A Decent Home* (Washington, D.C.: U.S. Government Printing Office, 1968), p. 54. For an abbreviated historical review of federal housing policies, see Appendix A.

12. Lyndon B. Johnson, "The Problems and Future of the Central City and Its Suburbs," The President's Message to the Congress on Urban Problems, March 2, 1965.

Banking and Currency, differing with the Administration's view, argued that the program should support the home-building component of the economy by confining all rent supplement payments to specific buildings under contract to FHA.[13] The congressional viewpoint prevailed, the debate ending with the supplements tied to FHA-insured mortgages for new construction or substantial rehabilitation rather than channeled directly to the tenant. In effect, the private developer enjoys a guaranteed rent-roll; when coupled with mortgage insurance, this provides a powerful inducement for new construction starts.

The Housing and Urban Development Act of 1968 actually established national housing production targets[14]—the construction or rehabilitation of 26 million units over the decade 1969–1978. Of this total, 20 million were to be built through the workings of the private market, while an additional 6 million subsidized low- and moderate-income units were pledged toward relief of the "bad housing" problem. Here, in the most explicit terms, the government subsumed its redistributive objective under an aggregate housing production goal.

The conscientious reader of newspapers and periodicals might well carry away the impression that national housing policy is less lopsided in favor of new construction than is, in fact, the case. A number of legislative authorizations do exist for housing rehabilitation and indirect income supplementation (leased housing, rent supplements), and local efforts utilizing these programs have received disproportionate amounts of publicity. However, these efforts have generally been limited in scale, never receiving a fraction of the funds available for conventional public housing and other builder-oriented subsidy programs. The true imbalance emerges from an assessment of the composition of the subsidized housing stock, with 90 percent of all subsidized units between 1968 and 1972 being newly constructed,

13. Majority Report, House of Representatives, Committee on Banking and Currency, Committee Hearings, Eighty-Fifth Congress (Washington, D.C.: U.S. Government Printing Office, 1965).
14. George Romney, the former Secretary of the U.S. Department of Housing and Urban Development first responsible for achieving this goal, actually established a Housing Production Award for outstanding achievement by local FHA insuring offices in surpassing local production quotas.

totally dwarfing the 10 percent made available by rehabilitating dwellings from the existing private housing stock.[15]

Limitations of Existing Production Subsidies

Clearly, the United States needs a housing production strategy to preclude housing shortages and to dampen the inflationary spiral of higher and higher dwelling costs, as well as to help achieve overall economic growth and stability. But as a means for attacking the "bad housing" problem, the current preoccupation with builder-oriented subsidies is inappropriate. It ignores the fact that the total housing stock grows at a slow rate (less than 3 percent annually) and that the shelter needs of most people, not merely the poor, must be satisfied with the housing already in existence.

A somewhat perverse case might be made defending the vagueness of national housing objectives as "good politics." Vagueness, in this view, allows elected representatives from diverse constituencies and ideological persuasions to rally behind the same policy, albeit for different reasons. The less explicit the trade-offs, the easier the formation of the political coalitions necessary to secure any results from our governmental system. A clear separation of redistributive from productive objectives, according to this line of argument, would sacrifice much of the support from special-interest groups which made the housing legislation of the sixties a reality.

The danger inherent in this brand of political "realism" lies in its readiness to dilute substance in the interest of palatability. With respect to housing policy, political support has been purchased at the cost of reducing the residual benefits left over for the poor themselves after the developers, contractors, lawyers, and other middlemen have claimed a "piece of the action." A number of other economic, social, and political factors—highlighted in the following sections of this chapter—confirm the need to redirect our present federal housing policy.

The Supply Shortage Argument

Proponents of construction subsidies contend that there is a shortage of standard housing for the poor. That such shortages exist is indisputable, but the construction advocates fail to make a basic conceptual distinction

15. See Message from the President of the United States, *Fourth Annual Report on National Housing Goals* (Washington, D.C.: U.S. Government Printing Office, 1973).

between the "supply" of dwelling units and the "supply" of residential services.[16] The supply problem is not a purely quantitative one, in the sense of an absolute shortage of housing units, but rather a shortage of "residential services," resulting from a decline in the quality of structures, neighborhood environments, and municipal services. The latter type of shortage can be overcome, therefore, only by upgrading the quality of existing structures, neighborhood environments, and municipal services, not by adding new units to the stock.

As illustrated in Table 1.1, the dynamics of decline have followed a similar pattern in most of the older cities of the Northeast and Midwest. In broad outline, this pattern is as familiar by now to the casual readers of the Sunday supplement as to the social scientists who originally charted its course: the mass exodus from the central city of its more affluent and mobile residents in search of greener suburban pastures; left behind, a residual population, increasingly nonwhite and economically destitute, and a city government frantically trying to accommodate the resultant demand for expanded services with a relatively shrinking or stagnant tax base.

The population of many of our older cities has declined faster than the removal of the older substandard housing stock. It is the loss of housing demand associated with an absolute decline in population, as well as more concentrated poverty—rather than the inadequate supply of housing stock—which is at the heart of the older central cities' housing problems. Between 1960 and 1970, St. Louis lost 17 percent of its residents, while its nonwhite population grew by 19.1 percent; Detroit lost 9.5 percent, with a 38.0 percent increase in the number of nonwhites; for Buffalo the corresponding figures were 13.1 percent and 25.3 percent, respectively. Compar-

16. For a clear distinction between the concepts of housing stock and residential services, see Morton Isler, "The Goals of Housing Subsidy Programs," in U.S. House of Representatives, Committee on Banking and Currency, papers submitted to Subcommittee on Housing Panels, 92nd Congress, 1st Session (Washington, D.C.: U.S. Government Printing Office, 1971) . "Housing stock" denotes the existence of a physical facility such as a furnace or a building shell, whereas the concept of "housing services" designates what the physical facility produces, such as heat or space. Public services (such as trash removal), access to work, and quality of local schools are among the residential services available because of the location of a home. As Isler indicates, many automatically associate new construction with solutions to housing problems of the poor because subsidies have been traditionally tied to the long-term goals of capital stock development instead of the day-to-day provision of residential services.

Table 1.1 Urban Housing Markets, Selected Characteristics (percentages)

	Total Population Change, 1960–1970a	Nonwhite Population Increases, 1960–1970a	Percent Households Unable to Afford BLS Standard Low-Rent Budgetb	Excessive Rent Burden Change, 1960–1970b	Vacancy Rate Low-Rent Units 1970c	Percent of Stock Built Prior to 1939b
St. Louis	−17.0	19.1	29.2	− 9.8	20.4	72.5
Cleveland	−14.3	15.7	25.0	− 8.3	13.7	75.3
Boston	− 8.1	40.1	38.3	19.0	14.4	75.4
Chicago	− 5.2	38.3	29.4	4.9	11.4	69.6
Buffalo	−13.1	25.3	27.2	11.6	7.3	83.7
Providence	−13.5	49.5	32.5	−18.2	12.8	82.1
Newark	− 5.6	53.9	38.0	29.8	7.8	64.7
Philadelphia	− 2.7	25.2	20.3	40.8	8.9	69.4
Detroit	− 9.5	38.0	18.1	28.3	14.2	70.6
Baltimore	− 3.6	29.6	26.7	22.0	9.1	65.2

a. U.S., Bureau of the Census, *General Population Characteristics, U.S. Summary*, 1970, Tables 66 and 67.
b. Derived from U.S., Bureau of the Census, *Metropolitan Housing Characteristics*, 1960, 1970, Tables D-2 and D-3. Households were considered unable to afford the Bureau of Labor Statistics (BLS) low-rent budget in their own SMSA if they would have to expend more than 25 percent of their gross income for this standard of housing. More than 25 percent was considered an excessive rent burden.
c. Derived from U.S., Bureau of the Census, *Metropolitan Housing Characteristics*, 1970, Tables D-7 and D-9. Low-rent units refer to all dwelling units renting for less than $99 per month.

able situations prevailed in Cleveland, Chicago, Providence, Newark, Philadelphia, and many other core cities. The impact of these transitions upon the urban housing market has been an enervating one. Demand has slackened. The units vacated by middle-income whites have been occupied by families whose rent-paying ability is insufficient to command a decent level of maintenance and repair. At the same time, the inflationary costs of operating properties has exacerbated the problems caused by slack demand. As fixed costs such as property taxes, insurance, fuel, and utilities keep climbing, landlords invariably cut back their budgets for variable costs such as maintenance and building services—particularly in a market that does not allow them to increase rents proportionately (that is, pass cost increases onto the tenants).

While Washington persists in its single-minded emphasis on housing production, hundreds of thousands of existing dwelling units are deteriorating or being withdrawn from the standing stock.[17] On a citywide basis, for example, 45 percent of Newark's housing units have been judged substandard. In Baltimore about 28 percent of the entire inventory is either deteriorated or dilapidated, including 50 percent of the rental stock occupied by nonwhite families.[18] The New York City housing market is something of an anomaly, not as a result of scale alone, but because its unique urbanity and role in the national economy keeps housing demand high in select areas of the city. Nonetheless, while its inventory of sound housing grew by 24 percent during the 1960s, its dilapidated inventory increased by 44 percent, and its deteriorated stock by 37 percent. Unless measures are taken to counteract the processes of economic and psychic disinvestment at work behind such figures (such as opening a broader range of suburban opportunities while shoring up the core areas), the older cities will increas-

17. Although housing abandonment statistics are often cited as evidence of the deterioration of the urban housing market, the fact of abandonment itself does not signify a serious public policy problem. Housing—like old cars and old refrigerators—must be replaced at the end of its useful life. Housing abandonment, in some cities, may merely reflect an efficient response to changing housing market conditions. On the other hand, when housing abandonment causes harmful spillover effects (involving the loss of decent housing or leaving a residual population of only those unable to flee), then abandonment is a cause for serious concern.

18. The terms "dilapidated" and "deteriorated" refer to dwelling units that either lack full plumbing or have other structural deficiencies.

ingly become isolated preserves for the elderly, the poor, the blacks, the Puerto Ricans, and others unable to escape to the suburbs.[19]

There is another category of cities which, for different reasons than the older central cities of the Northeast and Midwest, have an oversupply of housing, and where production programs seem equally inappropriate to local needs. In Phoenix, Baton Rouge, Albuquerque, Seattle, and other growth centers of the South and Far West, population has increased substantially over the past decade, but, because of the boom mentality, new housing has been built even faster, outstripping the demand. The mayor of Seattle expresses a typical view:

> ... and to save the central city, the government has to do something about central city housing. The present federal programs don't. In fact, they do just the opposite. Take the Seattle situation, where we have an oversupply of housing, the last thing I want is money for new housing. I want money for Section 23 leasing type of housing aid, because new housing goes against our priorities rather than meeting them.[20]

In these cities over one-third of the standing stock has been built in the last ten to fifteen years. With most of the demand for new housing falling in the middle or high price range, a rapid turnover of the standard stock should set off a chain of moves which finally reaches the poor. But, as discussed in Chapter 2, the spatial location of new units as well as the structure of housing vacancies has limited the benefit of "filtering" for the poor.[21] In the older central cities of both the Northeast and the Midwest (where housing demand has slackened) and the growing cities of the South and the Far West (where speculative construction has resulted in housing surpluses), a continuing preoccupation with production subsidies seems inconsistent with local market conditions.

19. Abandonment is just the tip of the iceberg; it is the overall process of disinvestment which is so alarming. For a review of some theories of slum housing, as well as the major source of the foregoing data, see Michael A. Stegman, *Housing Investment in the Inner City* (Cambridge, Mass.: MIT Press, 1972), pp. 50–57.
20. The view expressed by the mayor of Seattle, Washington, was cited in an article on federal housing subsidies by William Lilley III. See William Lilley III, "Urban Report/ Federal Housing Subsidies Under Attack," *National Journal*, Vol. 3, No. 30, pp. 1535–1542.
21. While there are a number of different concepts of the filtering phenomenon, the term is used in this section to denote the change in the relative socioeconomic status of occupants of the same dwelling unit. For a fuller discussion of the conceptual debate over the meaning of "filtering," see Edgar Olsen, "A Competitive Theory of the Housing Market," *American Economic Review*, September 1969, and William Grigsby, *Housing Markets and Public Policy* (Philadelphia: University of Pennsylvania Press, 1963).

"Getting the Most" for Our Subsidy Dollars

The public monies made available for the remedy of social ills invariably fall far short of the sums required for a meaningful solution. Perhaps if poverty responded to innoculation, we could hope for some "breakthrough" vaccine that, at a minimal expenditure per capita, would make it all go away. Alas, such is not the case: even in some rose-colored future, housing and neighborhoods will continue to age, markets to perform erratically, income to be distributed unequally, and minimum acceptable standards to be adjusted upward with the average level of affluence.

For planning purposes, when dealing with congressional appropriation committees, scarcity must be accepted as axiomatic. Given the limited funds available to meet our national housing objectives, then, one naturally hopes that those strategies will be selected which promise the greatest impact per dollar of U.S. Treasury funds (or, in economic terms, per dollar of scarce economic resource). A useful criterion for contrasting the impact of alternative housing programs would be the number of inadequately housed families moved into decent shelter for any given expenditure of public funds. By this criterion, new construction appears highly inefficient. In fact, our comparative analysis of the major federal housing subsidy programs reveals that building new units is far more costly than using the existing housing stock, irrespective of whether the costs are calculated from the viewpoint of the federal government—direct HUD expenditures and forgone tax dollars—or in terms of total resource costs. Our calculations indicate that *twice* as many poor families can move from substandard to standard housing when the government leases existing units from private landlords than when it either sponsors new construction or guarantees the mortgage for a private developer to build new units.[22] The cost of leasing used housing or providing direct housing allowances is small when compared to the capital cost of adding new units.

A second cost consideration when contrasting federal subsidy programs is the extent and duration of the U.S. Treasury's commitment which they entail. With respect to government-subsidized production programs, such commitments are staggering. As the President's *Third Annual Report on National Housing Goals* (1971) bemoans:

22. For a detailed treatment of these cost comparisons, see Chapter 7.

. . . it is estimated that subsidized housing units started or projected for the three fiscal years 1970–72 have already obligated the Federal Government to subsidy payments of perhaps $30 billion over the next 30 to 40 years. And assuming the completion of the six million subsidized units for low- and moderate-income families called for in the 10 year housing goals by 1978, present estimates suggest that the Federal Government will by that year be paying out at least $7.5 billion annually in subsidies. Over the life of the mortgage this could amount to the staggering total of more than $200 billion.

As the major housing lobbyists correctly observe, the future commitment of housing subsidy dollars has to be seen in the perspective of the nation's overall economic growth. If the national economy can afford such a commitment, and if social needs warrant it, then there is nothing inherently inappropriate or wasteful about a $200 billion commitment to housing the nation's low- and moderate-income population. But in justifying the size of the commitment to housing in comparison to other social, economic, and national security goals, there is no implied defense of any particular housing strategy. Thus, the observation of the major housing lobbyists would apply to housing allowances as well as production subsidies.

Who Benefits from Federal Subsidies?

As experience with existing federal subsidy programs accumulates, it has become increasingly evident that they perpetuate serious inequities. These inequities are two-dimensional—one vertical, the second horizontal.

The first of these, the issue of vertical equity, refers to the fact that a disproportionate share of program benefits actually finds its way into the pockets of individuals above the poverty level, rather than the poor themselves. This diversion of subsidy dollars is inherent in the structure of the federal government programs. In the case of conventional or turnkey public housing, the federal government raises capital through the sale of tax-exempt housing authority serial bonds. Exempting the interest payments on these bonds from federal income taxation imposes a net cost on the U.S. treasury.[23] Similarly, for the privately produced units under the various FHA mortgage-insurance programs, accelerated depreciation allowances provide high-income investors with a means of sheltering income from the federal income tax. Syndication of these tax shelters is an exceedingly

23. For the actual calculation of this net cost to the U.S. Treasury, see the Technical Note to Chapter 7.

costly method of raising development capital.[24] Altogether, the use of intermediaries and high capital costs consume 35 percent of every subsidy dollar, seriously reducing the actual expenditure on bricks and mortar to
house the poor.

The second—and potentially more explosive aspect of the equity issue—
centers on the problem of horizontal, as opposed to vertical, equity: the fact
that persons in essentially the same circumstances receive widely varying
treatment. Given the current structure of federal housing programs, and
their levels of funding, only a small fraction of those eligible for assistance
receive any government aid at all. In addition, many households whose
incomes hover just beyond eligibility requirements pay market prices to
occupy substandard housing, while other families with only marginally
lower incomes are provided new standard housing at below-market rents.

According to government estimates, nearly 2 million households receive
benefits from federal housing subsidy programs. The amount of assistance
per household varies up to a maximum limit of nearly $2,400 per year.
Yet under present law as many as 25 million households could qualify for
aid under one or more of the major subsidy programs.[25] Smolensky and
Gomery, for example, have estimated that the present tenants of public
housing comprise only 2.9 percent of those whose income status satisfies
the program's eligibility requirements.[26] And some households at the very
bottom of the income scale cannot be helped at all either because of the
maximum limit on the amount of subsidy per family or because of the need
for local housing authorities to remain fiscally solvent—in other words, even

24. For an analysis of less costly methods to raise development capital, see Stanley S. Surrey,
"Federal Income Tax Reform: The Varied Approaches Necessary to Replace Tax Expenditures with Direct Government Assistance," *Harvard Law Review*, Vol. 84 (December
1970), and James E. Wallace, "Federal Income Tax Incentives in Low- and Moderate-
Income Rental Housing," in *The Economics of Federal Subsidy Programs*, Part 5,
Housing Subsidies, Joint Economic Committee, U.S. Government Printing Office, October
9, 1972.
25. President of the United States, *Third Annual Report on National Housing Goals*
(Washington, D.C.: U.S. Government Printing Office, 1971). This calculation does not
include, of course, the many millions of homeowners who benefit from favorable Internal
Revenue Service treatment, FHA and VA mortgage-insurance programs, and other indirect
government subsidies. For an excellent analysis of who benefits from these federal policies
see Aaron, *Shelter and Subsidies.*
26. Eugene Smolensky and J. Douglas Gomery, "Efficiency and Equity Effects in the
Benefits from Federal Public Housing Programs in 1965," Working Paper No. 2 (Madison,
Wis.: Institute of Poverty, 1971), p. 24, n.d., processed.

if supplemented by the maximum subsidy, the incomes of these families could not cover the cost of a unit in standard condition.

Not only do a mere fraction of the needy actually receive aid, but even for those assisted the levels of benefits are dramatically different. Since subsidized tenants make rent payments based on a percentage of their income rather than on the market price of the unit they occupy, those with comparable incomes pay essentially the same monthly amount. However, despite these equal payments, the participants may inhabit housing and neighborhoods of markedly different quality, some newly constructed or renovated, others in poor condition, perhaps still others in violation of code standards. The use of new construction strategies aggravates this form of inequity, since far more is spent to rehouse any single family than is required to meet their minimum needs; only the leasing of existing dwellings provides standard housing at resource costs comparable to the rent levels of low-income standard housing on the private market and thereby allows a maximum number of families to be aided for any given federal expenditure. New construction for the few means less assistance for the many.

Effect on Economic Growth and Stability

One of the most persuasive arguments for securing congressional and general public support of new construction subsidies for the poor has been the assertion that these programs create significant employment opportunities while adding to the total stock of housing. However, closer scrutiny casts serious doubt on this argument. In a full-employment economy the construction of subsidized housing does not create any *net* employment benefits but merely shifts workers from existing jobs. Despite the fact that government investment in low-income housing first won approval during the depression years as a stimulus to the economy, its limited value as an anticyclical instrument has since been recognized. During periods of economic slack, monetary and fiscal policies have proved more effective means for stimulating economic activity. Furthermore, the long interval elapsing between authorization of new housing developments and their actual construction and occupancy, as well as the possible lack of geographic coincidence between high unemployment rates and housing needs, severely limits the usefulness of federal housing programs as anticyclical measures.

Of equal importance is whether or not federally subsidized construction programs, in fact, have contributed to a net increase in total housing starts.

Although the number of subsidized starts exceeded 300,000 in both 1971 and 1972, there is some evidence that these assisted starts may merely have replaced unassisted starts without adding to the total.[27] In fact, the net effect of subsidized housing starts in both the short as well as the long run is still uncertain. Yet, while a questionable instrument for economic growth, subsidy programs do offer a potentially effective means for redistributing income and expanding equal employment opportunities. Both the Demonstration Cities and Metropolitan Development Act of 1966 and the Housing and Urban Development Act of 1968 provide for the employment of persons from the communities in which assisted projects are located. In addition, program guidelines require proof of "affirmative action" in the recruitment and training of minorities in the construction trades. The Office of Federal Contract Compliance in the Department of Labor assists local contractors, building trades, and minority communities in formulating "hometown" strategies to promote minority hiring on local construction jobs. Unfortunately these affirmative action programs have produced token results at best,[28] with the Administration backing away from its earlier commitments as the political volatility of the hiring issue became apparent.

Impact on Property Taxes

The general public assumes that federally assisted housing in blighted central city areas will invariably make some net contribution to the local tax base. This holds true for only the smallest subsidy programs. Privately owned properties subsidized under the Section 236 rent supplement and leasing programs do have a positive property tax effect where the construction or improvements made possible by the subsidy are accompanied by some increase in assessed valuation; however, the significantly larger public housing programs represent an actual drain on the local treasury. A city with 5,000 units of conventional public housing receiving federally mandated property tax exemptions suffers a loss of nearly $1 million in forgone

27. In order to estimate the net effect of subsidized housing starts, it is necessary to use a sophisticated econometric model of the national economy. One of the difficulties inherent in this type of anlysis is to distinguish the short- versus the long-run effects. For a preliminary estimate of the net effects see Craig Swan. "Housing Markets: An Aggregate View," Working Paper No. 40, Federal Home Loan Bank Board, November 1972, processed.
28. See, for example, Peter B. Doeringer and Michael J. Piore, "Equal Employment Opportunities in Boston," *Industrial Relations*, Vol. 9, No. 3 (May 1970), and Irwin Dubinsky, "Trade Union Discrimination in the Pittsburgh Construction Industry," *Urban Affairs Quarterly*, March 1971.

tax revenue per year. This figure assumes that the local housing authority (LHA) is making some payments in lieu of taxes—an assumption that appears increasingly problematic as more and more local authorities confront the specter of fiscal insolvency. In any event, the local revenue loss grows over the years, because an LHA's payment in lieu of taxes rarely, if ever, keeps pace with increases in regular property tax returns.

The property tax exemption for public housing has the anomalous effect of narrowing a municipality's tax base while placing a greater burden on the poorest of local taxpayers, who must take up the slack through the narrow and regressive real property tax.[29] This form of tax subsidy is not only inequitable but inefficient as well, since a municipality with an eroding tax base is less able to provide necessary services. Yet it is the central cities —which already assume a disproportionate share of the metropolitan property tax burden—that both house and subsidize the same public housing population (and other low-income tenants) whom the suburbs exclude. These are the cities least able to absorb additional fiscal erosion.

Locational and Environmental Liabilities

Because of cost and site selection constraints, many federally subsidized new construction projects have taken the form of large, highly visible multistory developments. Projects of this scale have almost inevitably suffered from two serious liabilities: first, vulnerability to political pressures in their site location and, second, the dehumanizing physical and social environments they create.

As job opportunities have rapidly suburbanized over the past decade, housing policy has had to adjust its priorities to emphasize the widening of locational choices for low-income households. With a few noteworthy exceptions, however, proposals to locate newly constructed housing for the poor outside blighted ghetto areas have met vehement resistance from the more affluent central city neighborhoods and suburban communities alike. One has only to recall the deliberate exclusion of subsidy programs by Forest Hills, New York, by Black Jack, Missouri, by Newton, Massachusetts, and by myriad other communities to recognize the tremendous social

29. The regressive nature of the property tax has been documented by many public finance and urban economists. For an excellent summary of the regressivity argument, see Dick Netzer, *Economics of the Property Tax* (Washington, D.C.: Brookings Institution, 1966), and George E. Peterson and Arthur P. Solomon, "Property Taxes and Populist Reform," *The Public Interest,* Winter 1973.

and political barriers that new construction programs face—particularly when they try to advance racial and socioeconomic integration. In a landmark case, Federal District Judge Richard B. Austin responded to these exclusionary forces by ordering the Chicago Housing Authority

... to build 75 percent of all new public housing projects in predominantly white communities and at least one mile from the edge of the nearest black ghetto; to limit future projects to no more than three stories, and to avoid clearing the selection of project sites with the alderman of the wards involved.[30]

Unfortunately, this type of forthright judicial action has remained the exception rather than the rule. Advanced legislation—such as the Massachusetts anti-snob-zoning statute, which places the responsibility for housing low- and moderate-income families on local communities that have not already provided a minimum amount of such housing—has proved relatively ineffective in practice.

New construction is a particularly cumbersome means for dispersing low-income households. Proposals for large federally subsidized developments are highly conspicuous and, wherever local interests are aroused, soon become embroiled in controversy, leading to long delays, and, in the end, damaging compromise or cancellation. Successfully completed developments of any size, with the notable exception of projects for the elderly, have almost always been located either in the midst of an existing slum or in an isolated, undesirable location, already discarded as worthless by the private land development market and cut off from adequate public transportation, schools, and retail facilities.[31]

The second liability associated with large-scale subsidized new construction is its poor environmental qualities. In physical terms, most new housing does, of course, comply with local building and sanitary codes; it contains hot running water, private toilet and bath; it is not dilapidated, deteriorated, or overcrowded. Experience shows, however, that by itself a sound physical structure does not guarantee a suitable living environment; clean and amenable surroundings, playing space for children, provision for

---

30. See citation in Leonard Freedman, *Public Housing: The Politics of Poverty* (New York: Holt, Rinehart & Winston, 1969), pp. x–xi.
31. Columbia Point in Boston and Pruitt-Igoe in St. Louis are two of the more notorious examples of isolated projects in unwholesome environments.

personal safety and security, and access to work and shopping areas are just a few of the many environmental qualities separating a workable neighborhood from an institutional project. But many new federal housing developments tend to reinforce the social disorganization and despair (as evidenced in welfare dependency, vandalism, street crime, and so forth) that plague the inner city today.[32]

In assessing the locational effect of such developments, however, one must distinguish between subsidized developments that create deleterious environments for their own tenants and those which, built in the midst of slums, inherit a preexisting physical and social sterility. Of late, most subsidized moderate-income rental units (such as Section 236) have been built in the outermost sections of the central city or on scattered sites, thereby escaping the most unwholesome environments. And one can point to a few inner-city developments that are well designed and physically integrated into the larger community. Yet, no matter how well conceived inner-city developments may be in architectural terms, they are insufficient to upgrade a declining neighborhood. This is true for rehabilitation programs as well, since it is impossible to regenerate a slum area by physical change alone. But in some neighborhoods modest renovations and repairs will prolong the life of the existing stock. Yet, unless public policy confronts the knottier problems of poverty and racial discrimination, larger and larger areas of our older central cities will become uninhabitable. Under such conditions, a more comprehensive upgrading of the public services, neighborhood infrastructure, and housing stock would aid everyone, whereas the isolated construction of single developments hardly benefits even the few subsidized tenants they actually house.

Organization of the Study

Chapter 1 has provided an overview of the book. Its specific function was to highlight the arguments for redirecting national housing policy. The rest of the book provides the analysis for this conclusion. Specifically, the study offers a systematic comparison of alternative strategies for housing the urban poor. Taking as given the stated objectives of redistributive housing pro-

---

32. For an interesting and thoughtful treatment of the impact of physical design on personal safety, crime, and mobility, see Oscar Newman, *Defensible Space: Crime Prevention Through Urban Design* (New York: Macmillan, 1972).

grams, along with some normative standards prescribed by welfare economics, it empirically contrasts the performance of new construction,
rehabilitation, and programs for using the existing stock. For this purpose,
the conventional public housing and Section 236 programs are used to illustrate the new construction approach, Section 236 and public housing with
leasing (Section 23) the rehabilitation strategy, and the leasing of unimproved private dwellings as the prototype for housing allowances and
other consumer-oriented approaches for using the existing housing stock.
By setting forth clear objectives and then analyzing alternative strategies
for their attainment, we sharpen our awareness of the gains and costs associated with policy choices and lessen our reliance upon undocumented rhetoric and subjective opinion.

Chapter 2 examines the major strategies for solving the "bad housing"
problem. After reviewing the alternative strategies, it sets forth a framework for analyzing and comparing them. In order to measure the social
impact of each strategy, such questions as the following are addressed:
Which housing strategy contributes the most to aggregate economic welfare? What is the least costly method for providing the urban poor with
decent shelter and environment? Who benefits from the respective subsidized housing programs? Which strategies are most responsive to changing
conditions in the housing market?

Since many of the urban poor live in deteriorated, dilapidated, or overcrowded dwellings, sometimes paying as much as 30–35 percent of their
income, it is important to analyze how much the alternative housing strategies improve the housing and financial position of the poor. Chapter 3
examines how these consumption benefits vary according to local housing
market conditions. Since this is such an important feature of program
performance, a considerable portion of the chapter is devoted to selecting
an appropriate measure. Finally, the comparative results are presented and
discussed.

While the preceding chapter concentrates on the magnitude of the benefits received by subsidized tenants (as well as nonsubsidized tenants), Chapter 4 determines how the benefits are distributed. How much of the total
subsidy dollar actually reaches the poor? Do the federal subsidy programs
reach the privileged few and fail to serve the most disadvantaged? How
are the benefits of subsidy programs actually distributed?

Chapters 5 and 6 examine two of the economic effects of federal subsidy programs. Since there is such widespread concern about the regressive and burdensome nature of property taxes and the quality of local public services, Chapter 5 examines the municipal fiscal effect of government-assisted housing. Whenever a federal subsidy program results in an increase in municipal revenue, the local government is able either to reduce property taxes or to spend more on local schools, health and hospital care, or other types of service. Conversely, if the federal housing programs are a drain on local revenues, then they produce the opposite effect. Since some federal programs require local governments to accept payments in lieu of taxes instead of full property taxes on government-subsidized real property, our estimates take these measures into account in comparing the municipal fiscal effects of alternative housing strategies.

Chapter 6 focuses on the employment impact of new construction, rehabilitation, and direct assistance programs. The creation of job opportunities under varying economic conditions is examined. Moreover, since the net employment benefit of housing investments depends upon the primary resource requirements that final demand generates, a step-by-step procedure for this analysis is outlined. Then the on-site and off-site manpower requirements as well as those associated with the management, maintenance, and operation of the housing units are compared.

The cost of federal housing programs differs considerably because the various subsidy schemes are tied to newly constructed, rehabilitated, and existing housing units. Chapter 7 estimates the capital, operating, and administrative cost of each strategy from the viewpoint of both the U.S. Treasury (direct expenditures plus forgone tax revenues) and the overall economy.

In Chapter 8 a qualitative assessment of the social and environmental impact of the alternative housing strategies is presented. This chapter addresses such questions as: What is the effect on landlord-tenant relations? How much discretion does the subsidized tenant have in his choice of dwelling unit, neighborhood, and jurisdiction? What is the impact on economic and racial integration? How adaptable is the strategy to local conditions? Do the programs provide an acceptable living environment?

On the basis of the performance of alternative strategies to deal with the "bad housing" problem, analyzed and compared in earlier chapters, the final chapter sets forth a new direction for national housing policy.

The Choice of a Housing Policy

The most frustrating aspect of public life . . . is the endless hours spent on policy discussions in which the irrelevant issues have not been separated from the relevant, in which ascertainable facts . . . have not been investigated, in which consideration of alternatives is impossible because only one proposal has been developed and, above all, discussions in which nobility of aim is presumed to determine effectiveness of program.

Charles L. Schultze,
The Politics and Economics of Public Spending

Although the first national housing law was not enacted until the 1930s,[1] since then the scope of federal activity has grown so that today Internal Revenue Service regulations and national credit conditions shape the economic environment in which all housing investment decisions (public and private) are made. Federal support of the mortgage market, for example, has dramatically increased the availability and lowered the cost of home financing. While the federal government itself seldom acts as builder or owner, it does offer an array of direct subsidies for both the production and the occupancy of low- to moderate-income housing. Moreover, federal highway funds, water and sewer grants, support for community facilities, and other infrastructure have a decisive influence on the pattern of land-use activities and urban growth, on the quality of neighborhood environments, and indirectly on the conditions of the housing stock itself.

Despite the impressive scope of national housing policies, a changing political and institutional environment has brought them under intensive scrutiny in recent years. First of all, revelations of scandalous misuse of housing funds in certain cities has crystallized a more pervasive dissatisfaction with the cost and performance of subsidy programs. At the same time, a parallel reevaluation of the welfare system and its proposed replacement by some form of income maintenance or earmarked allowances has raised questions about the future role, if any, for housing subsidies. If a reasonable floor is placed under all incomes, will there still be a residual need for a categorical assistance program such as rent supplements or mortgage insurance? Moreover, with the recent proposal of special revenue sharing for

1. The Housing Act of 1934 created the country's first nationwide residential mortgage institutions, the Federal Housing Administration, the Federal Savings and Loan Insurance Corporation, and the Federal National Mortgage Association.

community development, state and local officials suddenly confront the prospect of greater discretion, as well as responsibility, in the expenditure of housing-related funds.[2] These officials are concerned about how they might best take advantage of this new programming freedom, while federal administrators worry about how to ensure local accountability to national objectives without compromising the flexibility central to the revenue-sharing concept.

Whether the locus of decision making remains at the national level or is shifted to the states and municipalities, the classical dilemma at the heart of welfare economics remains: How should scarce resources be allocated? The housing problem lingers stubbornly on, government appropriations are necessarily limited, and numerous schemes for sheltering the poor compete for public attention and a share of whatever funds are available. As always, trade-offs must be made. How much additional money should be invested in new construction? How much in preserving the existing housing stock? What is the most appropriate form of housing subsidy? What measures, if any, should the government take to achieve a greater dispersal of subsidized units? Who should benefit from public expenditures for housing?

While recognizing that political considerations will always influence, if not dominate, such choices, we can still move toward a more rational decision-making process; any gain in rationality brings its own compensation in the form of greater social benefits for a given dollar expenditure. This study, then, is premised on the belief that applying objective criteria to an evaluation of policy alternatives can clarify options and reduce reliance upon ideological assertions, political horse trading, and undocumented rhetoric.

Although there are many political factors that inhibit fully rational and explicit policy deliberations, the present chapter sets forth a normative decision model for determining national housing policy. (See the Technical Note at the end of this chapter for a formal presentation of the benefit-cost model). The model uses a rational choice paradigm that assumes the

2. Currently, states and local communities receive categorical grants and aid for housing assistance and community development, for example, public housing, Section 236 FHA mortgage-insured rental housing, or Model Cities grants. Under revenue sharing, these would be replaced by more discretionary, unearmarked federal block grants.

end of decision making to be the maximizing of national housing objectives, within existing constraints. Under this paradigm, the selection of an optimum housing strategy involves the following steps:

1. *Specify national housing goals and objectives:*
Federal legislation and administrative guidelines have set forth a number of national housing objectives. These multiple objectives (such as providing decent shelter and a suitable living environment for every household, eliminating economic and racial discrimination in the housing market) fall into broad economic, social, and environmental categories.

2. *Formulate alternative strategies:*
There are a range of federal housing programs and alternative courses of action that may be combined in various ways to achieve national goals. Among the available options are housing allowances, subsidized construction programs, mortgage insurance, preferential tax treatment, rehabilitation loans and grants.

3. *Determine the constraints:*
In practice, there are constraints—political givens, institutional weakness, constitutional and other legal provisions, limitations on physical resources and production technologies, and budget ceilings—which delimit the set of feasible alternatives and the success with which each can be pursued.

4. *Evaluate the alternatives:*
The implementation of each alternative generates a stream of costs and benefits that accrue over time. For comparative purposes we calculate the costs of the resource inputs (land, labor, and capital) and the benefit of the *socially* valuable outputs (decent shelter, employment income, degree of social and economic integration, and so forth).

5. *The decision rule—choose the optimal strategy:*
A rational choice of a housing policy requires the selection of the strategy alternative for which the net value (benefits minus costs) is highest. In other words, in choosing the optimal strategy, policy makers should try to provide the greatest amount of social welfare possible from the resources allocated to government housing activities.

The Nation's Housing Goals
In any decision process, the choice and evaluation of objectives constitute the point of departure. Thus the national commitment to "a decent home

and a suitable living environment for every American" is the goal against which any housing program must be measured. Inherent in this goal are three standards: a shelter that meets minimum health, safety, and sanitary code requirements; a neighborhood free of blight, secure from crime and violence, and adequately supplied by public services; and an equal opportunity for every household to seek such a shelter and neighborhood in any location, according to its individual needs and preferences.

Most Americans do, in fact, occupy decent homes in suitable living environments and enjoy unrestricted access to a wide variety of housing styles, tenure arrangements, and geographic areas. But there are many families, however, who cannot obtain housing that satisfies the minimum standards set forth in our national housing goal either because of inadequate incomes, discriminatory practices, or institutional barriers. The persistence of physical squalor, even in times of unequaled prosperity, continues to frustrate the designers of federal housing policy. As the search for solutions has evolved, this policy has come to embrace an ever more diverse set of economic, social, and environmental objectives—some explicit in the enabling acts themselves, others implicit in the manner of their execution. These objectives, and their corresponding measures of performance, are outlined in Table 2.1.

For the purpose of our analysis, economic welfare consists of both aggregative and redistributive effects. The government's investment in low-income housing increases real national income (real individual consumption) through its direct and indirect effects on housing consumption, municipal revenue, and employment. Besides contributing to economic growth, these housing investments redistribute income from corporate and higher-bracket taxpayers to the poor.

First among the social benefits to be examined are the changes in housing consumption resulting from the impact of housing programs upon the price and quantity of dwelling units.[3] (See Chapter 3.) Both direct tenant

3. Since the theoretical foundation of the formal decision model is from welfare economics, we examine how each of the economic benefits derives from welfare considerations. In Western nations economic welfare accrues to individuals, not the state. Thus the net social benefit of a particular housing subsidy program is the value, at the time of the decision making, of the net addition to individual consumption which will result from the project. This is the definition of net social benefit (NSB) presented by Martin S. Feldstein, "Net Social Benefit Calculation and Public Investment Decision," *Oxford Economic Papers,* March 1964.

Table 2.1 Major Objectives of Federal Housing Subsidies

Impact of Housing Subsidies	Objectives	Measurements
Economic	Increase aggregate real income (mitigate poverty)	Housing services added
		Municipal services added
		Employment income added
	Redistribute income	Housing services distributed equitably
Social	Enhance consumer sovereignty	Scale of satisfaction
	Encourage fair housing opportunities	Segregation index
	Foster social stability	Sociometric scale
Environmental	Upgrade deteriorated neighborhoods	Fire insurance rates, property assessments, capital investments
	Stabilize neighborhood environment	Vacancy and turnover rates, abandonment
	Decrease social costs of slum living	Crime statistics, morbidity rates, fire damage

benefits and indirect spillover effects on the rest of the housing market are included. The subsidized tenant experiences an improvement in his housing condition (the move from substandard private dwellings to standard public or private housing), a reduction in housing expenditure, and a corresponding increase in his disposable income for nonhousing goods and services. Normally the unit vacated by the subsidized tenant filters down to another low-income family who, in turn, improves its housing consumption. Also, social benefits accrue if the federal assistance increases the supply of standard housing—by inducing either new construction or rehabilitation of an abandoned unit—since theoretically, at least, the equilibrium price of other low-income housing units falls as a result.

The second aggregate measure of social benefit derives from the value added in municipal revenue. (See Chapter 5.) Strengthening the fiscal capacity of central cities—the predominant users of housing programs—tends to offset some of the inefficiencies and inequities that stem from jurisdictional balkanization. Central cities provide services to suburban dwellers without receiving sufficient revenue in compensation; because of the arbitrariness of municipal boundaries, core-city governments also find themselves saddled with the problems of the impoverished and disadvantaged, even though these problems arise from conditions in the same regional economy from which all the residents in a given metropolitan area draw their sustenance and shelter. Moreover, any net additional revenue allows an increase in the level of municipal services—a result normally consistent with the preferences of local consumers.

The final aggregate contribution of housing expenditures to social welfare is the creation of net gains in employment income. (See Chapter 6.) Under full-employment conditions, with only frictional unemployment, the demand for labor generated by the government's housing investments merely shifts workers among jobs without lowering unemployment (that is, without adding any real income). However, when housing programs generate additional demand for idle workers—or provide more stable, higher-paying employment for victims of discrimination, part-time laborers, or other underutilized workers—a genuine social gain occurs. Thus in depressed regions or geographically delimited ghettos characterized by high unemployment, government-assisted housing investments tend to increase aggregate national income.

The income distributional effects are overlooked in the aggregate measures of traditional welfare economics, which implicitly assigns an equal value to each dollar of income added by a government program. Some economists defend this equal valuation by arguing that government fiscal programs, such as housing subsidies, should aim for maximum efficiency, while income redistribution objectives are best accomplished through tax or transfer schemes.[4] But as Stephen Marglin[5] and Arthur Maass[6] point out, communities are not indifferent to the means by which income redistribution is achieved, nor is there a realistic likelihood of enacting an adequate transfer or tax program in the immediate future. On welfare grounds, those families with the most urgent housing need should be selected for

4. This approach, called the Wicksell-Lindahl tradition by Richard A. Musgrave, argues that a more useful theory of public finance can be developed by separating efficiency and equity questions. See Richard A. Musgrave, "Cost-Benefit Analysis and the Theory of Public Finance," *Journal of Economic Literature,* September 1969, pp. 797–806.
5. Stephen Marglin, *Public Investment Criteria* (Cambridge, Mass.: MIT Press, 1967).
6. Arthur Maass, "Benefit-Cost Analysis: Its Relevance to Public Investment," *Quarterly Journal of Economics,* May 1966.

admission, since a marginal dollar of benefit brings more satisfaction (utility, value, worth) to them than to more privileged households. (See Chapter 4.)

In addition to economic objectives, housing subsidies serve a variety of important social and environmental ends as well. (See Chapter 8.) Program performance with respect to these noneconomic objectives has received increasing public recognition in recent years but is difficult to measure, particularly in monetary terms. While the housing census documents that the number of dwelling units lacking full plumbing facilities and having other structural deficiencies has declined continuously over the last twenty years, more inner-city neighborhoods than ever seem to have become uninhabitable—plagued as they are by financial disinvestment and social disruption. This fact has led some critics to claim that the contemporary housing problem is not one of inadequate shelter but of unlivable environments, that housing relief cannot be separated from overall community development, and that any subsidy program that helps upgrade deteriorating neighborhoods, or at least slows down the rate of decline, is contributing to social welfare.[7] Such a contribution—insofar as it takes the form of increased personal security, less drug abuse, greater neighborhood cohesiveness and stability, and so on—is all but impossible to value in monetary amounts yet nonetheless may be worth as much, if not more, than benefits that can be easily measured in dollars and cents.

Common experience suggests that one's physical environment (space, light, air) has some effect on the quality of social relationships, child-rearing practices, and physical and mental health, even if the causal relationships are hard to establish empirically, and the benefits of environmental improvements too elusive to measure. Locational mobility is yet another social objective espoused by national housing legislation that frustrates precise quantification; nevertheless, since equal opportunity to secure a home anywhere throughout a metropolitan housing market determines one's access to jobs, educational opportunities, neighborhood amenities, and other goods and services, any evaluation of housing programs should assess their ability to foster consumer choice and residential integration. Conversely, the isolation of subsidized tenants within concentrated ghetto areas im-

7. See, for example, George Sternlieb and Robert Burchell, *Residential Abandonment: The Tenement Landlord Revisited* (New Brunswick, N.J.: Transaction Books, 1973).

poses costs on society as a whole as well as on the tenants themselves. Tight housing market conditions and neighborhood (or suburban) resistance have often undermined efforts to disperse subsidized units, yet the ability of housing policies to promote equal residential opportunities, and thereby relieve impacted areas, is an important welfare contribution.

Strategies for Housing the Urban Poor

National housing objectives, once identified in operational terms, must be the basis for selecting an optimal strategy (or combination of strategies) for their attainment. There are at least five major alternative housing strategies:

1. Eliminate all federal government support for housing, and rely solely on the private market.
2. Abolish direct federal housing subsidies, but retain favorable income tax and mortgage-insurance provisions.
3. Continue to rely on new construction programs for the poor.
4. Develop subsidies for using the existing housing stock such as direct consumer subsidies or management and maintenance incentives.
5. Develop a mixture of subsidies for new construction and use of the existing stock.

Elimination of Government Subsidies

The first alternative calls for the elimination of all subsidies, direct and indirect, including favorable income tax provisions and mortgage-insurance programs. Surprisingly, this alternative, which reflects total distrust of federal involvement, emanates from both extremes of the political spectrum. Conservatives such as Edward Banfield [8] complain that insofar as housing subsidies, urban renewal, and other forms of government "meddling" have any effect whatsoever, it is to aggravate the very problems they are supposed to solve. Banfield would argue that the "so-called" housing crisis is, in fact, largely nonexistent and that whatever residual problems may remain are solvable, if at all, through the natural workings of the private market.

Radical critics, on the other hand, contend that housing ills are deeply rooted in our present economic system, based as it is on the concentration

8. See Edward C. Banfield, *The Unheavenly City* (Boston: Little, Brown, 1970), pp. 14–16.

of property and the means of production in the hands of a few. Little use is seen in treating a symptom while the disease remains.[9] Radicals contend that the state is merely an instrument of capitalist interests so that government activities will necessarily profit those in control at the expense of those in need.

While agreeing with the radical critique that the solution to housing problems is ultimately bound up with more fundamental issues such as the maldistribution of wealth and income, I would still argue that—pending a political millennium—some government action is better than none, even if the treatment is merely palliative, the relief stopgap, and the results insufficient. Indeed, ministering to symptoms is often the humane imperative when the ambulance is nowhere in sight and major surgery must be postponed. As for the conservative case, one need only note that the government originally entered the housing field with reluctance and only after serious and chronic deficiencies in the private market had shown no evidence of healing themselves. Since the first decision to intervene, government housing activities—no matter how inefficient, wasteful, and, at times, even corrupt—have demonstrably improved living conditions for millions of households. Moreover, government intervention finds support in the notion that housing is a merit good[10]—like education and medical care—which should at least meet the minimum standards embodied in municipal building, health, and housing codes. Since housing supplied by the private market does not always meet these minimal standards, collective action is justified.

Also, housing generates significant side effects or spillovers not fully reflected in market prices. The provision of better housing for the poor, for example, can generate additional housing improvements while reducing the social cost of blight.[11] A further rationale for public action derives from the existence of housing market imperfections. Discrimination, restrictive zoning, and collusive real estate practices limit the free flow of information

9. Although not a radical himself, Michael Stegman has articulated this view in a recent article. See Michael A. Stegman, "The New Mythology of Housing," Society, Vol. 7, No. 3 (January 1970).
10. Richard Musgrave has justified government activity that assists in meeting the minimum standards as the provision of a merit good. See Richard A. Musgrave, The Theory of Public Finance (New York: McGraw-Hill Book Co., 1959), pp. 13–55.
11. For an account of the social externalities created by slum housing, see Jerome Rothenberg, Economic Evaluation of Urban Renewal (Washington, D.C.: Brookings Institution, 1967).

and accessibility, two necessary prerequisites for an efficient housing market. Much economic and racial stratification is the direct consequence of explicit institutional and real estate practices, which accounts for some of the differences in prices paid for the same quality of housing and residential services.

Relying on the Filtering Process
The second alternative—the elimination of direct federal subsidies for low- and moderate-income housing, but retention of favorable tax laws for the affluent—relies entirely on the "trickle-down" process to provide shelter for the poor. All new construction would be for households in the upper half of the income scale, while those of poor or moderate means would upgrade their housing by moving into the units previously occupied by higher-income families. Although it is true that the normal turnover of housing improves the quality of shelter for many low-income households, a number of recent studies reveal basic shortcomings in the filtering or trickle-down process as a strategy for improving the living conditions of the poor.

Bernard Frieden, in an article on housing and national urban goals, reviewed the spatial aspects of the filtering strategy.[12] As a large number of middle-income people moved from the central city to new suburban developments in the 1950s and 1960s, the units they vacated were occupied by lower-income whites, blacks, and other minorities. This led to increasing segregation of the population along racial and economic lines and left the core cities with a multiplicity of employment, fiscal, health, education, and other problems. As Frieden concludes, it is fair to say that this approach to the national housing problem causes or, at least, exacerbates many of our other urban problems. Other limitations of the filtering process were cited in two recent empirical studies, which suggest that the segmentation of local urban housing markets along racial and class lines prevents the full benefits of housing turnovers to reach the black poor or other inner-city residents. Lansing, Clifton, and Morgan provide well-documented evidence from their surveys that new construction opens up some improved housing for

12. Bernard J. Frieden, "Housing and National Urban Goals: Old Policies and New Realities," in James Q. Wilson, ed., *The Metropolitan Enigma* (Cambridge, Mass.: Harvard University Press, 1968).

poor whites, but that blacks improve their housing conditions much less than their incomes would lead one to expect.[13] Similarly, Brueggeman, Raester, and Smith, in a study of various housing programs in Columbus, Ohio, found that the higher the value of the new homes built in the suburbs—where most new housing is located—the smaller the proportion of units experiencing turnover in the inner city.[14] Higher-income households usually vacate units in the suburbs, and, for the most part, the chain of moves triggered by new construction peters out before reaching central-city residents. Thus, whatever role the filtering process may play in metropolitan housing markets as a whole, it has dubious value as a strategy designed to aid urban families concentrated in the older neighborhoods of central cities. Moreover, even this residual value continues to decline as the locus of new construction follows the sprawl of the urban fringe in its advance outward into the open countryside.

Subsidizing New Construction for the Poor

The third strategy—subsidizing the cost of new construction—has been the approach traditionally adopted by the federal government—for example, through its direct mortgage subsidies and land write-downs (as in conventional public housing and Section 236 developments); its efforts to encourage new construction technology (such as Operation Breakthrough), to unify local building codes, and to promote land banking; and its secondary mortgage operations. All these activities aim at reducing the price for the basic factors of production—labor, land, materials, and capital. Those who favor subsidies for the direct construction of low- and moderate-income housing claim such an approach serves several critical ends:[15]

—Expansion of the total supply to relieve pent-up housing demand and help keep prices from rising;

—Dispersal of poor families throughout the metropolitan area, particularly

---

13. John Lansing, Charles W. Clifton, and James N. Morgan, *New Homes and Poor People* (Ann Arbor: Survey Research Center, Institute for Social Research, University of Michigan, 1969).

14. William B. Brueggeman, Ronald L. Raester, and Halbert C. Smith, "Multiple Housing Programs and Urban Housing Policy," *Journal of American Institute of Planners*, May 1972.

15. See Anthony Downs, "Federal Housing Subsidies: Their Nature and Effectiveness and What We Should Do About Them: Summary Report" (Chicago: Real Estate Research Corporation, October 1972), processed.

in those rapidly growing suburbs having few available units on the market;
—Creation of certain types of units not available in the existing inventory
and, without subsidies, unlikely to be built by private developers;
—Stimulation of increased construction activity and maintenance of employment in the building trades;
—Provision of dramatic, highly visible upgrading in older deteriorated
areas as a spur to private reinvestment.
Defenders of federally assisted construction programs premise their case on
the debatable assumption that the availability of subsidies actually increases production above levels that would prevail in their absence. More
skeptical observers maintain that subsidized housing starts merely replace
building activity that would have otherwise occurred, in effect, shifting
laborers, machinery, capital, and entrepreneurial energy from purely private to publicly supported developments. Thus, in debating the efficacy of
construction, it is the *net* impact of federal policy that emerges as the major
area of contention. And, as previously noted, macroeconomists have just
begun to research this issue.

Using the Existing Stock
If the government chooses to move toward a demand-side approach, the
fourth housing strategy alternative, it could enhance the purchasing power
of the poor in several ways: by subsidizing the actual rents paid by low-
income tenants (as in the public housing leasing program); by providing
a general income maintenance subsidy (an unearmarked cash transfer);
or by making available an earmarked income transfer for housing (a restricted cash transfer through housing allowances, rent certificates, or rent
vouchers). Advocates of demand- or consumer-oriented strategies argue that
cash transfers or housing allowances would offer several distinct advantages
when compared to existing production subsidies:
—They would be less costly since tax shelters, developer profits, and increases in municipal service requirements would no longer be involved.
—With fewer administrative intermediaries, more of the subsidy dollars
would actually reach the target households.
—The choice of housing type, structural quality, and location would be left
with the individual beneficiary.
—The increased rental payments would promote better use of the existing

housing stock, by offering inducements to landlords to upgrade their structures, and thereby reduce housing deterioration and abandonment.
—They would overcome many of the hurdles blocking the construction of subsidized units in the suburbs and thus offer a greater potential for the geographic dispersal of the poor.
—They are more equitable and less politically explosive for local communities.

Demand subsidies contain an implicit argument for conserving the existing housing stock and stabilizing demand in otherwise declining areas. Yet the use of housing allowances, rent certificates, or other consumer-oriented strategies assumes a reasonably competitive housing market in which landlords will respond to higher rental payments by improving their housing units. A critical question, then, is whether or not landlords will respond as predicted or will merely raise prices instead.

A Mixture of Programs
The fifth and final of the strategy alternatives is to adopt a mixture of housing programs. Given the range of federal housing objectives, some contend that it is unrealistic to assume that any single strategy will be preferable for all housing market conditions, for all phases of the economic cycle, and for all geographic locations. Such a perspective might argue for special revenue sharing for housing programs, with each state and local community choosing a complement of housing and community development activities best suited to its own circumstances.

Policy Constraints
In theory, rational decision makers can maximize benefits at a given cost through the choice of appropriate housing policies. In practice, however, a variety of institutional, financial, legal, and political constraints prevent federal housing programs from achieving policy objectives in an optimal manner.

One of those constraints is the availability of land. For example, in most central cities, particularly the older ones, little vacant land remains for new multidwelling construction. Available sites are limited by established patterns of land use, neighborhood resistance to public housing projects, and the controversy that often accompanies the use of eminent domain powers.

On the other hand, it is questionable whether construction labor constitutes a real constraint. During the short run, labor shortages may occur in specific skilled trades in particular localities, but over longer periods the construction labor force normally adjusts in response to changing demand. Estimating the short-term labor constraint in a single construction subsector (for example, high-rise residential) in a single central city presents difficult conceptual and empirical problems. These problems arise from considerations of both the supply and demand for construction manpower. On the supply side, we confront several definitions of the construction labor force.[16] While one can make an assumption about the most appropriate definition, it is extremely difficult to account for geographic, occupational, and industrial mobility. There is little empirical knowledge regarding labor flows into and out of the construction industry, between the major construction sectors, and among local labor markets. And actual measurement of the cross-elasticities of supply is limited. Statistical series on mobility, employment, and unemployment by craft are nonexistent, and the ability to project changes in labor productivity is minimal.

Establishing the labor constraint for residential rehabilitation is even more complex than for new construction. While the product is just as heterogeneous, there is even less information about labor supply requirements. The relationship with other construction sectors is limited. As an industry, residential rehabilitation is weakly organized, in most cities dominated by small nonunion specialty firms. The absence of a formal industrial relations system, work rules, or institutionalized entry ports further discourages us from predicting future labor conditions.

The most binding constraint on housing subsidy programs, however, is the annual federal budgetary appropriation. Labor and land constraints may be binding in the short run, but theoretically, at least, they can be removed whenever the government is willing to pay the necessary price for

16. Anyone who has read John T. Dunlop and D. Quinn Mills, "Manpower Construction: A Profile of the Industry and Projections to 1975," in the *Report of the President's Committee on Urban Housing*, Vol. 2 (Washington, D.C.: U.S. Government Printing Office, 1968), will recognize my indebtedness to their analysis of construction manpower. They indicate that one can define the construction labor force as the current employees of construction contractors, the unemployed whose last job was in construction, persons with building trade skills working in other occupations, those reporting any earnings in contract construction, or workers whose longest period of employment during the year was in the construction sector.

attracting enough craftsmen or purchasing adequate sites. As Samuelson points out in his basic economics text, these constraints, as experienced by a single producer, are not ones of supply or capacity but of cost.[17] On the other hand, the annual appropriation is a binding constraint, since we assume that dollar scarcities will continue to be the rule throughout the economic life of federal housing programs. Exceedingly high mortgage interest rates discourage private construction and, in turn, limit the number of possible rent supplement or leasing units in new private developments. And federally regulated ceilings on the interest rate associated with long-term serial bonds may prevent a local housing authority from borrowing development capital and thus frustrate plans to construct public housing.

Other institutional, political, and financial constraints further circumscribe the feasible policy choices. For example, community demands for construction jobs pose legitimate issues whose resolution can dilute economic efficiency, since the training and supervision of unskilled laborers generally entails higher construction costs, at least over the short run. Institutional factors such as the categorical nature of federally assisted housing programs, or the limited capabilities of LHA personnel, can also inhibit the optimal allocation of federal housing appropriations.

Financial realities comprise yet another set of boundary conditions, as is the case with limitations on the availability of mortgage capital. With conventional public housing, for example, the semiannually adjusted ceiling on the interest rate associated with long-term serial bonds may prevent the housing authority from offering a rate of return competitive enough to attract the investment funds needed to finance new projects. On the other hand, exceedingly high mortgage interest rates, or a shortage of mortgage capital, may very well discourage private construction, thereby limiting the number of FHA mortgage-insured units.

Evaluating the Alternative Strategies
The policy contraints reviewed in the last section establish the limitations within which housing strategies are implemented. Once the respective strategies are carried out, they generate a stream of benefits and costs which provide the basis for our comparative analysis.

17. Samuelson refers to this situation as the "fallacy of composition." See Paul A. Samuelson, *Economics*, 8th ed. (New York: McGraw-Hill Book Co., 1970), pp. 11–12.

The theoretical foundation for the benefit-cost model used in our analysis is derived from traditional welfare economics; the model is normative rather than behavioral or descriptive and is intended to facilitate the systematic evaluation of alternative housing policies. Specifically, the model tells us how a purely private market system would allocate housing appropriations and examines the extent to which this solution represents the economic welfare optimum.[18] Properly used, it can prescribe the single housing strategy (or mix of strategies) most likely to maximize social benefits within any given budgetary constraint.

The basic structure of the decision model is straightforward. Housing programs are viewed as alternative production processes, with each program using a variety of inputs (land, labor, and capital) to produce certain socially valuable outputs (standard housing, municipal revenue, and employment opportunity). A decision is seen as a choice among this set of feasible production alternatives, delimited by a set of constraints (such as physical resources, production technologies, congressional funding, and legal prohibitions). The choice proceeds from the evaluation of both output (social benefits) and input (resource costs) for each alternative followed by the application of a rational economic criterion for selecting the optimum combination of programs.[19] Although set forth in linear programming terms, the existence of only one binding constraint allows for the use of a benefit-cost calculation.

The approach used in this analysis differs from the traditional welfare model in several respects. First, while most benefit-cost models rank programs only in terms of their economic efficiency or contributions to aggregate national income, this model incorporates other public policy goals as well—above all, equity considerations such as the redistribution of income to low-income groups. Second, the study goes beyond previous attempts to attach a higher social value to the benefits received by specific subgroups;

18. In this study "economic welfare" is defined as the difference between the present value of the economic benefits associated with the housing programs' output and the present value of the associated input costs.
19. For a detailed theoretical explication of the public expenditure approach, see Otto Eckstein, "A Survey of the Theory of Public Investment Criteria," in James M. Buchanan, Public Finances: Needs, Sources and Utilization (Princeton, N.J.: Princeton University Press, 1961), and Richard Zeckhauser and Elmer Schaefer, "Public Policy and Normative Economic Theory," in Raymond A. Bauer and Kenneth J. Gergen, eds., The Study of Policy Formation (New York: The Free Press, 1968).

weighting schemes have generally relied on a single attribute—the recipient's income—while the present methodology uses several additional characteristics (race, family size) to determine a distributive weight. As a result, the model is better attuned to assessing program performance with respect to congressional directives and federal regulations specifying that federal housing programs are intended to benefit not simply those of low income but those who are *most* disadvantaged in the private housing market.

Third, while the formal model is confined to economic measures of benefits and costs, program effects not amenable to quantification have been added to the analysis to account for the fact that policy makers consider both economic and noneconomic objectives in their decisions, for example, racial and economic dispersal or environmental impact.[20]

Measuring Housing Policy Performance: Benefits and Costs

BENEFITS

The economic benefit attributable to any particular housing strategy is represented as the value of the net addition to individual consumption that results from its implementation. Government investment in low-income housing increases real national income (aggregate real individual consumption) through its direct and indirect effects on housing consumption (see Chapter 3), municipal services (see Chapter 5), and employment income (see Chapter 6). To this end, we apply a distributive weight—based on the socioeconomic characteristics of the tenants served—to the consumption benefit of each housing program. (See Chapter 4.) [21] The respective distributions of housing benefits, then, are used to weight the aggregate social benefits of each program. Since a nation's economic welfare involves the distribution as well as the magnitude of its national income, integrating the efficiency (aggregative) and equity (redistributive) objectives yields a more appropriate measure of national economic welfare. The gross contribution of housing programs to national economic welfare, then, can be expressed as

20. By restricting the formal model to economic benefits, I do not mean to minimize the relative importance of social and environmental factors but only to limit the formal model to factors of dollar value. For the other benefits an ordinal scale is developed (see Chapter 8).

21. For each program we establish weights that reflect the probability that an average subsidized tenant would live in substandard housing in the absence of government assistance.

$$B^G = (1 + X)B^H + B^M + B^E \qquad\qquad (2.1)$$

where

B^G = the gross economic benefit of a housing program,

X = the distributive weight on housing consumption (Chapter 4),

B^H = the housing consumption benefit (Chapter 3),

B^M = the municipal service consumption benefit (Chapter 5),

B^E = the employment income consumption benefit (Chapter 6).

COSTS

On the cost side of the equation, it is important to understand the basic distinction made by economists between social (or opportunity) cost and contractual cost.[22] Social cost is the overall cost to society of a particular resource use, as valued in terms of the alternative uses to which it could have been put (that is, the amount that users of displaced goods or services would have been willing to pay for the goods or services forgone). Contractual costs, on the other hand, are actual payments between a buyer and a seller.

In an ideal market situation (one characterized by perfect competition, mobility, and free access to information), the social value of a given resource is equivalent to its market price. But where the market is imperfect or nonexistent, disparities may emerge between the market price and the social value of a resource and therefore between any given program's opportunity and contractual costs. For example, where slum dwellings generate negative spillovers (fire hazards, family disorganization, crime), collective and private interests differ, and the market price of the property may well exceed its social value.[23]

The social cost that results from the disparity between private and collective interest may be best addressed through government action. But federal

22. See any of the public expenditure analysis literature, such as Feldstein, "Net Social Benefit Calculation"; Stephen A. Marglin, "The Opportunity Cost of Public Investment," *Quarterly Journal of Economics,* May 1963; Otto Eckstein, "A Survey of the Theory of Public Investment Criteria," in Buchanan, ed., *Public Finances.*
23. For a detailed discussion of the social costs of deteriorated housing, see Jerome Rothenberg, "Urban Renewal Programs," in Robert Dorfman, ed., *Measuring Benefits of Government Investments* (Washington, D.C.: Brookings Institution, 1965), pp. 306–307.

expenditures also involve social costs. Taxation and the sale of bonds (the primary sources of federal funding) lead to a reduction in household consumption and a decline in corporate investment and hence to forgone opportunities in the private sector. Moreover, the displacement of alternative government programs by a particular resource allocation results in unrealized consumer benefits.[24] To determine the effectiveness of government intervention, then, it is necessary to estimate the social as well as the contractual costs of federal financing. (See Chapter 7.) In general, if the benefits of a program exceed the social or opportunity cost, government investment in that program represents an efficient use of resources. If, on the other hand, the economic benefits generated by a housing investment fall below its opportunity or social cost, then capital would be more efficiently allocated if it remained in the private sector.[25]

Looking specifically at the resource inputs for federally subsidized housing—capital, labor, and land—we note some disparities between social and market prices. Because the market for building supplies is reasonably competitive, the price of materials and equipment used in subsidized housing reflects their social value. In the case of labor, however, there is often a divergence between social and contractual costs. When pockets of local unemployment or underemployment exist or when construction activity is slack, for example, the social cost of hiring underutilized labor is less than the prevailing wage. In depressed regions, then, the cost to society of constructing new housing falls below the nominal development cost. On the other hand, during periods of high construction activity and labor shortage, the wages of skilled craftsmen are less than their social value, since the levels of compensation are fixed for several years under collective bargaining agreements.

Finally, the market value of low-rent housing projects on urban land is usually lower than the value of the site and improvements in its alternative private use. This means that in the absence of federally assisted housing

24. The satisfaction or benefits of public projects depend on both the direct increases in the consumption of individual project tenants and the indirect increases in the consumption of others due to the private investment induced by project outputs.
25. When a budget constraint exists, the social value of a dollar of government expenditure usually exceeds the value of a dollar in private use. Where this is not the case, the government should tax the private sector until the marginal social value of a dollar of government expenditure equals the marginal social value of the forgone private expenditure.

the land parcels would yield a higher property tax payment to the city. Social costs are included in our discussion because a conceptually meaningful model should take into account the overall costs of housing programs to society at large. These overall costs can be categorized into federal and associated expenditures (private as well as state and local government):

$$C^G = C^F + C^A \tag{2.2}$$

where

C^G = the gross economic cost of a housing program,

C^F = the federal government expenditures (Chapter 7),

C^A = the nonfederal or associated expenditures (Chapter 7).

The Decision Rule

So far, the model has been presented in a static manner, as if all costs and benefits occur in the same year. However, since federal housing programs generate streams of benefits and commit resources for the future, it is necessary to bring intertemporal considerations into the analysis. This is accomplished by selecting an interest rate that reflects the relative social value of marginal output and resource inputs at different points in time.

The social discount concept, which has been embraced by most economists, as well as the Joint Economic Committee of Congress, uses an interest rate reflecting the opportunity cost of displaced private spending.[26] Because it implies that investments in the public sector have to yield at least as high a rate of return as the funds would otherwise have earned in the private sector, this approach is consistent with welfare economic criteria. Since the funds drawn from the private sector for public investments involve both forgone investment and consumption, the opportunity cost must represent some weighted average of the two.

The actual cost of displaced private spending depends on the method of government financing—whether, in fact, public revenues are obtained through taxation or borrowing. In either case, the ultimate source of government funds must be traced so that we can estimate the rates of return

26. Report of the Subcommittee on Economy in Government, Joint Economic Committee, U.S. Congress, *Economic Analysis of Public Investment Decisions: Interest Rate Policy and Discounting Analysis* (Washington, D.C.: U.S. Government Printing Office, 1968).

on the forgone uses. For funds withdrawn from private investment, the respective rates of return are calculated in the affected sectors, while forgone consumption is valued at the interest rate used by households in their saving-spending behavior. The social discount rate, itself, represents a weighted average of those rates found applicable in the relevant private consumption and investment sectors.

By estimating the opportunity cost of displaced private investment and spending, we implicitly enter into the analysis the weighted average allowance for risk and uncertainty used in the private sector. Since we cannot establish probabilities for each possible outcome, we rely on the private sector's recognition of uncertainty, as well as our own sensitivity testing with a range of interest rates and time horizons.

The final task is to establish a decision rule (or test of preferredness) for comparing and ranking alternative housing strategies. If the costs and benefits of all housing programs could be valued in terms of a single unit of measure, such as dollars, it would be possible to make objective decisions on the basis of public expenditure efficiency criteria. We could compare, for example, the discounted present value of the benefit-cost ratios of the various housing strategies. Alternatively, it is possible to rank strategies by their net contribution to economic welfare (gross benefits minus gross costs) subject to the limitation of federal budgetary dollars. This welfare economic decision rule—ranking programs according to their net benefit per dollar of scarce federal funds—is a convenient approximation to the standard maximization problem and can be expressed as

$$\lambda = \frac{B^G - C^G}{C^F}$$

$$= \frac{[(1 + X)B^H + B^M + B^E] - (C^F + C^A)}{C^F} \tag{2.3}$$

The foregoing benefit-cost calculation ranks alternative housing strategies in terms of their economic efficiency or contribution to aggregate national income. Much of our comparative analysis reflects this traditional welfare economic approach. However, our analysis is not confined to economic criteria since federal housing subsidies have many social and environmental as well as economic objectives. (See Table 2.1.) Because the measurement of these noneconomic objectives is seldom amenable to quantification, non-dollar-valued effects are usually omitted from public expenditure analysis. Yet this is inappropriate since the effects of housing programs on racial and economic segregation, neighborhood stability, and environmental conditions are at least as important as, if not more important than, their relative economic efficiency. For a meaningful policy analysis, then, it is necessary to supplement the formal benefit-cost evaluation with a qualitative assessment as well. Since most of the social and environmental effects do not lend themselves to a market valuation, we compare their performance on the basis of an ordinal ranking scheme. The inclusion of this type of qualitative analysis means that the various measures of program performance are incommensurable (for example, how much racial integration can be traded off for each additional dollar of housing consumption). Therefore, it is impossible to formulate a determinate decision rule. In this situation each decision maker has to establish his own subjective weighting scheme for comparing and ranking the alternative strategies. It is the purpose of our analysis to facilitate this effort by making the social, environmental, and economic trade-offs as explicit as possible.

Technical Note: An Exposition of the Formal Welfare Economics Model
In this technical appendix the basic structure of the traditional welfare economics model is outlined. We provide an operational definition of economic welfare in the production of housing and examine the constraints which delimit a solution. Finally, we discuss the interest rate, time horizon, and decision rule appropriate for such a model.

The Production Function: Benefits and Costs
The objective or production function expresses the net social benefit (or economic welfare) contributed by each program. As Bergson[27] has suggested, the function for social economic welfare can be expressed as

$$W = \sum_{i=1}^{n} W_i, \tag{2.4}$$

where

27. Abram Bergson, "A Reformulation of Certain Aspects of Welfare Economics," *Quarterly Journal of Economics,* February 1968.

where

C_i^F = the gross economic cost of federal expenditures that accrue to individual i,[30]

C_i^A = the gross economic cost of associated expenditures that accrue to individual i.

The annual federal project cost consists of capital and operating expenditures. We represent these cost factors as follows:

$$C^F = \sum O_i^F + K_i^F, \tag{2.10}$$

where

O_i^F = the annual federal operation and maintenance cost for individual i,

K_i^F = the annual federal capital cost (principal and interest payment) for individual i.

The associated cost, required to make federal housing programs available, includes costs to state and local government as well as private expenditures and can be written as

$$C^A = \sum_{i=1}^{n} \left(O_i^P + K_i^P + O_i^L + K_i^L + T_i^F \right), \tag{2.11}$$

where

O_i^P = the annual private operating and maintenance cost for individual i,

K_i^P = the annual private capital cost for individual i,

O_i^L = the annual state and local government operating and maintenance cost for individual i,

K_i^L = the annual state and local government capital cost for individual i,

T_i^F = the annual federal forgone tax revenue—due to exemptions, accelerated depreciation provisions, and abatements—which results in real costs for individual i.

---

30. Since it is only the welfare of individuals that concerns us, we express the cost of federal housing projects in terms of the individuals upon whom the incidence of federal tax or debt revenue ultimately falls.

The Constraints

In a traditional linear programming model, the resource constraints are represented as factor inputs: land, labor, and capital.[31] For computational purposes, one can assume linear constraints or, in other words, fixed input coefficients for any given program. One should assume, however, that the input coefficients are fixed *only* for a particular central city at a particular time. For any location outside the designated central city (including suburbs within the same metropolitan area) or for any other time, the coefficients would be adjusted to reflect changes in technology, production techniques, or relative supply costs. Otherwise, the choice of fixed input coefficients for public construction seems reasonable, because of the fixed dollar ceilings per dwelling unit and the standard specifications for materials, prevailing wage rates, and other relatively stable construction conditions.[32] The notation for the factor input constraints is as follows:

LAND

The effect of land scarcity as a limitation on the production of subsidized dwelling units can be expressed as

$$\sum_{j=1}^{n} A_j \leqslant D, \tag{2.12}$$

where

A_j = a site of sufficient land area for the construction of one minimum size (a minimum of 100 units) development of federal program j,

D = the total number of sufficient-size development sites in the city for program j.

LABOR

In practice, for the reasons elaborated earlier in the text of this chapter, we are unable to measure the labor constraint; however, the formal concept of such a measurement can be expressed symbolically as

31. The amount of rehabilitation is also limited by the number of existing substandard dwelling units. But since there are large numbers of dilapidated or deteriorated dwellings within most of the nation's older central cities, we assume this is not a real constraint on program size.
32. Fixed input coefficients approximate the constraints on new construction more closely than those of rehabilitation, since rehabilitation requirements may vary substantially from dwelling to dwelling.

$$\sum_{j=1}^{n} \sum_{k=1}^{n} b_{kj} \leqslant L_k, \tag{2.13}$$

where

b_{kj} = the number of craftsmen of craft k necessary to construct or rehabilitate one dwelling unit of program j,

L_k = the total number of craftsmen available in craft k at a specific time in a particular city.

CAPITAL

Assuming, for purposes of simplification, that a city receives a single federal block grant for low-income housing programs rather than separate categorical grants,[33] one can express the budgetary constraint as

$$\sum_{j=1}^{n} C_j^F \leqslant Y, \tag{2.14}$$

when

C_j^F = the annual federal expenditure for debt service, rent assistance, administration costs, and other housing subsidies for one dwelling unit of project j in a given city,

Y = the annual federal budgetary appropriation allocated for a given city's low-income housing.

Interest Rates, Discounting, and Time Horizons

So far, our discussion of performance measures has been presented in a static manner, as if all costs and benefits occur in the same year. However, since federal housing programs generate streams of benefits and commit resources for future years, it is necessary to allow for the relative social value of resource inputs and marginal outputs at different points in time. Capital costs can be expressed in terms of level annual interest and amortization charges, but other costs, such as forgone federal revenue from accelerated depreciation, vary over a program's life, and still others, such as land write-downs, are incurred only once. Similarly, the

---

33. The categorical nature of federally assisted housing programs can itself be a constraint that limits the optimal allocation of resources.

value of program benefits, such as municipal revenue and services added, may fluctuate over time.[34]

Public expenditure analysis generally either uses a social discount rate to give future benefits and costs at present value or relies on the benefits and costs of a typical or average year. Because of the uncertainty inherent in any projections of operating expenses and consumer benefits, this analysis will use estimates of benefits and costs for an average year.

The Decision Rule

Having outlined the structure of the decision model, we must now establish a decision rule to rank alternative housing programs.

As in traditional normative economic studies, the decision rule reflects welfare considerations as well as the constraints and timing of benefits and costs. Programs are ranked by their net contribution to economic welfare—that is, by the difference between the money value of benefit streams and the costs incurred in their production. Thus the rule is to maximize the net social benefit of low-income housing programs, within the limits imposed by the availability of federal funds. We express this rule as

$$\lambda = \sum_{i=1}^{n} \sum_{t=1}^{T} \frac{B_{it} - (C_{it}^{F} + C_{it}^{A})}{C_{it}^{F}}, \tag{2.15}$$

where

λ = the net social benefit per dollar of federal budgetary funds,

B_{it} = the weighted economic benefit of the housing program to individual i in time t,

C_{it}^{F} = the economic cost of federal expenditures to individual i in time t,

C_{it}^{A} = the economic cost of associated expenditures to individual i in time t.

By separating federal project from associated costs, one is able to place in the denominator those project expenditures subject to the federal budget constraint—as a result maximizing the net benefits per dollar of scarce resources.

34. See John Krutilla and Otto Eckstein, *Multiple Purpose River Development* (Baltimore: Johns Hopkins Press, 1958); William J. Baumol, "On The Discount Rate for Public Projects," in *The Analysis and Evaluation of Public Expenditures: The PPB System;* Report of the Subcommittee on Economy in Government, *Interest Rate Policy and Discounting Analysis,* pp. 12–15.

CHAPTER 3

Improving Housing Conditions

According to the official national goal, every American household which
does not enjoy "a decent home and a suitable environment" is part of
the housing problem. Unfortunately, this statement utterly fails to convey the appalling living conditions which give the housing problem such
overriding urgency to millions of poor Americans. In fact, most Americans have no conception of the filth, degradation, squalor, overcrowding,
and personal danger and insecurity which millions of inadequate housing units are causing in both our cities and rural areas. Thousands of
infants are attacked by rats each year; hundreds die or become men-
tally retarded from eating lead paint that falls off cracked walls. . . .
Anthony Downs,
"Moving Toward Realistic Housing Goals,"
Agenda for the Nation

Housing conditions for the average citizen have steadily improved over the
last three decades largely as a result of rising real incomes, a high volume of
new housing construction, and an impressive amount of renovation. Since
the end of the Second World War the net supply of standard dwellings has
increased by 80.7 percent, far outstripping the 35 percent growth in population over the same period. The number of units needed to replace substandard housing—that is, housing which is physically dilapidated, lacks
hot water or complete plumbing facilities—had plummeted from 17.0 million in 1950 to 6.9 million by 1970, and the proportion of households living
in substandard housing, from 36.9 to 9.9 percent.[1] Moreover, our concept
of what constitutes a decent housing standard has expanded from a simple
"roof over the head" to a still minimal, but nonetheless heightened, expectation that includes indoor plumbing, central heat, full kitchen facilities,
and certain social and environmental requisites. The measures of progress
cited above incorporate these heightened expectations in the standards
they employ.

Middle- and upper-income families, in particular, have savored the fruits
of improved housing conditions. In the last five years alone, nearly three
million single-family homes were built for households in these higher-
income groups, located mainly toward the fringe of central cities and sub-

1. The foregoing data are from Anthony Downs, "Moving Toward Realistic Housing
Goals," in Kermit Gordon, ed., *Agenda for the Nation* (Washington, D.C.: Brookings
Institution, 1968).

urbs. Luxury apartment complexes now dot the landscape in and around all our major urban centers.

Although private enterprise has accounted for most of this housing development, government policy has offered hidden subsidies and significant incentives for new construction and homeownership through its mortgage guarantees, secondary credit facilities, and preferential tax treatment. In computing his federal income tax, for example, the private homeowner may deduct interest and property tax payments; and he is not required to report the imputed value of rent as a part of his income.

Despite this nation's remarkable housing production record and the relatively high living standards enjoyed by the vast majority of its citizens, we have made little progress in providing the poor and near poor with decent housing at rents and prices they can afford. Apologists for our past and present programs might point to the 2.4 million people sheltered by the public housing program since the 1930s and to the 100,000 units a year that are made available through such low-rent programs as rent supplements and leased housing. But the social and environmental acceptability of public housing is questionable at best, and the 200,000 units per annum provided in recent years under other subsidy programs house only a small fraction of the persons needing assistance. Still worse, under many subsidy programs, the most impoverished families have been virtually excluded.[2] An increasing number of low-income families in urban areas must, by necessity, spend more than a reasonable share of their income for rent in order to obtain acceptable shelter, particularly elderly citizens with fixed incomes vulnerable to inflation. In addition, urban renewal and other community development programs ostensibly designed to aid the poor have resulted in showcase plazas and spectacular business-apartment complexes for the rich and only residential dislocation for the poor.[3] Through highway construction, code enforcement, "equivalent eliminations" and demolitions on and near public housing sites,[4] urban renewal and other programs, government

2. This fact has been documented in many studies of federal housing programs. See, for example, the statistics on recipient characteristics presented in the Kaiser Commission Report, *A Decent Home* (Washington, D.C.: U.S. Government Printing Office, 1968).
3. The Douglas Commission estimated that under urban renewal there has been a net loss of 400,000 low-income units.
4. Under its enabling legislation the U.S. Housing Act of 1937 stated that for every public housing unit built a substantially equal number of unsafe or insanitary housing units had to be eliminated.

action has destroyed more housing for the poor than it has built. These facts offer a convincing and widely recognized rationale for redirected government and private action to improve the housing welfare of the poor.

Thus one of the explicit objectives—or, from a more cynical perspective, one of the ostensible justifications—of federal housing subsidies has been to improve the living conditions of the poor by directly constructing new low- and moderate-income housing. The Eighty-First Congress passed the National Housing Act of 1949, expressing the national housing objective in an oft-repeated phrase, for "the realization as soon as feasible of the goal of a decent home and suitable living environment for every American family." This same goal justified the passage of the Housing and Urban Development Act of 1968. The National Commission on Urban Problems emphasized that its fulfillment is not an abstract fancy but a "moral requirement for the Nation."

Expressing a worthy objective is easy enough; power conflicts and antagonistic self-interests are readily submerged in rhetoric but display an uncanny ability to frustrate substantive action. As we have seen, the critical difficulty for housing, as for any public policy, is to choose among competing strategy alternatives and to design and implement effective programs. Today—after more than forty years of federal intervention in the housing sector, and decades after improved shelter for the poor first received recognition as a legitimate objective of public policy—widespread misunderstanding remains as to the impact of housing subsidies upon the housing welfare of the poor. And despite the flood of housing literature since the urban crisis was "discovered," few satisfactory analyses of the aggregate effect of federally assisted programs have appeared. This is not entirely surprising, given the difficult theoretical and practical problems inhibiting such an analysis. Still, if we hope to alleviate the housing burden of the poor, we must first understand the impact that new construction, rehabilitation, and the leasing of housing units have on urban housing markets and consequently on low-income housing consumption.[5] We need to develop an

5. We define "housing consumption" in terms of the housing goods and services a household receives when it rents or purchases a home: a particular location, neighborhood environment, quality of schooling and other municipal services, as well as the specific physical structure. One unit of housing service is that quantity of service yielded by one unit of housing stock per unit of time. See Edgar O. Olsen, "A Competitive Theory of the Housing Market," *American Economic Review*, September 1969.

understanding of the structure of existing subsidy programs, the dynamics of housing market behavior, and, most important, the interrelations between the two. This chapter begins such an analysis and concludes by presenting a conceptually appropriate measure of the impact of federally assisted programs upon the housing condition of the urban poor.

Existing Programs: The Design of Available Subsidy Programs
As indicated in Chapter 2, the available strategies for housing the poor (new construction, rehabilitation, the leasing of existing units) have been combined in varying ways into three major programs: conventional and turnkey public housing, leased housing, and rent supplements.
Conventional Public Housing
Traditionally, public housing has been a program of new construction through which rental units are developed, owned, and operated by a local housing authority; as such, it has been the federal government's primary tool for the production of low-cost housing. The units are reserved for low-income families (generally those with an adjusted annual income of $6,500 or less for a family of four) who cannot afford the amount necessary to obtain safe, sanitary dwellings in their market area. With the exception of those families left homeless because of fire, public displacement, eviction, or some other emergency beyond their control, applicants for public housing in most cities must also demonstrate that they currently inhabit unsafe, unsanitary, or overcrowded quarters. The project rent (contract rent plus utilities) for each family in public housing cannot be less than one-fifth of net family income at the time of admission or, according to the so-called Brooke amendments[6] in the 1969 Housing Act, more than one-fourth of a household's income at any time of occupancy. For example, if a family's annual "adjusted" income comes to $4,800 or $400 per month, its project rent will not be less than $80 or more than $100 monthly. Furthermore, in order to preclude "unfair" competition with private realtors, rents must be at least 20 percent below the lowest rents charged for a substantial amount of a city's private, low-rent standard housing. The LHA (local housing authority) uses this 20 percent rent gap to establish a maximum rent schedule. For tenants with incomes below the maximum limits, the rent level is

6. Amendment sponsored by Senator Edward Brooke, Republican, Massachusetts.

a constant portion of net family income. Typically the rent/income ratio is 1:5, and average public housing rents are as little as half the market rates for comparable units.[7]

Leasing Existing Housing

With respect to legislative authorization, leased housing is a public housing program, funded out of public housing appropriations and administered through LHAs in accordance with public housing procedures. Unlike conventional public housing, however, leased units are obtained from private property owners at prevailing market rates and are drawn from among a city's older housing stock. These units must be in standard condition and, for the most part, are in conformance with local housing codes. Tenant families then pay only a fixed proportion of their income (usually 20 to 25 percent of net income) toward the rent rather than the full market price. The LHA provides a direct rent subsidy, using federal funds, to cover the difference between what the family can afford and the fair market value of the leased unit.

Instead of subsidizing the construction of new units, the government (through the LHA) directly enhances the effective "demand" of the poor by subsidizing their rents. Thus the low-income tenant can choose the neighborhood, local school district, and housing structure he prefers as long as the dwelling meets local code standards. Unlike the public housing tenant—too often stigmatized as a ward of the state—the recipient of leased housing assistance obtains and occupies his home in complete anonymity. His subsidy is a confidential matter between himself, the LHA, and the landlord. In these respects, the leasing of units on the private market more closely resembles the proposed scheme of housing allowances than do any of the other housing programs currently in operation.[8] The only major

---

7. In 1970 the median rent for families in public housing was $63 per month. Since the average rental for any project depends on operating and maintenance costs (which, in turn, depend on geographical area, project age, and other variable factors), rents vary widely from jurisdiction to jurisdiction. Despite these variations, however, there is little doubt that public housing rents are significantly lower than those of comparable private units in any given local housing market.

8. The housing allowance concept is presently the subject of several large and promising demonstration efforts funded by the Department of Housing and Urban Development (HUD). The demonstrations are designed to determine the likely impact of a national housing allowance on households (mobility patterns, housing consumption) and on the housing market (rent increases, landlord investment).

difference between leased housing and housing allowances is that, under the former, the tenant forfeits the subsidy once he moves from the unit he initially occupies. The subsidy remains with the dwelling rather than the tenant.

Section 236 with Rent Supplements

In the Section 236 multifamily rental program, the federal government lowers rent levels by subsidizing the interest rate on the mortgage, allowing sponsors to pay only 1 percent instead of the conventional rate on the loan. The below-market interest rate lowers the monthly costs sufficiently so that moderate-income households can afford to occupy the units. Through the rent supplement program, the federal government offers nonprofit organizations, cooperatives, and limited-dividend corporations supplementary rent payments for up to 40 years on a specified number of units. These supplements are confined to FHA-insured new or substantially rehabilitated projects and are computed as the difference between the fair market rent for a given housing unit and the needy tenant's rent payment (once again, 25 percent of the adjusted income). This additional subsidy brings the rents within the reach of low-income tenants. The assurance of government rent subsidies and FHA mortgage insurance reduces the risk to conventional lenders, thus increasing their readiness to finance privately sponsored developments in the low- to moderate-income market. Under tight monetary conditions, these assurances clearly stimulate the production of housing for lower-income families. For the units in a rent supplement project, the FHA establishes maximum gross rents, allowing up to a 25 percent increase in high-cost areas. However, as Table 3.1 shows, the limitation of the rent

Table 3.1 Maximum Gross Rentals and FHA Rent Supplement Ceilings

Number of Bedrooms	Rent Supplement Maximum Rents	Rent Supplement Limit
0	$125.00	$ 87.50
1	155.00	108.50
2	177.00	124.00
3	206.00	144.00
4 +	221.00	155.00

Note: The rent supplement limitation is set at 70 percent of market rent.

supplement to 70 percent of the actual market rent determines the real ceiling on government assistance under the program. The administrative regulation stipulating that rent supplements can amount to no more than 70 percent of market rents in effect determines the minimum rent; tenants must be able to pay 30 percent of the total rent. This means, of course, that the poorest families may not be able to qualify, since 30 percent of the actual rent may well exceed 25 percent of their incomes. The maximum is the same as that allowed for public housing, although after occupancy the tenant's income may rise above this maximum, without forfeiting the subsidy. However, the tenant's share of the rent changes with economic circumstances as the tenant contribution rises, until the household's income is sufficient to pay the full market rent for the occupied apartment. Once the household's income exceeds the program maximum, supplement payments cease, but the tenant is not required to leave his dwelling as he would be under the public housing program.

Federal Subsidies and Local Housing Markets
Subsidy programs have differential impacts on the housing conditions of the poor: some direct and immediate, others less so; some intentional, others unforeseen. By giving program participants an opportunity to live in standard housing at below-market rents, subsidies contribute directly to a reduction of poverty, as measured by levels of consumption and the quality of living environments. However, the selfsame programs may also cause less perceivable and sometimes negative spillover effects. For example, if existing private units are leased in an area with low vacancy rates, the rents of surrounding units may be driven up, causing nonparticipants to suffer over the short term while the market adjusts to the sudden increase in housing demand. Or if new units are added to the housing stock, as can happen under the public housing or rent supplement programs, demand may slacken for low-rent private housing.[9] Confronted with higher vacancy

9. During the depression—when the poor doubled up with relatives, lived in "Hoovervilles" and shanties, returned to rural areas, and in general failed to use the entire housing supply—it was recognized that if public housing construction increased the housing supply when vacancy rates were high, vacancy rates would increase still further and rents would drop. Since such a result was politically undesirable, the Wagner-Steagall Act (public housing's enabling legislation) included "the equivalent elimination" provision to avert the problem of oversupply.

rates, a landlord may choose either to upgrade buildings or to reduce rents in an attempt to recapture tenants; alternatively, he may simply cut back on maintenance and building services, hoping to conserve profit margins in the face of a shrinking rent-roll. Taken together, these decisions may have the further effect of hastening the filtration of "used" housing down to tenants in even lower socioeconomic groups.

Other benefits attributable to these subsidy programs may be more subtle. Housing programs may alter the overall investment psychology and neighborhood self-image in rundown areas. Private homeowners may be encouraged to freshen the appearance of their properties and make other improvements; outside capital may be attracted back to an area of physical and social decline. Landlords may profit from more tenant stability and less economic uncertainty. Nonparticipants from outside the area may benefit too—for example, the general taxpayer, who gains from any reduction in the social cost of slums (at least as translated into a lessened demand for public services), or the civic leader, who may derive a paternalistic satisfaction from aiding the poor.

Given the importance of these "spillovers" from housing subsidies, each program's true worth must be measured in terms of its aggregate impact, not simply its direct effects. This means that the consequences for nonparticipants (neighbors, taxpayers) and intermediaries (housing officials, construction workers) must be considered along with the more apparent benefits enjoyed by those with subsidy payments directly in hand (tenants, homeowners, and landlords).

Measuring the Consumption Benefit

The aggregate quantity and price of housing change when a shift occurs in either the supply or the demand for housing services. Housing demand varies with household income, size of family, stage in family life cycle, and the price of housing vis-à-vis other consumption goods. The supply of housing shifts with changes in the costs of labor, construction materials, land, and investment capital. To measure the impact of federally assisted housing programs, it is therefore necessary to trace the effect on the residential supply that results from the addition of subsidized units through new construction, extensive rehabilitation, and the leasing of used housing, and to estimate how prices have responded to these changes. Once the adjustments in supply and demand generated by housing programs have been estimated, the change in the equilibrium price and quantity of housing services consumed can be determined. This provides us with an aggregate measure of added housing consumption or, in other words, the change in overall housing conditions for the poor and nonpoor alike.

The calculation of supply-and-demand adjustments is a complex task. To estimate net changes in housing supply, for instance, we need data on input prices (of land, labor, capital) for new construction and rehabilitation, on abandonment and filtration rates, and on rates of return for alternative investment opportunities. Estimating changes in demand requires knowledge of income and population trends and the prices of alternative consumption opportunities. Without complete information, we must make certain assumptions about the behavior of the urban housing market, particularly with respect to the elasticity of housing supply and demand. These assumptions have critical implications for our housing consumption measure and, consequently, for our choice of the most appropriate housing strategy.

Supply Elasticities and Housing Consumption

Proponents of production-oriented programs warn that if poor families are given housing assistance in the form of cash transfers, the families may spend the money on items other than housing or that existing rents may merely be inflated, with no improvement in housing conditions. To assure that subsidies have their intended impact on shelter conditions, they must be converted into actual housing goods and services before reaching the poor—in effect, according to this line of argument, subsidies must be tied to specific housing units.[10] Under this approach, the subsidized family would have neither the temptation nor the opportunity to divert its housing assistance into food, clothing, transportation, or other expenditures.

Among economists, however, the consensus is that a substantial share of additional income—even if fully discretionary—would, in almost any event, be used for housing. In fact, most empirical studies demonstrate that the income and price elasticities of rental housing demand are approximately 1.0

10. Here we have the rationale for yet another elaborate and costly set of precautions designed to protect people from themselves. As has so often proved the case, such elaborate precautions are unnecessary, reflecting stereotyped and patronizing images of the poor rather than an objective understanding.

and −1.0, respectively.[11] This means that for any given percentage change in income there is an equivalent percentage change in housing demand (that is, the amount families are willing to spend on housing). Thus, for example, if a family has been paying $100 rent per month, a 10 percent increase in income, from $380 a month to $418 a month, will probably result in a 10 percent increase in demand, with the family then willing to pay $110 a month rent; conversely, a 10 percent increase in prices will probably result in a 10 percent decrease in housing demand. Existing information on income elasticities suggests that subsidies to the demand side (such as cash transfers, housing allowances, and the existing leased housing program) will result in households spending more on housing consumption. Whether or not the increased demand will stimulate landlords to undertake repairs and upgrade structural conditions is a more uncertain issue.

"Productionists" argue that cash transfers or earmarked housing subsidies will result only in windfalls for landlords, who will meet increased demand by raising rents rather than by upgrading substandard units or adding to the existing stock. This argument depends on an implicit assumption that housing supply displays a low elasticity—a function about which economists differ far more than they do with respect to demand elasticity. In one aggregate housing market study, for example, Muth found the long-run housing supply schedule to be quite elastic; an increase in housing demand resulted in a 90 percent adjustment in the housing stock within six years.[12] In a cross-sectional study of low-, medium-, and high-rent housing across metropolitan areas, de Leeuw estimated that long-run supply elasticities varied from 0.3 to 0.7.[13]

For our analysis, we shall assume a competitive housing market in which the supply schedule is almost perfectly elastic. This means that over the long run landlords are assumed to respond to an increase in tenant demand by upgrading their housing in an amount equivalent to the increase in demand. Undoubtedly, the elasticity of supply for low-rent housing is

11. See, for example, Frank de Leeuw, "The Demand for Housing: A Review of Cross-Section Evidence," *Review of Economics and Statistics,* February 1971, and Richard F. Muth, "The Demand for Non-Farm Housing," in Arnold C. Harberger, ed., *The Demand for Durable Goods* (Chicago: University of Chicago Press, 1960).
12. See Muth, "The Demand for Non-Farm Housing," pp. 49–52.
13. Frank de Leeuw and Nkanta F. Ekanem, "The Supply of Rental Housing," *The American Economic Review,* Vol. 61, No. 5 (December 1971).

somewhat less than perfect. Variations in the conversion costs of different structures, the existence of specialized markets (for poor or minority households), institutional barriers, and other such factors inhibit the responsiveness of landlords. Furthermore, the higher transaction costs in segregated submarkets may lengthen the time period necessary for the housing stock to adjust to changes in demand.

Several recent housing studies suggest, however, that even in blighted areas urban housing markets may be quite competitive.[14] Rather than several large slum landlords owning the vast majority of properties in low-income neighborhoods (the pattern commonly thought to hold true), Sternlieb, Stegman, and other investigators have revealed extensive fragmentation of ownership. In a submarket with a large number of potential suppliers of housing services, and with a premium placed on full occupancy, landlords will tend to compete for tenants who are likely to support a higher and more stable rent-roll. Over the intermediate and long run, competition leads to an upgrading of the housing stock through maintenance, filtering, and conversion. One should expect this to hold true, especially where the number of subsidized tenants is so small that their increased demand has little inflationary effect upon prices. For these reasons our assumption about supply elasticity seems a reasonable one.[15]

The effect of this assumption on the value of consumer benefits from federal housing subsidies can be illustrated graphically by contrasting the differential changes in real housing consumption which result from the leasing of existing units (a demand-oriented strategy) with those resulting from the construction of new public housing (a supply- or production-oriented strategy).[16] (See Figure 3.1.) Given a perfectly inelastic supply of housing, the quantity of services does not respond to a shift in demand. A

---

14. George Sternlieb, *The Tenement Landlord* (New Brunswick, N.J.: Urban Studies Center, Rutgers University, 1966); Michael Stegman, *Housing Investment in the Inner City* (Cambridge, Mass.: MIT Press, 1972); and George E. Peterson, Arthur P. Solomon, Hadi Madjid, and William C. Apgar, Jr., *Property Taxes, Housing and the Cities* (Lexington, Mass.: D. C. Heath, 1973).

15. As we shall see, this assumption overstates the relative advantage of leasing existing units with respect to the measure of housing consumption added; it has no effect on other measures of program efficiency and effectiveness.

16. The public housing program contains both supply and demand subsidies, but for our illustration, we shall assume that it is simply a supply strategy. Further, we assume that subsidized households do not reduce their own housing expenditures and that other factors affecting the supply and demand for housing remain constant.

Perfectly Inelastic Supply Model

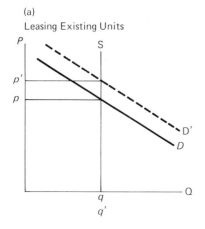

(a)
Leasing Existing Units

(b)
Public Housing Construction

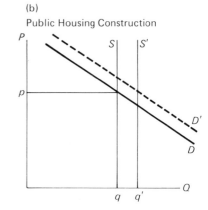

Perfectly Elastic Supply Model

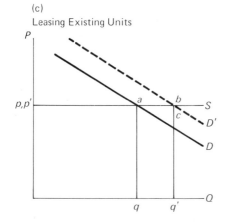

(c)
Leasing Existing Units

(d)
Public Housing Construction

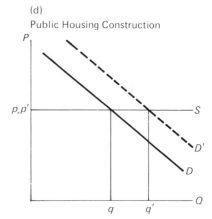

Figure 3.1   The Effect of Supply Elasticities on Housing Consumption Benefits.
In Figure 3.1c,
$abqq' = acqq' + abc,$
where
$abqq' =$ the housing services added as a result of the government subsidy,
$acqq' =$ the value which the tenants place on the housing services added (the direct
      tenant benefit),
$abc =$ the amount by which the cost of providing the additional housing (the gov-
      ernment subsidy) exceeds the tenant's valuation.

decrease in demand (an unlikely possibility except where there are localized population shifts or doubling up to beat costs) simply leads to a drop in prices, while an increase pushes them higher. As Figure 3.1a illustrates, when the supply of housing is fixed, the leasing of units has an adverse effect upon real housing consumption, since it causes rent inflation without adding to the housing supply. For example, a subsidy raising the demand of all poor families by 25 percent would result simply in an average rent increase of 25 percent with no change in the quantity of housing services received. On the other hand, direct government construction programs increase the availability of housing without inflating rents. Therefore a housing market characterized by perfect inelasticity of supply would confirm the logic of new construction programs. (See Figure 3.1b.)

By comparison, in a housing market having perfect supply elasticity, the equilibrium price of housing services remains constant, and every additional dollar of housing expenditure results in the provision of an additional dollar value of housing service. The total quantity of housing services grows, since, in the long run, owners of smaller amounts of housing services increase their maintenance expenditures, while owners of larger amounts allow their dwellings to filter down to a more profitable submarket, with shortages eventually reduced or eliminated through new construction.

In order to derive an empirical measure for the consumption benefit under conditions of perfect supply elasticity, we make two additional assumptions: first, that, on an aggregate basis, subsidized tenants do not reduce their housing expenditures; second, that the value that tenants place on *direct consumption benefits* plus the value that nontenants place on *indirect neighborhood effects* (reducing the social cost of slums, preventing the spread of blight, and so on) equals the cost of producing the additional housing services (the value of the government subsidy). This implies, of course, that the sum of the benefits to tenants and neighborhood residents equals the cost of the government subsidies even though their redistributive effects may differ.

Granted these assumptions, the long-run, aggregate effect of a government program upon housing consumption is then measured as the net change in the market value of housing services. This net change equals the market price of additional housing services minus the price adjustment in the nonsubsidized stock. In other words, the net effect is the difference between the total rental value of the housing stock with $(p'q')$ and without (pq) the government program. Symbolically, we express this housing consumption measure (B^H) as

$$\Delta B^H = p'(q' - q) - q(- p')$$
$$= p'q' - pq$$
$$= abqq' \quad \text{(see Figure 3.1c)}, \tag{3.1}$$

where

B^H = the housing consumption benefit,

$p'q'$ = the total value of the occupied federally subsidized unit,

pq = the total value of the unit occupied prior to participation in the federal housing program.

The value given by the tenants to this additional housing consumption, however, is only $acqq'$. The indirect benefit to nontenants equals the value of the triangle abc. This means that the total consumption benefit of programs that enhance the rent-paying ability of the poor is equivalent to the total value of the government rent subsidy $(abqq')$. Subsidized construction programs, however, have no effect on the equilibrium price in the housing market. (See Figure 3.1d.) The addition or improvement of a dwelling unit through government action merely preempts a comparable response by the private sector. Thus, if dwellings constructed or rehabilitated under government programs actually commanded market prices for their housing services, then the level of aggregate housing consumption would be completely unaffected. But since tenants are, in fact, charged less than the market price for the housing they receive, there is a housing consumption benefit associated with public housing and other construction programs. The value of this benefit is equal to the value of the government subsidy, just as it was for the consumer-oriented subsidies.

Calculating the Benefits

The value of a government rent subsidy (the housing consumption benefit) can be calculated by several methods; some of these rely on the value of factor inputs, others on the value of program outputs. Our analysis employs an output approach because it is the most consistent with a welfare economic framework. In all cases we assume that the local housing market approximates an equilibrium condition and therefore that variations in market rents correspond to genuine differences in housing structures, neighborhood environments, municipal services, and so forth. The housing consumption benefit for the leased housing and rent supplement programs will be computed as the difference between the rent paid by a tenant in a subsidized unit and the rent paid for a comparable unit on the private market. Consistent with this approach, we then calculate the benefit of public housing as the difference between the project rent-roll (under normal operation by a local housing authority) and the hypothetical rent-roll if the same public housing were to be owned and managed by a private firm.[17] Symbolically, the benefit is represented as

$$B^H = R_{pi} - R_{si},\tag{3.2}$$

where

B^H = the housing consumption benefit,

R_{si} = the project rent in a subsidized unit with i bedrooms,

R_{pi} = the private market rent for a comparable unit with i bedrooms.

Since local housing authorities generally utilize a constant rent/income ratio ($R/Y = K$), the rent for tenants admitted to subsidized housing is

$$R_{si}^j = KY^j \qquad j = 1,2,\ldots,n,\tag{3.3}$$

where

R_{si}^j = the rent in a subsidized unit with i bedrooms, for households within an eligible income class j,

K = the constant rent/income ratio,

Y^j = the income class j.

When the maximum rent schedule of a local housing authority is known, then the estimated rent for a comparable unit on the private market is computed as

$$R_{pi} = \frac{R_{si}^m}{(1-g)} \qquad i = 1,2,\ldots,n,\tag{3.4}$$

where

17. See the technical note on calculating the consumption benefit at the end of this chapter.

R_{pi} = the rent for a comparable private unit with i bedrooms,

R^m_{si} = the maximum public housing rent for a unit with i bedrooms,

g = the administrative rental gap (usually set between 0.20 and 0.25).

Thus the benefit is found to be

$$B^H = \frac{R^m_{si}}{(1-g)} - KY^j. \tag{3.5}$$

Having developed a procedure for measuring the housing consumption benefit, we can then estimate the impact of federal housing subsidies under alternative program concepts. Equation 3.4 is used to calculate the dollar benefits for two-bedroom units in the public housing, leased housing, and rent supplement programs, respectively. These calculations use data drawn from the operations of the Federal Housing Administration and the Boston Housing Authority; the city has taken advantage of all three programs and therefore offers the broad base of information needed for comparative analysis. Since housing prices in Boston are relatively high, the dollar benefits shown in our computations may be somewhat higher than they would be for other urban areas. In many crucial aspects, however, the Boston housing market is typical of other older central cities: it has experienced a substantial increase in nonwhite population over the last decade, while its total population has declined; vacancy rates in the low-rent housing submarket are high; the percentage of families unable to afford low-rent standard housing is increasing; and the cost of new construction has risen sharply. (For a statistical comparison of Boston and other central cities see Table 1.1.) Given these similarities, our ordinal rankings of program benefits should provide a generalized picture of comparative housing consumption benefits, despite variations in price levels and in the administrative features of federal subsidy programs from city to city.

Some Comparative Findings
The housing consumption benefits that have been derived for two-bedroom units in each of the three major low-income housing programs are presented in Table 3.2 together with corresponding tenant rent payments and the estimated private market rents for comparable units. It should be

Table 3.2 Housing Consumption Benefits, Boston, 1970 (dollars per two-bedroom unit per month)

Program	Market Rent (R_{pi})	Tenant Monthly Rent (R_{si})	Monthly Consumption Benefits $(B^H = R_{pi} - R_{si})$
New Construction			
Conventional public housing	$167	$69	$ 98
Leased housing	167	69	98
Section 236– rent supplements	180	73	107
Existing Housing Stock			
Leasing housing without rehabilitation	124	69	55
Leasing housing with rehabilitation	148	69	79
Section 236– rent supplements with rehabilitation	167a	73	94

a. The rehabilitation program in Boston involved substantial upgrading: replacement of some mechanical subsystems, changes in interior structures, and so forth. Consequently, the Boston figure is quite high. For more moderate rehabilitation, the market rents and consumption benefit would be lower.

remembered that, with our assumption of local housing market equilibrium, higher average market rents correspond to better-quality housing and more desirable neighborhood environs. The consumption benefit, computed as the difference between the market rent and the tenant payment, represents the change in overall housing conditions resulting from the government subsidy. The results in Table 3.2 indicate that new construction programs offer the largest housing consumption benefit.

At first glance, these findings may seem to contradict the critique of production programs, which forms a basic theme of this book. However, on closer examination, the very size of the consumption benefit offers one of the most clear-cut indictments of a production-oriented housing policy by graphically indicating the disproportionately large benefits accruing to each subsidized household. If the goal of national housing policy were simply to provide a maximum improvement in the housing conditions of a few poor households (the small percentage of those actually receiving government assistance) without regard to equity and cost factors, a reliance on new construction would indeed be a satisfactory policy. But, given both the scarcity of federal resources in relation to overall need and the large number of eligible families receiving no assistance, any definitive judgment regarding program alternatives must also consider their equitableness, cost effectiveness, and political acceptability.

The production strategies provide housing far in excess of minimum standards. Because of the existence of local building, safety, and health codes, newly constructed housing has to be built to excessively high standards. As discussed in Chapter 7, it is far more efficient to produce modest-quality housing through adjustments and conversions of the existing housing stock than through new construction. Moreover, when the amount of housing provided far exceeds minimum standards, the sum of tenants' and nontenants' valuation of the housing is less than the government's cost of producing it. This means that the social value of the consumption benefit for newly constructed units is probably overstated in Table 3.2.

Our findings also suggest two basic equity problems. First, subsidized tenants pay monthly rents on the basis of their income yet receive different levels of benefits: for example, a leased housing tenant with rent payments of $69 per month may enjoy benefits that range from $55 to $98 per month, depending on whether the occupied unit is newly constructed, rehabilitated, or unimproved. Second, a substantial gap exists between the number of families receiving the direct benefits of subsidized housing and the number of families eligible to participate in the federal programs. In the Boston area, for example, there are approximately 12,000 subsidized units, yet more than 65,000 families meet program eligibility requirements (and Boston has almost the highest per-capita number of subsidy units in the country). While federally assisted tenants pay less than market prices for new housing services, families with slightly higher incomes must live in used housing at full market costs.

To a certain extent these equity effects, which are examined more extensively in Chapter 4, reflect arbitrary features of program design and administrative structure rather than intrinsic qualities of the subsidy in question. For example, as noted earlier in this chapter, HUD has effectively set minimum income requirements for rent supplements by excluding families unable to cover 30 percent of the market rental with a quarter of their income. Consequently, a program intended to assist needy families excludes those most in need of help. Yet another inequity of the rent supplement program in its present form stems from the fact that government contributions make up the difference between market rentals and one-fourth of gross family income (less a $300 deduction for each dependent). Because rent payments are fixed portions of income, the lower the incomes of participating families, the larger the average rent subsidy and, in consequence, the smaller the number of families assisted. Moreover, since poor families possess the same sound consumer instincts as those who are better off, they try to maximize the housing benefits they receive by using the maximum allowable subsidy. Inasmuch as they are successful, rent supplement funds will be apportioned among a smaller number of families. Finally, since few suburban communities have workable programs for community improvement [18] as required by the rent supplement and several other community development programs, subsidized units are generally restricted to central cities where construction and debt service costs are higher, and thus the average subsidy required per unit is higher too. Again this results in assistance to fewer families.[19]

Keeping equity considerations and the scarcity of federal resources in mind, it becomes clear that new construction programs provide an "excessive" amount of residential services. In other words, both newly constructed and existing units offer standard housing, but the units provided by construction programs far exceed minimally acceptable standards. We can understand this discrepancy by comparing the monthly consumption benefits of subsidized housing with the average cost of a low-budget, standard

18. The Housing Act of 1954 prohibited federal aid for urban renewal or low-rent public housing projects unless the locality had first prepared a workable program. A workable program has been deemed by HUD to have five essential elements:
1. Development of a local planning process;
2. Development of specific plans for achieving effective citizen participation in planning and developing programs assisted by HUD;
3. Adoption of up-to-date housing and building codes and development of effective enforcement programs;
4. Local effort to expand the supply of housing for low- and moderate-income families;
5. Development of a coordinated relocation system for families displaced by urban renewal projects.
19. This is not to suggest that the rent supplement program offers no advantages. The FHA rent supplement formula is more flexible than other subsidies because the supplement level varies with each tenant in accordance with family need and local rental conditions. Rent supplement tenants retain an incentive to raise their earnings since only one-quarter of any increase goes toward rent, and, unlike those in public housing, tenants are allowed to remain in the same dwelling at full market rent once their income exceeds the program maximum.

two-bedroom unit.[20] The average monthly rent of such a unit adjusted for
Boston is about $115—roughly comparable to that for an existing leased
housing unit (either with or without rehabilitation). The monthly consumption benefit of existing leased housing, as a percentage of the Bureau
of Labor Statistics (BLS) low-budget standard rent, ranges between 47 and
68 percent, depending on the degree of rehabilitation involved. In contrast, the monthly rent for a new unit (for example, FHA Section 236 with
rent supplements) is $60 per month more than that for the BLS standard
low-budget unit, and the tenant's consumption benefit alone is 90 percent
of the BLS monthly rent.

In addition to the equity argument, a number of other factors point to
the need for greater reliance on the existing stock and for less dependence
on production strategies. Among these are the high cost of new construction,
the failure to achieve suitable living environments, and the problems of
externalities.

Exposure to market realities soon reveals that there is no such thing as
inexpensive new housing. New construction costs significantly more than
using the existing stock (see Chapter 7). Moreover, the subsidy of new
construction postpones the actual enjoyment of housing benefits (because
of the time lags and administrative delays inherent in the construction
process), whereas using the existing stock may make possible the moving of
larger numbers of families from substandard to standard housing in a relatively abbreviated period of time.

By employing local land-use controls, suburban communities and relatively affluent sectors of central cities have managed to exclude most low-
and moderate-income housing developments proposed for their areas. Last-
minute zoning amendments, anti-apartment ordinances (refusals to rezone
for multifamily use), excessive frontage, setback and minimum-lot requirements are among the devices through which communities have kept out
so-called undesirables in the name of sound land-use planning. Where a

20. The Bureau of Labor Statistics estimates budgets for an "average" family of four living
in urban America based on three standards of living: lower, intermediate, and higher.
For 1970, housing consumption costs (including shelter, household operations, and home
furnishings) were estimated to be $119 per month on the average, and $136 for Boston.
Estimating the costs of household operations and home furnishings to be 15 percent of
total costs, we have taken the monthly cost for shelter in Boston to be $116 per month.
This is a relatively low estimate; consequently, our findings may understate the inequities.

workable program or special approval is required before a project can be built (as with the rent supplement program), a community, simply by failing to meet the requirement, can help perpetuate existing patterns of exclusion. Consequently, new subsidized housing is seldom built where it is most needed—in suburban areas experiencing the greatest expansion in employment opportunities for low- and semiskilled workers. Low-income families are either cut off from these opportunities for economic advancement altogether or else forced to absorb daily transportation costs they can ill afford.

Unable to build new low- and moderate-income housing in either the suburbs or the better central-city neighborhoods, housing officials have concentrated subsidized units in blighted central-city areas, where the market for private construction has already collapsed and, for the most part, private financing has been withdrawn. In such neighborhoods, crime rates, vandalism, and social tensions already run high; under these conditions, housing maintenance is a dubious effort at best. Indeed, the economic life of new subsidized housing may expire before its 40-year mortgage can be retired. Even worse, its market value at completion may not even equal the cost of construction; the resale value of new subsidized housing, if sold on the private market without its federal subsidy, might be zero, or even negative, if annual unsubsidized costs exceed market rent. The result is instant slums, new wastelands on the model of St. Louis's notorious and ill-fated Pruitt-Igoe project,[21] where, ironically, public housing has exacerbated social and psychological problems rather than relieved them.

Technical Note: Alternative Methods of Calculating the Consumption Benefit

The method employed in this chapter for calculating the consumption benefit has been selected from among several alternatives. In one approach employing the value of factor inputs, the consumption benefit is computed from the subsidy implicit in the financing of the federally assisted housing units; the investment is socially justified only if the discounted present value

---

21. The Board of the St. Louis Housing Authority has recently decided to relocate the last remaining occupants of Pruitt-Igoe and then sell or demolish the structure. For an excellent sociological analysis of human interrelationships at Pruitt-Igoe, see Lee Rainwater, *Behind Ghetto Walls* (Chicago: Atherton-Aldine, 1971).

of the rent plus the implicit subsidy exceeds or equals the development cost. This may be expressed in equation form as[22]

$$I \leqslant \sum_{t=1}^{n} \frac{R_{st}^{G} + B_{t}^{H}}{(1+i)^{t}},$$

where

I = the total development cost,

R_{st}^{G} = the gross project rent receipts at time t,

B_{t}^{H} = the implicit subsidy or consumption benefit at time t,

i = the social time preference discount rate.

Alternatively, by using program outputs instead of factor inputs, the benefit can be calculated as the sum of two components—first, the additional consumption of housing services and, second, the reduction in housing expenditures. The benefit from additional consumption of housing services is the area under the appropriate demand curve between Q_s and Q_p, where Q_s is the amount of housing services provided by the subsidized housing. The value of the reduction in housing costs is simply the difference between housing expenditures prior to admission to subsidized housing ($P_p Q_p$) and the rent paid as an occupant of subsidized housing (PG). The consumption benefit for a unit with i bedrooms in any time period can then be written[23]

$$B^{H} = P_p Q_{pi} - P_s Q_{si} + \int_{Q_{pi}}^{Q_{si}} D.$$

Under another output approach, the housing consumption benefit can be computed from the difference between the rent a tenant pays for a subsidized unit and the rent paid for a comparable unit on the private market. In the case of public housing, the benefit is calculated as the difference

22. See Eugene Smolensky, "Public Housing or Income Supplements," *Journal of the American Institute of Planners,* March 1968.
23. This concept and its measurement are developed in more detail in Edgar O. Olsen and James R. Prescott, "An Analysis of Alternative Measures of Tenant Benefits" (Santa Monica, Calif.: Rand Corporation, 1970), mimeographed, pp. 2–5.

between the project rent and the estimated rent if public housing were owned and managed by a private firm. Using conventional real estate accounting techniques, we can compute the estimated rent under private ownerships as follows:

Tenants' monthly project rent in public housing
+ Adjusted debt service per unit month (**PUM**)
+ Full real estate taxes—payments in lieu of taxes **PUM**
+ Profit factor **PUM**
− Residual receipts

Tenant monthly rent in comparable private housing

Because an output approach is most consistent with a welfare economics framework, it has been used in this chapter to calculate the housing consumption benefit. Symbolically, the benefit measure is represented as

$$B^H = R_{pi} - R_{si},$$

where

R_{si} = the project rent in a subsidized unit with i bedrooms,

R_{pi} = the private market rent for a comparable unit with i bedrooms.

CHAPTER 4

Distributing the Housing Benefits

One of the reasons for governmental adoption of a housing policy is to alter the distribution of income. . . . Americans with low incomes are not the sole or even the primary beneficiaries of the most important housing programs. By far the largest and most significant form of public aid to housing is contained in the Internal Revenue Code, which in 1970 allowed nearly $10 billion in tax benefits to homeowners who were predominantly in the middle and upper income brackets. Low-rent public housing was a distant second.

Henry J. Aaron,
Shelter and Subsidies

The erratic political fortunes of the major federal housing programs can be attributed to many factors, including the lack of consensus about policy objectives, changing national priorities, fluctuations in the economy, and program mismanagement, to name only a few. Increasingly, however, public sentiment, in both its positive and negative expressions, also reveals an awareness that the choice of housing policy may significantly alter the distribution of family income and the incidence of social benefits.

Of course, economists have long recognized that whenever the public sector intervenes in the private economy, each family finds that, to some extent, its income position relative to others is altered by the tax payment it makes to support that intervention and by the value of the benefits it may receive in return from various government expenditures or transfer payments. Moreover, in a liberal democracy such as ours, most voters would concede that taxes and public spending should narrow rather than widen disparities in family living conditions and should reduce rather than aggravate inequalities brought about by the private market. However, the redistributive potential of housing subsidies has never been realized for a variety of reasons: the close identification of housing itself with social status and self-concept, the difficulty of attaching dollar values to housing conditions and to their social and environmental consequences, the extent of both legitimate and self-serving interests with a stake in the status quo and hence the politically volatile nature of redistribution issues associated with housing programs (or, for that matter, any government policy). These difficulties have found expression in a number of exaggerated but disquieting stereotypes: at one extreme, the corrupt housing administrator using his position to line his pockets, and the wily contractor spiriting off windfall profits from newly constructed "instant slums"; at the other extreme, the undeserving loafers and the welfare chiselers moving into "penthouses for the poor," free to loll about the swimming pools all day while honest men work for their living. Even though ethnic jealousies and racial antagonisms help shape these stereotypes, they also contain several elements of fact and, as such, reflect legitimate discontent. It is difficult for even the most benevolent of taxpayers to accept a program that moves a poor or moderate-income family into better-quality housing (at a subsidized rent) than he himself can afford. Nor can one find any ready justification for allowing a high percentage of tax dollars intended for needy families to be diverted into the hands of administrative intermediaries or of well-to-do professionals who purchase tax-exempt bonds or participate in real estate syndicates.

Even if an effective majority agreed that housing subsidies should not be used to widen disparities in family income and living conditions, it would be difficult to reach a consensus on the redistributive effect that subsidies should have or on the most effective means for achieving that end. When funds are too limited to go around, which poor families should get housing assistance—the poorest, who can contribute virtually nothing to rental costs, or the "moderately" poor, who can contribute a greater portion of their rents and be rehoused with smaller subsidies? Should the distribution of aid depend on socioeconomic characteristics—age, race, family size, welfare dependency, and the like—or should it be based solely on adjusted income? To what extent can the redistributive function of housing subsidies be used to achieve social and economic goals such as locational mobility, the integration of individual and minority groups into the larger community, the maintenance of social order and family stability, or the strengthening of neighborhood coherence? How efficient are present subsidy programs with respect to redistributive objectives? Is the use of existing housing a more effective means of achieving equality in living conditions than the construction of new dwellings?

As briefly noted in Chapter 1, the redistributive effects of housing programs can be measured in two ways: first, in terms of the extent to which persons of equivalent economic status are treated equally (*horizontal equity*) and, second, the extent to which persons of unequal status are treated in accordance with their relative position (*vertical equity*). If the intended beneficiaries of a given federal program are assumed to be in some sense "equal," housing assistance under that program may be considered horizontally inequitable to the extent that it provides some members of the target group with more assistance than others. Similarly, a housing program is judged vertically inequitable if a substantial proportion of its benefits are diverted to individuals outside the target population.

Horizontal Equity: Serving the Neediest Households
The initial difficulty in applying the concept of horizontal equity to housing (a difficulty going directly to the question of which families should be benefited) is selecting a standard of eligibility that categorizes the needy in an operational way. To a certain extent, the choice of a standard is necessarily a subjective one, but if we agree on the desirability of helping those families who without subsidy would in all likelihood be obliged to live in substandard housing, then there are some relatively objective measures of "need."

Those Least Able to Compete for Private Housing
Family income—the most inevitable criterion—has been a factor in the eligibility formulas of virtually all federal housing programs.[1] Most efforts to include equity considerations in public investment analyses have generally relied on the single variable of economic class (as measured by income status) to provide a distributive weight for benefit-cost calculations. However, other household characteristics besides income constrict a family's housing choice and therefore merit some consideration. One such characteristic is racial or ethnic identity; for example, most studies on residence and race distinguish one housing market for white families, allowing them to locate anywhere throughout the metropolitan area, and other, separate

1. Substandard housing is not inhabited solely by low-income households, but the proportion of families living in substandard conditions is highest among the lowest-income groups. In an analysis of U.S. housing needs for the 1968 Kaiser Committee report, for example, G. E. Tempo estimated that approximately 15 percent of white households and 36 percent of nonwhite households with less than $4,000 income per annum were occupying substandard housing. For marginally higher income groups the percentage occupying substandard dwellings was significantly lower.

markets for blacks and other minorities restricted to particular geographic areas where prices are higher for any given quality of housing.[2] In recent years the enactment and enforcement of fair housing laws have helped moderate the most blatant forms of discrimination such as racially restrictive covenants, but collusive real estate practices, restricted flows of information, and private exclusionary practices continue to frustrate the ability of nonwhites to find standard housing at normal market rents. In a recent study of housing market discrimination, for example, Rapkin found that blacks spending the same rent as whites for the same number of rooms obtain a significantly higher proportion of substandard units.[3]

Family size also restricts housing choice, especially among low-income consumers, as evidenced by the unusually low vacancy rates (the lowest of any identifiable submarket) for large-unit dwellings in both federally assisted and private rental housing. Families with a large number of children have special space requirements that can be satisfied only at the cost of higher rent payments. Moreover, such families often encounter resistance from landlords who fear the maintenance and management problems associated with minors and from local governments which anticipate added burdens on school facilities and public services. Private developers rarely feel that the costs of accommodating large families are offset by higher rentals; thus little if any housing is expressly constructed for this submarket, and existing supplies fall well below the demand. Even in government-supported housing, fixed development cost ceilings per room act to limit the supply of large units.[4]

Two additional factors that help to explain a household's living conditions are old age and welfare status. Elderly households are relatively immobile because of psychological and social attachments to a certain neigh-

---

2. See, for example, Davis McEntire, *Residence and Race* (Berkeley: University of California Press, 1960); Chester Rapkin, "Price Discrimination Against Negroes in the Rental Housing Market," in John F. Kain, ed., *Race and Poverty: The Economics of Discrimination* (Englewood Cliffs, N.J.: Prentice-Hall, 1969); John F. Kain and John M. Quigley, "Housing Market Discrimination, Homeownership, and Savings Behavior," *The American Economic Review*, Vol. 62, No. 3 (June 1972).
3. Rapkin, "Price Discrimination Against Negroes," pp. 116–117.
4. The inadequate supply of units with many bedrooms in public housing has been well publicized. The situation in some cities is so desperate that households with nine to twelve members are forced to live in three- and four-bedroom units.

borhood, health disabilities, and the need for access to public transportation, health facilities, and shopping. This immobility severely limits their housing options. In the case of welfare families, their ability to obtain decent housing is constrained by landlord hostility as well as the impermanence of the welfare status itself. Studies indicate that welfare tenants face discrimination not unlike that endured by blacks and other minorities; in many cases, the quality of housing they inhabit is significantly inferior to that obtained by unassisted households below the poverty line.[5]

By including all of these household characteristics (family income, race, family size, welfare status, and age) as independent variables in a statistical, generalized linear probability model, we can construct a profile of the households most disadvantaged in their housing search or, in other words, with the highest probability of living in substandard housing in the absence of governmental assistance.[6] The degree to which housing subsidies reach those in the greatest need provides some measure of the horizontal equity achieved in federal housing aid. It is this statistical measure, in fact, which provides the equity weight $(1 + x)$ for our formal benefit-cost calculation.

The actual results from our probability model, illustrated with the use of Boston data, are set forth in the technical note at the end of the chapter. The findings suggest that much of a tenant's housing disadvantage (the additional probability that he will occupy substandard housing if unaided) can be explained in terms of the two tenant characteristics that dominate the composite indices: race and welfare status. Since the rent supplement program has the highest percentage of blacks and welfare recipients—those with the most serious housing disadvantage in Boston—the average rent supplement family is the most likely to live in substandard housing in the absence of federal assistance. This means that, in terms of at least one measure of horizontal equity, the rent supplement program has been most

5. See George S. Sternlieb and Bernard P. Indik, *The Ecology of Welfare: Housing and the Welfare Crisis in New York City* (New Brunswick, N.J.: Transaction Books, 1973).
6. Other household characteristics such as consumer tastes and stage in life cycle also contribute to a family's housing demand. But the lack of pertinent data on these variables precludes their inclusion in the probability model. It is possible that the omission of these important independent variables may create some specification error.

equitable.[7] Public housing, however, was more effective in aiding unusually poor families, primarily because of the very low rents (that is, the larger subsidy per recipient) it makes available.

The rent supplement and public housing programs have both concentrated on new construction, primarily the development of large multiple-unit projects in undesirable areas of the city. As a result, they have reinforced the economic and racial segregation of those low-income families least able to bear the multiple disadvantages associated with poverty. Poor black and welfare families have been concentrated in the worst neighborhoods; thus many of the inherent problems of poverty and ghettoization are compounded.

By contrast, the leased housing program (and other schemes that allow for the use of housing already in existence) distribute both the burden of poverty and the benefits of subsidized housing more equitably. The standing stock costs less to use, and consequently a larger portion of the needy may be served for any given public expenditure. Since most leased housing is drawn from the existing stock (and therefore unconstrained by the cost ceilings applied to new public housing construction), it offers more opportunity for meeting the special needs of extra-large families. And perhaps most important, the use of existing units permits wider dispersal of the disadvantaged throughout the housing market, thereby minimizing the social costs of poverty for all. A family moving into a leased housing unit is indistinguishable from any other newcomer to a neighborhood and therefore is accepted matter-of-factly by the same local residents who would rally in arms at the suggestion that public housing be built in their midst.

Determining Eligibility

It might be argued that the measurement of horizontal equity, viewed solely in terms of the socioeconomic characteristics of the tenants, is an unsatisfactory method of evaluating subsidy programs. For one thing, the

7. Again, it should be noted that the Boston results are somewhat idiosyncratic. In Boston, since the rent supplement–rehabilitation units were part of a larger-scale FHA rehabilitation program, the selection of tenants was circumscribed by a local policy giving priority to displaced tenants. In other communities, where such a policy does not exist, the choice of tenants is the responsibility of the private landlord. We can surmise, therefore, that Boston's rent supplement projects are rehousing tenants with relatively more serious housing needs than are projects in other communities.

statistical probability that a subsidized tenant would live in substandard
housing in the absence of government assistance logically depends on
the conditions of the local housing market (housing supply) as well as on
the tenants' household characteristics (housing demand). However, since
the short-run supply of housing is relatively fixed, the individual household must deal with the housing supply as given, and one may reasonably
assume that the statistical probabilities depend on tenant characteristics
(that is, demand conditions) alone. Another possible criticism of our horizontal equity measure is that eligibility for housing subsidy programs is
primarily a function of household income. Therefore it may be unfair to
judge a program's equitability in terms of standards it was never intended
to meet. An adequate reply to this criticism requires a closer look at tenant
selection as actually applied over the years. For the most part, subsidized
housing programs do, in fact, serve a severely disadvantaged low-income
clientele. In 1970, 57 percent of the families living in public housing had
annual incomes under $3,000, and less than 1 percent earned more than
$7,500.[8] The average annual income for public housing tenants under sixty-
five years old was $3,636 in 1970. However, in 1970, only 1.4 percent of the
families eligible for low-rent public housing received any assistance. Combined, leased housing and rent supplements aided less than 0.1 percent in
the lowest income category.

The fact that only a limited portion of the poor have benefited from
existing subsidy programs suggests that income is not, and indeed has never
been, the sole criterion used for distributing housing aid. Other criteria
have reflected some widely held attitudes toward the poor, for example,
the tendency of our culture to equate chronic poverty with a failure of
moral will—the "God helps those who help themselves" tenet of the Prot-
estant work ethic. The public housing program, during its initial years
under the Roosevelt Administration, was aimed primarily at assisting "the
deserving poor"—in other words, those "honest" families betrayed by cir-
cumstance and only temporarily in need of assistance until "back on their
feet again."

A number of gaps in program coverage have their origin in the highly
charged and polarized atmosphere that envelops any legislative proposal

8. Derived from data supplied by HUD and cited by Henry J. Aaron, *Shelter and Subsidies*
(Washington, D.C.: Brookings Institution, 1972), Chapters 7 and 8.

having potential impact on the distribution of income. Most important
pieces of housing legislation have received congressional approval only as
the result of hasty compromise among a variety of interests. The effects of
this improvisation has revealed itself in the patchwork assembly of the
bills in their final form: omnibus in content; their provisions often inconsistent in spirit, scope, and level of detail; their language needlessly rigid
and specific in one place, vague and ambiguous in another.

Government Regulations

The legislative history of the rent supplement program amply illustrates
the politics of redistribution. Perhaps the most disputed issue that emerged
during congressional hearings concerned the definition of eligible tenants.
Initially, the Johnson Administration had proposed legislation to provide rent supplements to moderate- and middle-income families—that is,
those with incomes above the admission ceilings for public housing yet below the amount necessary to compete for standard units in the private
market. However, the Senate Banking and Currency Committee objected,
insisting that the income standards should be the same as those for public
housing. Ultimately the position of the Senate committee prevailed, resulting in a housing program for the poor rather than for the lower middle
class.

This congressional victory seemed to assure the redistributive character
of the rent supplement program, but the legislators—as a concession to
various political pressures—then proceeded to restrict eligibility to select
groups in the low-income population judged by specific criteria to be unfortunate or deserving. As the program now operates, prospective tenants
are required to demonstrate their neediness by meeting separate eligibility
tests with respect to total family assets, gross household income, and certain categorical restrictions.[9]

The income and asset limitations provide a test of financial need. A rent
supplement applicant must have a maximum gross income no higher than
the amount allowed for admission to public housing in the same locality,
that is, at least 20 percent below the income necessary to rent safe and

9. This discussion of tenant eligibility relies on a more exhaustive account found in
U.S., Department of Housing and Urban Development, Federal Housing Administration,
Rent Supplement Program: Public Information Guide and Instruction Handbook, Report
No. 2504 (Washington, D.C.: U.S. Government Printing Office, 1966), pp. 10–12.

sanitary housing in the local private market. In addition, his total assets cannot exceed $2,000 unless he is sixty-two years of age or older, in which case the total cannot surpass $5,000.[10] The higher asset allowance for the elderly takes into account their reliance upon savings, as a supplement to social security and retirement pensions, to pay current living expenses.

However, in addition to satisfying these financial criteria, the applicant for rent supplements must qualify under one of the following categories of the "deserving" poor: displaced by government action, head of household or spouse sixty-two years of age or older, head of household or spouse physically handicapped, living in substandard housing, or occupying dwelling units destroyed or extensively damaged by natural disaster. Here the rationale of Congress and HUD appears to be that these categories single out groups who are clearly the victims of circumstances, their housing plight a misfortune for which they cannot be held personally responsible. Little if any controversy attends housing assistance for persons within such categories; after all, who would begrudge the elderly, the handicapped, or the evacuee?

Local Politics

General eligibility requirements for each of the subsidy programs are prescribed by Congress, usually in terms of income limits.[11] Federal law prohibits racial discrimination and provides that priority be given to households displaced by urban renewal or slum clearance. But within these federal constraints, responsibility for establishing priorities and selecting tenants from the long lists of applicants is at the discretion of local authorities, subject, in some instances, to negotiation with private owners.[12]

10. Ibid., p. 11.
11. Public housing units are intended, for example, for families with an equivalent annual income of $6,500 or less for a family of four. The statutory and contractual requirements relating to leased housing eligibility are nearly the same as those applicable to public housing and other programs authorized under the U.S. Housing Act. Exceptions are the congressional waiver of the 20 percent rent gap requirement for Section 23 short-term leasing and the waiver of the Workable Program requirement. See U.S., Department of Housing and Urban Development, *Low Rent Housing Leased Housing Handbook,* Transmittal No. 2, RHA 7430. 1, November 28, 1969.
12. Normally, leased housing agreements provide for one of the following procedures: selection by the local authority; selection by the local authority subject to the approval of the owner; selection by the owner subject to the approval of the local authority; selection by the owner from a list of eligible applicants supplied by the local authority. See ibid., Chapter 3, Section 2, and Chapter 4, Section 1.

Standards of selection (and consequently the distribution of benefits) may vary considerably from city to city. Screening procedures are rarely made explicit and, even where clearly stated, may be altered or ignored in practice. Of course, this degree of administrative discretion allows opportunity for a humane flexibility but also risks favoritism, discrimination, and other forms of abuse. The short-term leasing program is particularly suited, for example, to meeting immediate relocation needs or emergency situations, such as fires or floods.[13]

Civil liberties groups have decried discrimination against welfare recipients, Negroes, and Spanish Americans, and even drug addicts and prostitutes.[14] On the other hand, tenant associations in public housing, when given a voice in management, have often demanded selection criteria designed to keep "troublemakers" out.

Most local housing officials place a high value on conventional good behavior by tenants, and, despite a congressional mandate to scatter the leased units throughout the community, many exclude "undesirable" families from middle-income areas. In some communities, housing authority staff and private owners clearly select those families considered acceptable to neighborhood residents. Even after a concerted attempt to eliminate the use of good-behavior standards (including stability of employment history, freedom from drug addiction, good housekeeping habits, presence of a father in the home), the New York City Housing Authority has continued to apply an admissions policy favoring "better families" and the maintenance of a "good family environment." [15]

Of course, the concern of local authorities and tenants is an understandable and, to some extent, a legitimate one. Concentrating a larger number of "problem families" (those with special disabilities, broken families, and

13. In 1970, 1,085 or 57.8 percent of the housing units under lease in Boston were used to house more than 700 families displaced during the FHA-sponsored Boston Urban Rehabilitation Program.
14. For a detailed discussion of the controversy in Congress that centered around tenant selection priorities in public housing, see Robert Moore Fisher, *Twenty Years of Public Housing* (New York: Harper & Row, 1958), pp. 241–242.
15. Gilbert Y. Steiner, *The State of Welfare* (Washington, D.C.: Brookings Institution, 1971), pp. 173–178. See also Roger Starr, "Which of the Poor Shall Live in Public Housing?" *Public Interest,* No. 23 (Spring 1971), and the reply by Al Hirshem and Vivian N. Brown, "Too Poor for Public Housing: Roger Starr's Poverty Preferences," *Social Policy,* May–June 1972.

several generations of welfare dependents) in a single project has, in many instances, proved self-defeating. However, in other cases, selection practices have been arbitrary, moralistic, unnecessarily exclusive, and unrelated to reliable indicators of potential problems.

Housing Authority Finances

Another outcome of the conflict between the redistributive intent of the housing programs and the local administrative stake in "good" results has been the use of selection criteria having more to do with the financial condition of the local housing authorities than with the relative need of the applicants.

The single largest subsidy program, conventional public housing, is run by the nearly 2,200 local housing authorities in the nation. Under this program tenant payments are expected to meet maintenance, replacement, and operating costs. But in recent years, an ever wider disparity between escalating operating costs and relatively stable rent-rolls has brought many local housing authorities to the verge of fiscal collapse (and, in the case of St. Louis, to an actual declaration of bankruptcy).[16]

In some extreme situations, local housing authorities are still paying off loans on housing projects that have become virtually uninhabitable because of neighborhood crime and vandalism. With operating costs increasing faster than tenant incomes, authorities have been left with the brutal choice of either concentrating assistance on the poorest families, who can't afford rents sufficient to cover management costs, but whose need is presumably greatest, or spreading assistance among families whose deprivation is less severe, but whose rent contributions will help stabilize the LHA's financial position.

Precarious finances, administrative anxieties, and conflicting political pressures are unavoidable facts of life for any subsidy program and, by themselves, do not comprise an indictment of present LHA operations. But the critical points are that many of the poorest families are excluded by existing programs, and that since the federal resources allocated to housing are not sufficient to aid all the needy, other criteria besides income alone have had to be used in selecting subsidy recipients from among the larger

16. For a lucid discussion of the fiscal plight of local housing authorities, see Albert Walsh, "Is Public Housing Headed for a Fiscal Crisis?" *Journal of Housing*, No. 2 (February 1969), p. 71.

target population. The supplementary criteria used in the past have not always been ideal from an economic and social point of view. It can be argued that since there is more social value in assisting those households least able to compete for standard housing on the private market, the government is justified in providing adequate housing for those with the most urgent needs. The argument that there is more social value in assisting households least able to compete for standard housing on the private market is consistent with principles of welfare economics, because it assumes that the very poor receive more satisfaction from a marginal improvement in their housing condition than do families relatively better off. Moreover, since the severely disadvantaged do not represent a market for real estate interests, this strategy minimizes one political problem inherent in housing programs: the potential competition between publicly subsidized rents and those supplied by the unassisted private market.

Differential Benefit Levels

As noted in Chapter 3, not only do the programs reach a small fraction of those in need, but even among those assisted the levels of benefits differ. Since the rent charged a subsidized tenant is based on his ability to pay rather than on the market rent of the unit he occupies, participants in the various subsidy programs pay roughly the same dollar amount for their housing. However, in exchange for these comparable payments, they obtain units (and neighborhoods) of markedly different quality. These variations in quality, as measured by differences in resource costs, reflect horizontal inequities in the design of the subsidy programs.

One way to measure the degree of such inequity is by comparing the market rental of units occupied by subsidized tenants with the mean rent for "standard" private dwellings paid by other low-income households in the same local housing market. Instead of assisting the maximum number of poor households possible with a given budgetary or resource expenditure, the new construction programs—Section 236 and conventional public housing—provide services far in excess of the minimum acceptable quality. As Table 4.1 indicates, only the leasing of existing dwellings makes standard housing available at resource costs comparable to rents of low-income standard units in the same private market (or to the Bureau of Labor Statistics' lower-income family budget).

Of course, ideally, one would like to offer to all families the highest hous-

Table 4.1 Horizontal Equity: Comparative Monthly Cost of Federally Assisted Rental Housing (Two-Bedroom Units), Boston, 1970

Program	Median Monthly Resource Cost	Monthly Resource Cost Divided by Boston Survey Low-Rent Standard Housing Cost ($129)
New Construction		
Conventional public housing	$215.50	1.7
Turnkey public housing	202.50	1.6
Leased housing	207.00	1.6
Section 236–rent supplements	190.00	1.5
Existing Housing Stock		
Leasing existing units	137.00	1.1
Leased housing with rehabilitation	174.00	1.4
Section 236–rent supplements with rehabilitation	180.00	1.4
Private Market Low-Rent Housing		
Standard housinga	129.00	1.0
BLS lower family budgetb	136.00	

a. Derived from the Boston Area Survey, M.I.T.-Harvard Joint Center for Urban Studies, *How the People See Their City: Boston 1969* (Cambridge, Mass., 1970).
b. U.S., Department of Labor, Bureau of Labor Statistics, "Three Budgets for an Urban Family of Four Persons, 1969–1970," Supplement to Bulletin 1570-5 (Washington, D.C.: U.S. Government Printing Office, 1970), Table A-1. Housing includes shelter, household operations, and household furnishings. All families with the lower budget are assumed to be renters. In spring 1970 the average cost of a lower budget for a family of four persons living in urban areas of the U.S. was $6,960.

ing consumption benefits possible. But it is hard to justify moving a fortunate few into brand-new dwellings while the vast majority of eligible families receive absolutely no direct relief at all. Wider awareness of these horizontal inequities has made subsidy programs for new construction increasingly controversial: newspapers across the country have exposed the grosser examples of maldistribution. HUD officials and members of Congress have received streams of complaints from families not receiving assistance and wondering why they must pay taxes to assist others in their neighborhoods who are in comparable financial circumstances.[17] Thus the

17. We assume that the political process behaves in accord with Pareto optimality; that is, we expect that indirect beneficiaries will not value increments in subsidized housing services beyond a certain amount. For example, nontenants will not receive psychological satisfaction if subsidized tenants are provided luxurious penthouses. In this case Pareto optimality is not achieved, since the combined benefit to tenants and nontenants falls short of the government subsidy cost. The Section 236 program with rent supplements for low-income families may be an example of this situation.

status of existing subsidy programs is compromised not only by the empirical measure of their inequities but also by their new political vulnerability in the wake of these disclosures.

Vertical Equity: Diverting Subsidies from the Poor

Any public policy calling for the redistribution of social welfare benefits (whether they are income or in-kind services such as housing) makes an implicit normative judgment that those fortunate enough to enjoy life's luxuries should help those denied its necessities. Almost by definition, this policy embraces as its means "taking from the rich to give to the poor," either by direct transfers or by transfers in kind. Vertical equity is the measure of a program's performance in assessing its costs on those most able to pay and distributing its benefits to those in sorest need.

With any redistributive program it is necessary to ask what proportion of the intended benefits actually reaches the poor and how much is siphoned off by individuals outside the target population. Is the net transfer effect progressive rather than regressive? How much so and with what qualifications? One of the telling arguments made for housing allowances, rent certificates, and income maintenance schemes is that virtually every dollar of government aid reaches the target group. Although these demand strategies require some expenditure on administrative support and program monitoring, the amount of resources deflected to the nonpoor should be minimal.

The Cost of Public Intermediaries

The analysis of how benefits are allocated under existing production programs provides some basis for assessing vertical equity since a large portion of subsidy dollars is diverted to intermediaries. In the case of conventional public housing, for example, the local housing authority negotiates, contracts, and monitors construction activities, and operates and manages housing units. Moreover, capital is raised through the sale of tax-exempt bonds to high-income investors. Under the leased public housing program, the same housing authority selects tenants, inspects dwelling units, and negotiates with landlords for the lease of private dwellings. With the Section 236–rent supplement program, a portion of the subsidy funds is kept to pay salaries and administrative expenses, as it passes through the hands of FHA administrators and local sponsors.

The Cost of Raising Capital through Preferential Tax Treatment
Diversion of federal housing funds to the nonpoor also results from the use
of high-income investors as a source of development capital. In the case of
conventional or turnkey public housing, the federal government raises capital through the sale of housing authority 40-year serial bonds. Interest payments on these bonds are exempt from federal income taxation in order
to facilitate their sale on the most favorable terms. The net cost of issuing
these tax-exempt bonds is the difference between the loss of federal revenue
on the tax-exempt interest payments and the interest cost saving that results
because the payments for retiring the bonds are less than those for retiring
fully taxable bonds.[18] For privately owned units—either constructed or rehabilitated in conjunction with the leased housing and rent supplement
programs—accelerated depreciation provisions offer high-income investors
a means of sheltering income from federal taxation. The syndication of
these tax shelters is a costly method of raising development capital and results in additional forgone federal revenue. Thus, as the data in Table 4.2
indicate, the share of the total direct benefits received by the poor (one
measure of vertical equity) varies among the alternative housing strategies,
with the target groups receiving their largest share of the subsidy dollar
through programs relying on the use of the existing housing stock.[19]

The Redistributive Goal
One of the major problems highlighted in the President's *Third Annual
Report on National Housing Goals* (1971) was "the need to deal with inequities which arise when some families receive subsidies and others do not,
the inevitable result of having to allocate scarce resources." To a limited
extent, Congress has sought to deal with these inequities in straightforward
terms, by imposing low-income limits for program eligibility and attempt-

18. For a detailed explanation of this cost estimate, see Arthur P. Solomon, "The Cost
Effectiveness of Subsidized Housing," Working Paper No. 5 (Cambridge, Mass.: MIT-
Harvard Joint Center for Urban Studies, 1972), Appendix A, mimeographed.
19. In a study of how the direct benefits of public housing are distributed, Bish found
that the poor and near poor received nearly 80 percent of the subsidy. See R. L. Bish,
"Public Housing: The Magnitude and Distribution of Direct Benefits and Effects on
Housing Consumption," *Journal of Regional Science*, Vol. 9 (December 1969), pp. 27–39.
This is an overestimate, however, since the cost of the income tax subsidy associated with
the interest payment exemption on the public housing serial bonds is not included in the
Bish analysis.

Table 4.2 Vertical Equity: Allocation of Federal Housing Subsidies to Tenants, Intermediaries, and Investors, Boston, 1970[a]

Program	Tenant Consumption Benefit		Government Intermediaries[b]		Investors and Syndicators[c]	
New Construction						
Conventional public housing	64%	($60.00)	24%	($22.00)	12%	($11.00)
Leased housing	79	(98.00)	17	(13.00)	4	(4.50)
Section 236–rent supplements	81	(107.00)	15	(5.50)	4	(4.50)
Simple unweighted mean	79					
Existing Housing Stock						
Leasing existing units	81	(55.00)	19	(13.00)	0[d]	(0)[d]
Leased housing with rehabilitation	79	(79.00)	13	(13.00)	7	(7.50)
Section 236–rent supplement with rehabilitation	83	(93.00)	10	(5.50)	7	(7.50)
Simple unweighted mean	82					
Housing allowances[e]	90					

a. The allocation of benefits is derived from Chapter 3.
b. The amount diverted to federal and local intermediaries is based on the program's respective administrative costs.
c. The share of the total costs diverted to high-income investors and financial syndicators is based on estimates of forgone federal revenue from accelerated depreciation and tax-exempt bonds.
d. Because many structures containing existing units have been under the same ownership for at least five to ten years, it is assumed that the cost of any tax shelter from an earlier syndicate is no longer incurred.
e. In the case of housing allowances, the direct tenant consumption benefit is likely to approach 80–90 percent, depending upon the type of administrative and monitoring mechanisms adopted.

ing to ensure that the neediest families receive priority. But lowering eligibility limits without simultaneously increasing the amount of the subsidy may, in effect, force local housing authorities into insolvency.

Ideally, the equity problems should be solved by increasing appropriations sufficiently to provide an adequate subsidy for all those eligible by some reasonable definition of need. As the President's Committee on Urban Housing (the Kaiser Committee) concluded, government assistance should be provided to all persons—regardless of family size, age, mental status, or health—who are unable to afford the cost of modest, decent, safe, and sanitary housing. However, as long as the nation is either unwilling or unable to allocate the funds required to meet this goal, the equity problem must be approached through improved allocation of whatever resources happen to be available. While recognizing that there is no single, unambiguous measure of poverty or individual need, we must try to channel limited funds to those most disadvantaged by the private housing market. This will require careful analysis of the probability that, in the absence of government aid, a family with given characteristics would be condemned by the market to live in substandard housing. It will also require a major restructuring of our housing subsidy programs—away from the existing miscellany of selection criteria, which leaves many needy families without any assistance whatsoever, and away from the new construction orientation, which grants excessive benefits to a few and deposits too much of the subsidy dollar into the pockets of the nonpoor.

Technical Note: The Housing Condition Probability Model
Through the application of a statistical, generalized linear model, it is possible to determine the likelihood that a household, with a specified set of characteristics, will live in substandard housing in the absence of government subsidies. The results of this type of analysis provide some measure of the extent to which federal housing subsidies are reaching those with the highest probability of living in deficient units, one of our measures of horizontal equity.

For this purpose a dichotomous dependent variable of housing condition, which takes on the value of zero (0) when the housing units are classified as standard and one (1) when the units are deteriorated or dilapidated, is regressed across the independent variable representing the household characteristics discussed in the chapter. The following equation is used:[20]

$$X = \alpha + b_1 Y + b_2 N + b_3 B + b_4 W + b_5 E + b_6 L + b_7 P, \qquad (4.1)$$

where

X = the probability of living in substandard housing,

α = the intercept or mean value of the independent variables that are not included in the housing condition model,

20. The variables for mean household size (N) and extra-large families (L), and for mean gross income (Y), and unusually poor families (P) are highly collinear (that is, as the values of both variables change, the values remain proportional). However, the dummy variables for extra-large and unusually poor households are included because the federal government provides local housing authorities with additional financial support for these specially disadvantaged groups. Welfare status and income are also highly collinear.

$b_1 \ldots b_7$ = the regression coefficients for the respective household characteristics,

Y = the gross income of the household,

N = the household size,

B = a dummy or dichotomous variable for tenant race (1 = nonwhite head of household; 0 = white head of household),

W = a dummy variable for welfare status (1 = household receiving some welfare assistance; 0 = no welfare assistance),

E = a dummy variable for the elderly (1 = household head 65 years of age or over; 0 = household head under 65),

L = a dummy variable for extra-large families (1 = 6 members or over; 0 = under 6),

P = dummy variable for unusually poor families (1 = under \$3,000 gross income; 0 = \$3,000 or over).

Numerical values for the explanatory or independent variables are taken from the tenant application forms for each household. The regression coefficients indicate the additional probability of living in substandard housing as explained by the associated independent variable once other variables have been accounted for. If, for example, the coefficient for a continuous variable like family size is 0.04, then the probability of living in substandard conditions increases by 4 percent with each additional family member. With a dummy variable like race, if the coefficient is 0.12, then the probability of a nonwhite family living in substandard housing is 12 percent above that of a white family, all other factors being equal. (These interpretations, of course, assume linear relationships.)

Using the data for the city of Boston,[21] we show some representative output from the generalized least-square model [22] in Table 4.3. Most regression

21. Data used for the regression are from the Boston Area Survey, MIT-Harvard Joint Center for Urban Studies, *How the People See Their City: Boston 1969* (Cambridge, Mass., 1970).
22. For a binary regression analysis we cannot use ordinary least squares (OLS) since it violates the homoscedasticity criterion as the variance of the error term is not random. Instead, the variance of the error term varies with the predicted value of each observation, for example, if the predicted value is E_{yt}, then the variance is $E_{yt}(1 - E_{yt})$. However,

Table 4.3 Families Living in Substandard Housing, Boston, 1970

Tenant Characteristic	Percentages and Averages	Regression Coefficients	t-Statistic	Indices
Family size	3.0	0.002	0.296	0.0060
Nonwhite families	20.0%	0.078	3.275[a]	0.0165
Welfare status	21.0%	0.162	3.604[a]	0.0340
Family income (in dollars)	$7,700	−0.000004	3.250[a]	−0.0310
Extra-large families	11.0%	0.057	1.392	0.0063
Unusually poor families	8.0%	0.034	1.739	0.0030
Elderly households	10.0%	0.062	3.341[a]	0.0620
Total (composite index)				0.0959[b]

Intercept 0.1743 (t-statistic 5.103)[a]

Degrees of freedom 0.1792

a. Coefficient different from 0 at 0.01 level. The t-statistic provides a measure of statistical confidence for each independent variable. (For a technical definition of the use and meaning of the t-statistic, see any elementary statistics text.)
b. The composite index is computed by multiplying the value of each independent variable by its associated regression coefficient (the fitted coefficients from the housing condition probability model) and summing the individual indices.

coefficients in our model are statistically significant, and their signs are consistent with expectations. Greater family size and lower income as well as minority, elderly, and welfare status each correlate positively with substandard housing conditions.

Using socioeconomic data and the estimated regression coefficients for a particular city, we can estimate the probability of an average urban household living in substandard housing. This probability—when compared to that of the average subsidized tenant living in substandard housing if he were to be denied government assistance—offers a means for evaluating the performance of existing programs with respect to reaching those with the most serious housing needs.

First, appropriate percentages and mean values for each household characteristic (average family size, mean family income, and so forth) are calcu-

---

we are able to correct for homoscedasticity by using a generalized least-squares regression model. Another difficulty worth mentioning is the unit probability problem associated with the type of model used in this study. Admittedly, with the use of this equation, the probability of living in substandard housing for given individuals might fall outside the zero-to-one range; however, our estimates concern groups rather than individuals. If we use the mean socioeconomic characteristics of the tenants in each subsidized program, it is highly unlikely that the equation would result in a probability falling outside the zero-to-one range.

lated for a given city and then multiplied by their respective regression coefficients. The products are summed to determine a composite index for the city. The addition of this index to the intercept (the mean value of excluded variables) determines the probability of living in substandard housing. In Boston, for example, adding the value of the intercept, 0.1743, to the composite index for the city, 0.0959, indicates a probability of 0.27; in other words, the average household in Boston has about one chance in four of living in substandard housing (see Table 4.3). Next, the probability that the average tenant in each of the three subsidy programs would live in substandard housing in the absence of government assistance is computed in a similar manner. Each of these probabilities is then subtracted from the mean probability for the average household in the city. The difference between the probability for the average household in a city and the probability for the average tenant in each federally assisted housing program represents the "additional" probability that a subsidized tenant would live in substandard housing without government assistance. In other words, the additional probability of subsidized tenants living in substandard dwellings—over and above that of the average city dweller—reflects the relative disadvantage those tenants would face in competing for standard housing on the private market. This provides a statistical measure of distributive equity, the measure used for weighting the housing benefit in the benefit-cost model. To illustrate, calculations are made using Boston data as summarized in Table 4.4. The degree of local discretion permitted in the selection of tenants for the subsidized housing programs suggests that the distributive weights determined for the Boston programs will not be universally applicable. However, the results do contribute to understanding how benefits are distributed in one particular city, and, more important, the methodology used is generally applicable to other cities and housing markets.

By applying the regression coefficients for Boston to the respective tenant characteristics and then summing the products, composite indices are derived for the city's public housing, leased housing, and rent supplement programs. (See Table 4.5.) The intercept for Boston (0.1743) is added to each index to find the probability that the average subsidized tenant would live in substandard housing in the absence of government assistance. Since the intercepts are the same, the distributive weight is computed by subtract-

Table 4.4 Tenant Characteristics, Boston, 1970

Tenant Characteristic	City	Public Housing	Leased Housing	Section 236–Rent Supplements
Mean family size	3.0	3.1	3.1	3.8
Percent nonwhite	20.0	41.0	72.0	100.0
Percent welfare recipients	21.0	32.0	52.0	89.1
Median household income	$7,700	$3,680	$3,353	$3,468
Percent extra-large families	11.0	17.0	20.0	19.2
Percent unusually poor families	8.0	69.0	48.0	53.9
Percent elderly	10.0	31.0	24.0	6.8

The sources of these statistics are as follows:
Public Housing: Boston Housing Authority, "Federally Aided Developments Tenant Status Report," June 1969, mimeographed.
Leased Housing: Boston Housing Authority, "Report on Leased Housing Programs as of April 1970," mimeographed, and BHA Tenant Application Forms.
Section 236–Rent Supplement: FHA Boston Insuring Office, Application for Tenant Eligibility for Rent Supplement, FHA Form No. 2501.

Table 4.5 Distributive Weights for Subsidized Housing Programs, Boston, 1970

Tenant Characteristics	Regression Coefficient	Public Housing Indices	Leased Housing Indices	Section 236– Rent Supplement Indices	Boston Indices
Mean family size	0.002	0.0062	0.0062	0.0076	0.0060
Nonwhite households	0.078	0.0320	0.0562	0.0780	0.0165
Welfare families	0.162	0.0518	0.0842	0.1141	0.0340
Mean family income	−0.000004	−0.0015	−0.0134	−0.0139	−0.0310
Extra-large families	0.057	0.0097	0.0114	0.0108	0.0063
Unusually poor families	0.034	0.0235	0.0163	0.0184	0.0030
Elderly households	0.062	0.0192	0.0149	0.0043	0.0620
Composite indices		0.1439	0.1758	0.2492	0.0959
Distributive weight (composite index for housing programs)		0.0480	0.0799	0.1533	

ing the composite values for each program from the composite value for the entire city. For example, if the probability for the average Boston household is 0.27 and the probability for the average rent supplement tenant is 0.42, then, in the absence of the government subsidy, the average family in a rent supplement unit has a 15 percent (0.42–0.27) higher likelihood of living in substandard housing than does the average Boston household.

CHAPTER 5

Estimating the Municipal Fiscal Effect

Few state or local governments are without fiscal problems. . . . But the
problems seem most severe for local governments serving the larger and
older metropolitan areas of the country. . . . In part, their difficulties
reflect the concentration of the urban poverty and race problems in the
large older cities. Also, the very fact of age creates problems associated
with physical and functional obsolescence. In addition, there are difficulties stemming from extremely rapid growth rates on their urbanizing
fringes.
Dick Netzer,
"Financing Urban Government"

Our federal system is unique because of the authority granted to local governments, especially the power given to raise revenue from local property
taxes for education and other public services. As a result, the debate on
any proposal affecting local land use tends to focus as much on the fiscal
impact (its impact on the balance between municipal revenues and expenditures) as upon the locational effects (the impact on the quality of life
within the immediate neighborhood). Inevitably, land-use decisions pose
questions regarding how many ratables the new activity will add to the
tax base and whether it will put more children in the schools as well as
require other municipal outlays.

Municipal Revenue—with and without Subsidized Housing
Given the centrality of the property tax base to municipal finance, the preoccupation of local policy makers with the likely fiscal effect of any proposed
change in land use is an understandable one. Insofar as any public program, such as subsidized housing, causes a net increment in local revenue,
it enables city hall either to increase its provision of services or to reduce
property taxes. For the affected households, this means either an increase
in public services or, with a tax reduction, an opportunity to consume additional private goods. Conversely, when a public program leads to a net loss
in municipal revenue, service levels may be lowered or taxes increased,
thereby reducing consumer benefits.

Applying a welfare economics approach, we compute the local fiscal benefit of government-assisted housing as equivalent to the aggregate value
added in municipal revenue, with any addition assumed to represent a net

gain in consumer well-being. In this chapter we first establish a meaningful procedure to measure the difference in municipal expenditures and revenues, with and without federally assisted housing.[1] Using this procedure, we then develop empirical estimates of the local fiscal effect associated with each of the housing subsidy programs and compare these results in terms of their implications for major policy alternatives (particularly new construction versus use of the existing stock).

Municipal Service Requirements

We shall assume that federally assisted housing has a negligible effect on municipal expenditures. In the case of the leased housing and Section 236-rent supplement programs, tenants occupy private units that receive the same municipal services as do other dwellings in their immediate neighborhood. For this reason it is doubtful that the introduction of subsidized tenants necessitates any incremental costs. With regard to public housing, the situation is less clear. Some argue that construction of public housing brings increased service costs (for police protection, garbage collection, health care, and so on) when tenants move from private substandard dwellings into public housing in the same community or from one community to another in search of better public services.[2] Other observers would contend that, to the contrary, such expenditures are largely associated with poor families wherever they live in the community rather than because of their concentration in public projects. Some additional municipal cost, however, may result from the competition between local housing authority bonds and other municipal obligations. (Since housing authority and municipal bonds are similar in duration, cost, and tax exemption, they compete in the same financial market; this may increase the interest rate on municipal

1. Inappropriately, some housing and urban renewal studies measure change in aggregate property values by estimating values before and after the introduction of a federally assisted housing program. Such "before" and "after" comparisons make the implicit assumption that the land use existing prior to the introduction of subsidized housing remains unchanged for the full economic life of the development. This assumption is unreasonable since in reality land use does change over time in accord with the standard life cycle of neighborhoods, community development activities, and shifts in industrial and residential locations. Thus it is conceptually appropriate to measure the difference in aggregate property values with and without subsidized housing rather than before and after its introduction.

2. See, for example, Jay Forrester, *Urban Dynamics* (Cambridge, Mass.: MIT Press, 1969).

bonds and consequently raise local government debt costs.) However, because data are unavailable, we have assumed that public housing does not affect the cost of municipal debt.[3] To the extent that actual differences in service costs do result, this assumption causes us to overestimate the net value added in municipal revenue from conventional public housing.

Changes in Real Property Values

Turning from expenditures to the revenue side of the municipal ledger, we find clear evidence of net changes caused by federally assisted housing programs. These changes are measured by first computing the impact of each program on the aggregate value of the housing stock and then using the result to determine the change in property tax revenue. Since property taxes are the major source of local revenue, this method provides a reasonable estimate of the effect of subsidized housing on the municipal treasury.

Realtors, appraisers, and housing economists generally use one of three measures for calculating property values: the sales price of comparable properties, the estimated replacement cost minus depreciation, or the capitalization of the net rental income stream. Given the ready availability of data on rent receipts, the capitalization method is the most feasible for our purposes. When applying this method, we assume that real property is assessed at 100 percent of market value. In the absence of federal housing, the market value can then be expressed as

$$V_j = \sum_{t=1}^{n} \frac{R_{jt}}{(1+i)^t},$$ (5.1)

where

3. In disregarding expenditure effects, we also assume that a community's use of federal housing subsidies does not alter the amount of land devoted to residential as opposed to other uses, or the overall pattern of population density, or the population mix (by driving away middle-class families or attracting poor households from other jurisdictions). Although little hard evidence exists on these questions, experience with local housing programs suggests that these assumptions are reasonable ones. However, certain exceptional situations might occur, for example, where a subsidized housing development preempts a site that could clearly be marketed for a more economically productive nonresidential purpose. Also, if metropolitan or state housing agencies should prove more successful in overriding local vetoes and building low-income developments in suburban communities, then the expenditure side of the net revenue effect might warrant more detailed consideration.

V_j = the market value (assessment value) of property j in the absence of federal housing,

R_{jt} = the net rental income from property j in year t,

i = the appropriate return to an investment of this particular degree of risk and liquidity (the discount rate),

n = the number of years in the economic life of the property.

We compute the total value of the housing stock by aggregating the estimates for each parcel. Of course, in the case of owner-occupied properties, it is necessary to impute a rental value. In the absence of government-assisted housing, then, the property value of the total stock is estimated as follows:

$$V = \sum_{j=1}^{J} V_j, \qquad (5.2)$$

where

V = the aggregate value of the total housing stock in the absence of federally assisted housing.

If the aggregate value of real property in each year is multiplied by the appropriate tax rate and discounted over the property's economic life, we obtain the present worth of the total tax yield. This amount is the present value of municipal property *without* government-assisted housing:

$$T = \sum_{t=1}^{n} \frac{r_t V}{(1+i)^t}, \qquad (5.3)$$

where

T = the discounted present value of the aggregate property taxes paid in the absence of government-assisted housing,

r_t = the property tax rate for year t,

i = the discount rate.

Through an understanding of how subsidy programs affect the housing market, we can isolate their marginal effect upon the value of the housing stock. As our analysis of the housing consumption benefit has indicated (in Chapter 3), the increase in the supply of housing services caused by the alternate housing strategies is, in each instance, equivalent to the value of their respective rental subsidies. Thus, to the extent that the capital value of real estate represents the stream of expected net rental income, the addition of the government subsidy creates an increase in aggregate property values. With federally assisted housing, then, the marginal effect on the value of the housing stock equals the capitalized value of the rent subsidy. This figure, added to the value of the total stock without subsidized units, gives us the aggregate value of the housing stock *with* the presence of federally assisted units:

$$V' = \sum_{j=1}^{J} \sum_{t=1}^{n} \frac{R_{jt} + S_{jt}}{(1+i)^t} , \qquad (5.4)$$

where

V' = the aggregate value of the housing stock *with* federally assisted housing,

R_{jt} = the net rental income from property j in year t,

S_{jt} = the value of the total rent subsidy for property j in year t.

If owners of subsidized units pay full taxes, then the present value of municipal revenue from real property is estimated by multiplying the aggregate value of the housing stock by the appropriate tax rate and discounting over the economic life:

$$T' = \sum_{t=1}^{n} \frac{r_t V'}{(1+i)^t}, \qquad (5.5)$$

where

T' = the discounted present value of the aggregate property taxes paid in the presence of government-assisted housing,

r_t = the property tax rate for year t.

The aggregate value of municipal revenue with (T') and without (T) federal housing is then computed as

$$B^M = T' - T = \sum_{t=1}^{n} \frac{r_t V' - r_t V}{(1+i)^t} \tag{5.6}$$

$$= \sum_{j=1}^{J} \sum_{t=1}^{n} \frac{r_t(R_{jt} + S_{jt})/(1+i)^t - r_t R_{jt}/(1+i)^t}{(1+i)^t}$$

$$= \sum_{j=1}^{J} \sum_{t=1}^{n} \frac{r_t S_{jt}/(1+i)^t}{(1+i)^t}.$$

Thus the marginal fiscal benefit is equal to the present worth of the tax yield from capitalizing the rent subsidy. In other words, since the capitalized value of the rent subsidy represents the value added to the housing stock, the tax yield from this added property value represents the municipal revenue benefit.

The measure of the municipal benefit given above must be modified, however, when applied to low-income housing programs receiving property tax concessions (for example, conventional public housing, FHA-sponsored Section 236). As a condition for funding under some programs, the federal government requires participating municipalities to forgo the levy of a conventional property tax and to accept in its stead a payment in lieu of taxes (PILOT). In such cases, the municipal fiscal benefit is the difference between the tax yield from capitalizing the rent subsidy and the actual payments made in lieu of taxes.

Conventional Public Housing

The impact of newly constructed public housing upon municipal revenue results from its implicit rent subsidies as well as from the statutory and administrative regulations for financing the projects. As our previous discussion indicates, the capitalized value of the rent subsidy is equivalent to the net change in aggregate property values.[4] If full real estate taxes were

4. Although our welfare economics computation is made on an aggregate basis, it would be interesting to consider also some of the disaggregated effects of public housing (spillover effects, filtering, and so forth). However, our theoretical understanding of the

imposed on conventional public housing, the municipal benefit would be the present worth of the tax yield from capitalizing the subsidy. However, federal regulations require that public housing receive a property tax exemption as part of the local government contribution.

Participating local governments are required to make an annual contribution equal to 20 percent of the federal subsidy. Typically, this contribution takes the form of a tax exemption on the local housing authority's real property, with the authority still rendering some lesser payments in lieu of taxes. Prior to 1944, the amount of these payments was negotiated, but in that year the federal government adopted a uniform policy[5] calling on each LHA to convey 10 percent of its shelter rent receipts (gross rent minus cost of utilities) to the local government. This sum can be represented as

$$P_{jt} = \sum_{j=1}^{J} \sum_{t=1}^{n} \gamma R'_{jt},\tag{5.7}$$

where
P_{jt} = the PILOT for property j in year t,
γ = a constant 0.10 of shelter rent,

R'_{jt} = the shelter rent for subsidized housing property j in year t.

Federal regulations provide for some additional payment to the city during the period between land acquisition and the actual occupancy of the units, but only for that part of the acquisition year remaining after the local housing authority deed has been recorded. Thus there is an interval over which a public housing site yields neither real property taxes nor payments in lieu of taxes, and the municipality loses revenue it would other-

behavioral relationships that underlie the supply and demand sides of the metropolitan housing market is limited, and there is little actual empirical analysis of market dynamics. Among the notable exceptions are Leo Grebler, *Housing Market Behavior in a Declining Area* (New York: Columbia University Press, 1952), and William Grigsby, *Housing Markets and Public Policy* (Philadelphia: University of Pennsylvania Press, 1963).
5. There is no conceptual justification for the uniform PILOT policy since it neither reflects considerations of economic efficiency nor corresponds to the cost of municipal services (benefit or user tax) or the market value of the developments (ad valorem tax).

wise have collected from the private property owners.[6] Though often ignored in fiscal evaluations of public housing or urban renewal,[7] any such analysis should include the value of revenue forgone during the development period.

Taking into consideration both rent subsidy and tax exemption effects, we measure the present value of municipal revenue from public housing (the overall fiscal impact) as the present discounted value of the stream of payments in lieu of taxes minus the revenue forgone during the construction period, minus the tax yield from the capitalized value of the rent subsidy. For the purpose of this analysis, municipal benefits are calculated for one year only. Since we want the computation to represent an average year of operation, rather than one including the construction period, it is necessary to exclude the period between land acquisition and occupancy.

To calculate the average annual municipal effect per tenant for public housing in Boston in 1970, we subtract the estimated tax yield at full taxation from the actual PILOT. Using Equation 5.7, we compute the PILOT as 10 percent of shelter rent.[8] The tax yield at full property tax rates is estimated by capitalizing the rent subsidy according to the formula used by the city of Boston[9] for income-producing properties. This formula gives the capitalization rate as the sum of the annual tax rate, a 2 percent depreciation allowance, and an 8 percent rate of return (profit) allowance. The value of the government's public housing rent subsidy in Boston was computed in Chapter 3 ($50 per month or $720 per annum for a two-bedroom unit); by incorporating these results, we can compute the fiscal benefit (B^M) per tenant household as

6. Under other low-income housing programs this situation does not exist because the subsidized properties remain under private ownership.
7. See, for example, Boston Redevelopment Authority, *The Prudential Center, Part One: Its Direct Impact on Boston,* September 1969, p. 3.
8. Shelter rent is assumed to be 90 percent of the gross rent.
9. Because our analysis is performed on an aggregate basis, without regard to the geographic location of the value added, the choice of a capitalization formula is arbitrary. The formula used here is the one employed by the Office of the Assessor in Boston. Since operating costs are assumed to be 45 percent of gross rents, the net effective income added by the government's rent subsidy is equal to 55 percent of the value of the government subsidy.

$$B^M = T' - T = \gamma \overline{R'} - r_t \frac{\overline{R}}{r_t + d + y}$$

$$= \gamma(0.9\overline{G}) - r_t \frac{\overline{G} - \overline{C^o}}{r_t + d + y}$$

$$= \gamma(0.9\overline{G}) - r_t \frac{\overline{G} - 0.45\overline{G}}{r_t + d + y}$$

$$= 0.10\,(0.9)(720) - 0.1568 \frac{0.55(720)}{0.1568 + 0.02 + 0.08}$$

$$= 64.80 - \frac{0.1568\,(396)}{0.2568}$$

$$= -\$177 \text{ per annum}$$

$$= -\$15 \text{ per month}, \tag{5.8}$$

where

γ = a constant 0.10 of shelter rent,

$\overline{R'}$ = the average shelter rent (assumed to be 90 percent of the gross rent subsidy),

$\overline{R}$ = the average net rent,

$\overline{G}$ = the average gross rent subsidy[10] ($720),

$\overline{C^o}$ = the average operating costs (assumed to be 45 percent of the gross rent subsidy),

r_t = the property tax rate in year t (0.1568),

d = the depreciation allowance (0.02),

y = the profit allowance (0.08).

Our results indicate that by constructing conventional public housing, municipalities reduce the aggregate value of their real property tax base. Moreover, it is important to recognize that the revenue loss increases over

10. The monthly rent subsidies for all public housing units are calculated in Chapter 3 and summarized in Table 3.1.

the years because the local housing authority's payment in lieu of taxes (PILOT) does not increase as rapidly as the tax yield with full property tax payments. The reason for this increasing differential is simple: the PILOT is a function of shelter rent, which, in turn, is based on the slowly rising income of public housing tenants (an increasing proportion of whom subsist on relatively fixed welfare or social security payments); full tax payments, on the other hand, are calculated, in part, on the basis of property tax rates that have risen continuously since the 1930s and at an accelerated rate in recent years (in part because of inflationary pressures on all municipal costs and also because of the demand for higher levels of public service).

Leased Housing: Using the Existing Stock

To analyze the effect of leased housing on the fiscal status of local government, it is first necessary to break the program down by the type of stock and the term of lease. This is important since we are comparing housing strategies—new construction versus use of existing stock—rather than specific programs. Essentially, three types of housing stock are leased: existing units as they are, existing units with rehabilitation, and newly constructed units.[11] With regard to the lease provisions, the federal government requires a real property tax exemption for units leased under the Section 10(c) long-term program but explicitly denies any exemption for Section 23 short-term commitments.[12]

In Boston, the Housing Authority–City of Boston Cooperation Agreement allows long-term leased property to remain on the tax rolls. The private owner of the property still pays full real estate taxes, but the municipality makes a contribution to the housing authority in the form of a credit against the payment in lieu of taxes (PILOT) that the authority owes on its other low rent housing projects. This credit is equivalent to the full

11. The United States Housing Act of 1937, as amended, confines the leasing program to existing structures, but local authorities are free to enter into agreements to lease in advance of rehabilitation or new construction. According to the Leased Housing Statistical Report of the Boston Housing Authority (April 30, 1970), mimeographed, the Boston program includes 1,710 existing units, 140 rehabilitated units, and 55 newly constructed units.

12. The Department of Housing and Urban Development will not make any annual contributions for a Section 10 (c) long-term program unless the program is exempt from all local property taxes or the city makes a contribution in the form of cash or tax remission. Under Section 23 short-term leasing, the property in which units are leased is privately owned, the LHA has only a short-term agreement for leasing, and the landlord pays full real estate taxes to the city.

amount of taxes less 10 percent of the shelter rents charged for the leased units. Therefore, under the long-term leasing provisions, the local government, in Boston as elsewhere, receives 10 percent of shelter rent in lieu of full real estate taxes. The municipal fiscal effect of the long-term Section 10(c) program is measured as the PILOT minus the full taxes associated with capitalizing the value of the subsidy. For 1970, the municipal fiscal effect of the long-term leasing program for a two-bedroom unit is computed as[13]

$$B^M = T' - T = \gamma \, \overline{R'} - \frac{R}{r_t + d + y}$$

$$= \gamma(0.9 \, \overline{G}) - r_t \frac{\overline{G} - \overline{C^o}}{r_t + d + y}$$

$$= 0.10 \, (0.9)(1{,}176) - 0.1568 \, \frac{1{,}176 - 0.45 \, (1{,}176)}{2{,}568}$$

$$= 106 - 383$$

$$= -\$277 \text{ per annum}$$

$$= -\$23 \text{ per month.} \tag{5.9}$$

In the case of the Section 23 short-term leasing arrangement (which enjoys no special tax exemption), we determine the program's impact upon municipal revenue simply by applying the appropriate 1970 property tax rate to the change in aggregate property values. As in previous calculations, the amount of this change is found by first capitalizing the rent subsidy. Applying the same formula used for our conventional public housing estimate (Equation 5.8), we find that the net effect of the short-term leasing of existing housing in 1970 is $222 per annum or $18.50 per month (when the value of the gross rent subsidy $\overline{G}$ is $55 a month).

We measure the fiscal impact of leasing rehabilitated units under a short-term lease in the same manner, the only difference being the larger value of the rent subsidy (and therefore the property value) associated with the

13. Rent subsidies for the public housing leasing program are summarized in Table 3.2. The value of the gross rent subsidy (G) for the leasing of newly constructed units, for example, is $1,176 per annum.

rehabilitated units.[14] Substituting the value of the yearly rent subsidy for a rehabilitated two-bedroom unit ($948) for $\overline{G}$ in Equation 5.8, we find that the municipal effect of a rehabilitated unit leased over the short-term is $518 per annum or $43 per month.

Our empirical findings on the municipal fiscal effect of the leased housing program are noteworthy. Although the value added in real property is largest for newly constructed dwellings ($395), the required exemption from local real estate taxes under the long-term leasing program (and a long-term commitment is necessary to induce the construction of new units) actually results in a loss of municipal revenue. Since the property tax exemption is related neither to the cost of municipal services (like a user tax) nor to the market value of the subsidized units (like an ad valorem tax), it is questionable whether this form of government subsidy is an appropriate means of assisting low-income housing. The questionable nature of this form of local government subsidy is treated in more detail in the final section, on comparative findings.

Section 236 with Rent Supplements

As noted earlier, the rent supplement program is tied to FHA-insured mortgages for the new construction or substantial rehabilitation of privately owned dwellings.[15] Since market rents and the associated subsidies for these units depend upon their structural and environmental qualities, the value of the Section 236 and other FHA-insured multifamily dwellings may vary considerably, even within the same community. If, for example, a rent supplement sponsor constructs a new project on a vacant parcel in a blighted neighborhood or rehabilitates an abandoned dwelling, negative externalities will severely limit the increment in property value. Conversely, the increment will be substantially higher if a development with rent supplement units is built in a middle-income area or is part of an overall neigh-

14. Since tenants pay a fixed proportion of their income for rent, with the LHA paying the difference between the tenant's share and the market rent, the larger rent subsidy in the improved units is to be expected.

15. Most rent supplements (90 percent of the subsidized units) are linked to new construction. But in high construction cost areas, such as Chicago and New York, close to 80 percent of the FHA rent supplement projects under payment, contract, or reservation involve rehabilitation instead. (See U.S. Department of Housing and Urban Development, Federal Housing Administration, *Rent Supplement Rental Project Operations*, Washington, D.C., September 1969) . According to the FHA insuring office in Boston, another high-cost area, 731 of 769 rent supplement units or 95 percent of the total are rehabilitated units.

borhood renewal program.[16] In general, from a fiscal point of view, rent supplement dwellings have proved an attractive alternative for local communities because of their positive contribution to the tax base.

To compute the program's fiscal value, we employ the same methodology used for short-term leasing. Since rent supplement projects do not involve a property tax exemption, the municipal revenue effect can be estimated by applying the appropriate property tax rate to the capitalized value of the average rent subsidy. For the rent supplement units in rehabilitated dwellings, the per-unit municipal benefit, where the value of the monthly rent subsidy was $94, was $378 per annum or $31.50 per month.[17]

The increase in the aggregate value of the housing stock and the associated tax revenue from newly constructed rent supplement units is estimated in the same manner. The municipal benefit is somewhat higher, of course, since the rent subsidy associated with newly constructed units exceeds that of the rehabilitated units. The actual municipal revenue contribution for each new dwelling unit was $36 per month.

The per-unit contribution to the municipal tax base from the rent supplement program is more than that from the leased housing program. This difference can be explained in two ways, one reflecting local policy, the other federal. First, landlords under the rent supplement program pay full real estate taxes, while owners of units under the long-term leased housing program receive a tax abatement. Second, the dwellings subsidized under the rent supplement program are usually of higher quality because they are linked to FHA-sponsored moderate-income housing.

Net Effects on Municipal Treasuries
The municipal benefits of the three major housing programs, as measured by the amount of property tax revenue added per unit per month, are compared in Table 5.1. The figures in this table provide a basis for comparing the impact on the local tax base associated with alternative forms of housing subsidy. With respect to new construction strategies the net fiscal effect

16. In both cases it is clear that the availability and choice of development sites, neighborhoods, and structural quality of rent supplements units—the factors that affect market rents—are critical determinants of a program's municipal fiscal effect.
17. For a summary of rent supplement subsidies by number of bedrooms and type of stock, see Tables 3.1 and 3.2.

Table 5.1 Municipal Revenue Effect of Subsidized Housing, Boston, 1970 (dollars per two-bedroom unit per month)

Program	Payments in Lieu of Taxes	Full Real Estate Taxes	Property Tax Effect (per annum)	Property Tax Effect (per month)
New Construction				
Public housing[a]	$ 65.00	$242.00	— 177.00	—$15.00
Leased housing[a]	106.00	383.00	378.00	— 23.00
Section 236–rent supplements	—	431.00	431.00	36.00
Existing Housing Stock				
Leased housing with existing units	—	222.00	222.00	18.50
Leased housing with rehabilitation	—	318.00	318.00	26.50
Section 236–rent supplements with rehabilitation	—	378.00	378.00	31.50

a. These are the federally assisted housing programs that require a local tax exemption.

varies widely, depending on whether or not the property receives a local tax abatement. For example, a large city having an inventory of 5,000 conventional public housing units, which receive property tax exemptions, would incur a loss of nearly $1 million in forgone revenue for 1970 (5,000 units × —$177 per unit per annum).

Moreover, this fiscal erosion increases over the years because of the public housing property tax exemption formula. Without federally assisted housing, the estimated tax yield from any given property (with the exception of properties whose market value declines precipitously) would tend to keep pace with the municipal tax rate as it has climbed steadily over the years. On the other hand, the actual payments in lieu of taxes (PILOT) are based on relatively fixed tenant incomes, precluding any comparable increase in municipal revenue. Thus the disparity between actual payments and estimated payments—the local subsidy—widens as the years pass. This problem arises in conjunction not only with public housing but also with any housing construction program that utilizes payments in lieu of full taxes that are tied to tenant incomes and rents. For example, Section 10(c) long-term leasing, in conjunction with federally assisted new construction, also requires a tax exemption and, in consequence, has a negative effect on local fiscal capacity. Conversely, the construction of new FHA-insured dwellings, when occupied by rent supplement tenants, may make a substantial contribution to the local tax base since owners must still pay full property taxes. Similarly, programs that utilize the existing stock (rent supplements with rehabilitation, Section 23 leased housing, and housing allowances) would make a positive contribution to the municipal treasury since the value of the rent subsidies would be capitalized into higher property values, consequently more property tax revenue.

These results raise some interesting policy questions: Is the local tax exemption on real property a desirable form of subsidy for low-rent housing? Does the subsidy (or PILOT) derive its rationale from any persuasive concept of efficiency, equity, or redistribution? Even if it does, can such indirection (that is, the use of tax relief rather than the outright transfer of funds) be reconciled with our notions of accountability in the political process? This is an important consideration since the actual cost of the tax subsidy—in terms of property tax revenue forgone—never appears in the municipal budget where it can be readily scrutinized by taxpayers and their elected representatives.

As we have seen, the municipal revenue effect is the difference in tax payments, with and without the federal housing programs. With construction programs which rely on PILOT, the result is a narrowing of the city's tax base, leading in turn to pressure either to raise the tax rate or to cut back on public services. This form of local subsidy is thus inequitable as well as inefficient; the greatest burden to compensate for the loss in local revenue falls on other local property owners through the narrow and regressive real property tax. Moreover, most subsidized housing (and hence most of the accompanying tax exemptions) occur in those very central cities least able to endure fiscal erosion—the same cities already forced to assume disproportionate responsibility for those households unable to provide for themselves.

The loss in revenue for municipalities participating in these programs should be interpreted, not as a condemnation of public housing (or other housing subsidy programs), but as grounds for devising a more efficient and equitable form of subsidy. Such a subsidy should eliminate disincentives for participating communities, distribute the cost of the subsidy over a larger geographic area, and rely upon a progressive rather than a regressive tax for its source of financial support.

CHAPTER 6

Subsidized Housing, Jobs, and Employment Benefits

The labor picture in the construction industry is markedly different from that of industry generally. The place of employment continually shifts. . . . Jobs at any one site are usually of limited duration. Contractors are continuously in the process of creating or liquidating job organizations and working crews. Job opportunities vary a great deal both seasonally and geographically . . . [yet] homebuilding has long been a major entry port for mechanics into construction employment generally.

John T. Dunlop and D. Quinn Mills,
Report of the President's Committee on Urban Housing

Just as municipal revenue losses often constitute a hidden cost imposed by federal housing programs, new job creation may be a hidden benefit. The construction, rehabilitation, and management of subsidized housing requires a diverse set of manpower skills and draws on an extensive cross-section of the labor force. During construction and rehabilitation, jobs are created for on-site supervisory, engineering, craft, and custodial workers and for off-site architects, cost estimators, building material and equipment manufacturers, distributors, and many others. Once occupied, subsidized housing requires a permanent staff of management and maintenance personnel. Furthermore, the spending of employee wages and contractor profits adds to the general level of consumer demand in the economy, generating additional job opportunities. This chapter is devoted to a comparison of the alternative housing strategies in terms of their impact on labor conditions, with emphasis on deriving, in each case, a measure of the aggregate employment benefits.

Net Economic Gains and Idle Capacity

In a traditional welfare economics study, the employment benefit of public expenditures is measured as the value added in after-tax earnings over and above what these earnings would have been without the expenditure. Any net gain to the economy is included, regardless of the location of the factor resource.[1] When the economy is operating at "less than full employment," government subsidies generate net additions to employment income, there-

1. This assumes, of course, that the after-tax earnings are used for consumption, not savings. This is not a trivial assumption, since savings are equivalent to deferred consumption and would have to be discounted in order to determine their present value.

by creating an increase in individual consumption. In a full-employment economy, however, any increase in the demand for labor simply shifts employed workers among jobs. Thus, to estimate the full-employment benefit of housing subsidies within a welfare economics framework, it would be necessary to trace the primary resource requirements generated by final demand through several stages of production. Moreover, to estimate the social value of these primary resources, it would be necessary to match resource requirements with prevailing and projected patterns of idle industrial capacity and occupational unemployment. Ideally, we would use a six-step procedure derived from the public expenditure model of Haveman and Krutilla[2] to estimate the net increment in after-tax earnings from federal housing subsidies:

1. Determine the final demand for goods and services created by government-assisted housing construction.
2. Transform final demand into requirements for the inputs of specific industries using the Office of Business Economics input-output matrix.
3. Translate industrial requirements into occupational needs, using the industrial-occupational coefficients from the 1966 Bureau of Labor Statistics Industry-Employment Occupational Matrix.
4. Add gross nonconstruction labor to gross construction-associated labor to yield an estimate of total first-round labor requirements.
5. Apply appropriate wage and salary data, then deduct federal income tax from gross employment income to determine after-tax earnings.
6. Estimate the social value of the after-tax earnings by comparing them with the earnings forgone in the "next-best use" of the employed workers.

Zero Effect with Full-Employment Economy

The empirical task of tracing sectoral demands through each phase of production is extremely difficult. Indeed, since our ability to trace final demand through to its primary labor requirements is confined to capital construction and our capacity to estimate the social value of employment by projecting future economic conditions is limited, we are unable to make a

2. The Haveman-Krutilla model can be used to estimate the employment benefit of public expenditures under conditions of less than full employment. See Robert Haveman and John Krutilla, "Unemployment, Excess Capacity and Benefit-Cost Investment Criteria," *Review of Economics and Statistics,* August 1967.

welfare computation. Thus, for present purposes, we assume the conditions of a full-employment economy operating at reasonable efficiency. This is a fair assumption since the economy has operated at close to full employment, with a few notable exceptions, since the end of the Second World War. The price of labor inputs and the value of employment income are then equivalent, and the *net* employment effect equals zero.

Once a full-employment economy is assumed, it is also appropriate to exclude the indirect employment effects of rent assistance as well as the second- and third-round multiplier effects of construction activity. This makes sense, since, in a full-employment economy, workers are merely shifted among jobs without any incremental change in real national income. Hence, our calculation of the employment benefit confines itself to the gross value of the first-round wage bill. Even though the net employment benefit is zero, it is still necessary to calculate the gross employment benefit and the gross employment cost (the value of the labor input). These calculations are made—despite their zero net effect—for two reasons. First, they allow our methodology to be usefully applied in ghetto areas and depressed regions where the net employment benefit is positive for those who work on housing construction and would otherwise be idle or underemployed. Second, to obtain empirical estimates for the net benefit of each program, we need a gross employment benefit from which to subtract the gross cost of labor. The gross employment effect of each program is made for an average year so that our calculations will be consistent with those of other chapters.

Public Housing Construction

From its inception, the public housing program has been supported as much for the jobs it creates as for the shelter it provides. In fact, it was the employment effect of public housing which supplied the initial justification for federal involvement in low-income housing during the early 1930s. At that time Congress enacted the Emergency Relief and Construction Act and the National Industrial Recovery Act, which, among its provisions, established a Federal Emergency Public Works Administration; the PWA's Housing Division was to initiate residential construction projects as a means of relieving unemployment.[3] The first major housing legislation, the Na-

3. See Robert K. Brown, *Public Housing in Action: The Record of Pittsburgh* (Ann Arbor: University of Michigan Press, 1939).

tional Housing Act of 1934, was passed not only to provide low-rent housing but also to create jobs.

Once economic conditions had improved and more effective anticyclical instruments had been devised, the use of public housing investment as an employment generator was de-emphasized. This policy continued until the mid-sixties, when the emphasis again shifted to the employment impacts of government-assisted housing. However, unlike the programs of the depression era, present efforts focus on structural problems in the labor force rather than on cyclical problems. As a result of subsidizing housing, public works, and public facilities construction, the federal government commands considerable political and economic leverage at the local level, which it can use to reduce discriminatory employment practices and to expand training and job opportunities for low-income community residents.[4]

The value of the employment opportunities generated by public housing depends upon national and local economic conditions. For our analysis, we have assumed conditions of full employment during which the jobs made available by public housing construction and management merely shift workers among openings. Hence, to the extent that we disregard the hiring of persons who would otherwise be unemployed or underemployed, our methodology will tend to undervalue the employment benefit of public housing.

The first-round wage bill—our measure of the gross employment effect— is calculated in four steps. First, we estimate the on-site and off-site labor requirements per $1,000 of construction costs. Second, since we want our analysis to reflect the average annual effect over the life of a housing project rather than simply the year of construction, we compute the annual principal payment on the average public housing project and then use it to arrive at an annual construction labor requirement. Third, we estimate public housing administrative, managerial, and maintenance requirements. Finally, using appropriate wage and salary rates, we calculate the first-round wage bill per unit per annum:

4. Both the Demonstration Cities and Metropolitan Development Act of 1966 and the Housing and Urban Development Act of 1968 contain provisions for the employment of low-income persons in connection with assisted projects. In addition, the federal government has promulgated administrative regulations regarding affirmative action in the recruitment and training of minorities in the construction trades.

$$B_P^E \qquad = P\left(W_1 O + W_2 F\right) + W_3 A + W_4 M + W_5 N, \qquad (6.1)$$

where

B_P^E = the gross employment benefit of public housing,

P = the annual principal payment for public housing,

$W_1, \ldots, W_5$ = the mean hourly wage or annual salary rates associated with specific occupations,

O = the on-site labor construction requirement in man-hours,

F = the off-site labor construction requirement in man-hours,

A = the administrative labor requirement in man-years,

M = the managerial labor requirement in man-years,

N = the maintenance labor requirement in man-years.

Our estimate of the labor inputs for construction relies on a Bureau of Labor Statistics (BLS) national survey that provides on-site and off-site man-hour requirements for labor and materials by job classification per $1,000 of housing construction cost. For the most part, we use BLS Northeast regional data for reinforced-concrete structures, since in Boston—as in other large central cities of the Northeast—high population density, limited vacant land, and high labor costs make multistory reinforced-concrete projects the preferred mode of construction.[5] The scale of Boston Housing Authority public housing projects is relatively uniform,[6] so for computational purposes the manpower required by the average-size development (667 units) is used. We also assume that man-hour requirements per $1,000 of construction have remained constant over time, but we make adjustments

5. This type of design and structure provides more opportunity to substitute laborsaving equipment and to use land intensively.

6. Because contractors can achieve labor economies of scale on large projects where there are more opportunities to substitute capital (cranes, conveyors, etc.) for labor and to organize and manage work performance, size of development can be a source of variation in manpower requirements. A BLS study found that the impact of project size was most important for very large and very small projects, while there was not a strong relationship for intermediate-size developments. See U.S., Department of Labor, Bureau of Labor Statistics, *Labor and Material Requirements for Public Housing Construction*, Bulletin No. 1402, Washington, D.C., 1964, p. 11. If the size of the developments in our Boston sample were skewed in either direction, our results would be biased.

to reflect changes in productivity, material, and labor costs, as well as fluctuating profit margins.[7] Man-hour requirements for the average-size development are listed by job classification in Table 6.1, together with a summation of construction man-hours per $1,000.

We compute the level annual principal simply by dividing the total development cost by the length of a project's economic life. In the case of conventional public housing developments in Boston, economic life is 40 years, and the average level principal payment is $267,334 per project. Where the turnkey approach to public housing construction is employed,[8] we assume a 15 percent cost saving because of the efficiencies of private development; this allowance brings the level principal payment down to $227,234.

The administration, management, and maintenance of public housing represent another source of employment for those with the requisite technical, managerial, and clerical skills. Information on annual labor requirements and corresponding wage rates by job classification is taken from Boston Housing Authority sources and reproduced in Table 6.2.

With a full-employment economy and efficient labor markets, prevailing wages reflect the social value of employment income. Therefore, using the average annual principal payment ($267,334) and the labor requirements computed from information given in Tables 6.1 and 6.2 (along with the weighted mean wage and salary rates), we can compute the first-round wage bill in 1970 as

$$B^E = \frac{\overline{B}(W_1 O + W_2 F)}{10,000} + W_3 A + W_4 M + W_5 N$$

$$= \frac{267,334 \ (6.08 \times 95.9 \text{ man-hours} + 3.78 \times 122)}{1,000} + (9,700 \times 5 \text{ man-}$$

$$\text{years} + 8,750 \times 6 + 8,483 \times 19)$$

$$= 279,061 + 262,177 \tag{6.2}$$

7. To inflate construction contract costs, we use Robert J. Gordon's Price of Structures Index. The average development has an adjusted construction cost in 1970 dollars of $14,085,000. For a thorough review of existing price indices as well as a proposed new construction index, see Robert J. Gordon, "A New View of Real Investment in Structures, 1919–1966," *Review of Economics and Statistics,* Vol. 50 (November 1968).
8. Through a memorandum to former Secretary Robert C. Weaver, President Johnson approved a pilot program for stimulating private enterprise to build and manage low-income public housing. This private development and management approach was designated Turnkey 1.

Table 6.1 Labor Requirements and Prevailing Wages for Construction of Public Housing Projects with Average Size of 667 Units

Job Classification	Man-Hours/$1,000 of Construction Contract[a]	Prevailing Wage per hour[b]
On-Site Construction		
General supervisors	2.2	$7.20
Professional, technical, and clerical	2.1	7.40
Asbestos workers	0.6	6.35
Bricklayers	6.6	7.15
Carpenters	13.0	6.95
Cement finishers	4.0	6.75
Electricians	5.1	7.50
Elevator mechanics	0.8	7.25
Glaziers	0.4	6.25
Lathers	6.0	6.60
Operating engineers	2.5	6.45
Ornamental ironworkers	2.0	7.45
Painters	3.4	6.20
Plasterers	4.4	6.60
Plumbers	11.3	7.75
Reinforcing ironworkers	1.5	7.45
Roofers	0.5	6.30
Sheetmetal workers	0.6	7.75
Soft floor layers	0.2	6.50
Structural ironworkers	0.1	7.45
Tile setters	0.1	6.50
Truck drivers	0.6	5.15
Helpers and tenders	6.3	5.20
Laborers	16.6	5.00
Custodial workers	2.6	2.95
Other	2.5	6.65
Subtotal	95.9	
Weighted mean wage		6.08

a. Source: U.S., Department of Labor, Bureau of Labor Statistics, *Labor and Material Requirements for Public Housing Construction*, Bulletin No. 1402, 1964.
b. Source: Robert Snow Means Co., *Building Construction Cost Data*, 1970, Duxbury, Mass., 28th Annual Edition. The R. S. Means Company, an engineering and estimating

Table 6.1 (continued)

Job Classification	Man-Hours/$1000 of Construction Contract[a]	Prevailing Wage per Hour[b]
Off-Site		
Construction	12.0	
Administration		$7.10
Estimating draftsmen		5.10
Engineering		6.80
Clerical		2.60
Manufacturing	64.0	
Fabricated products		3.80
Equipment		4.35
Raw materials		3.80
Transportation, trade and services	36.0	
Materials distribution		2.95
Warehousing		3.10
All other	10.0	3.80
Subtotal	122.0	
Weighted mean wage		3.78
Total man-hours	216.2	
Total number of annual jobs[c]	1.2	
Total number of workers[d]	1.6	

firm, has for many years published a book on building construction costs. Their labor rates are averages of the 30 largest cities in the United States as reported by the U.S. Department of Labor, and are approximately the same as those listed by the *Engineering News-Record*.
c. We assume that construction employees work an eight-hour day, 180 days a year.
d. According to a study by John T. Dunlop and D. Quinn Mills, each 100 contract construction jobs in 1967 were filled by 188 workers. See John T. Dunlop and D. Quinn Mills, "Manpower and Construction: A Profile of the Industry and Projections to 1975," *The Report of the President's Committee on Urban Housing*, Vol. 2, Technical Studies (Washington, D.C.: U.S. Government Printing Office, 1968).

Table 6.2 Manpower Requirements and Wage Bill, Public Housing Administration, Management, and Maintenance for Average-Size Development of 667 Units

Job Classification	Annual Man-Years[a]	Mean Salary or Wage[d]	Wage Bill
Central Office[b]			
Administrative services	3	$12,100	$ 36,300
Secretary-clerical	2	6,100	12,200
Subtotal	5		48,500
Management Office			
Manager	0.5	13,000	6,500
Assistant manager	1.5	10,900	16,350
Cashier	1	8,900	8,900
Senior clerk	1	6,100	6,100
Clerk typist	1	5,400	5,400
Resident custodian	1	8,200	8,200
Subtotal	6		52,500
Engineering and Maintenance[c]			
Superintendent of maintenance	0.5	13,000	6,500
Assistant superintendent	0.5	11,900	5,950
Maintenance clerk	1	8,200	8,200
Fireman	4	8,700	34,800
Laborer	10	6,600	66,000
Carpenter	2	9,700	19,400
Glazier	1	8,800	8,800
Painter	5	8,600	43,000
Plumber	2	11,200	22,400
Appliance man	1	7,100	7,100
Electrician	1	11,400	11,400
Subtotal	29		233,550
Total	40		$344,550

Source: Derived from the Boston Housing Authority Annual Operating Budget and Manning Tables, 1970.
a. The personnel schedule for the average development is estimated from the actual schedules for those developments which fall within a range of 500–800 apartment units.
b. The central office personnel are allocated among all the developments on the basis of each development's proportion of the total number of federal and state apartments (14,645). The administrative service staff includes all professional employees in finance, tenant selection, personnel, and other supportive sections.
c. Temporary summertime personnel who cover for permanent employees during their vacation are excluded.
d. We use the mean wage for 1970 employees, since 1970 is approximately the middle year for the 40-year economic life. The mean salary for engineering and maintenance workers includes overtime as well as regular pay.

= \$541,238 per housing development (667 units)

= \$800 per unit per annum or \$67 per unit[9] per month.

Under the turnkey program where the annual principal payment is only \$227,234, the per-unit employment effect is \$738 per annum or \$61 per month.

Leased Housing: Using the Existing Stock

The framers of the leased housing program—unlike the housing legislators of the thirties—were not particularly concerned with cyclical fluctuations in the economy or, for that matter, with problems of structural unemployment. At the time of the program's enactment, as part of the 1965 housing bill, there was a surplus of rental housing and a low unemployment rate;[10] thus, by concentrating on the use of the available housing stock, Congress was being responsive to prevailing market conditions. Still, it would be shortsighted to ignore the employment effect of this program; any housing subsidy, even on the demand side, has some effect on investments in construction, rehabilitation, and repairs and consequently has both immediate and secondary impacts on job opportunities.[11] However, since most LHAs use leased housing funds to obtain existing units, the program seldom affects employment in a significant way.[12] Even though some units receive minor repairs to correct code deficiencies, the few jobs created are generally limited to administrative, management, and maintenance functions. Few economic incentives exist, particularly in low-income neighborhoods, for private owners to undertake substantial rehabilitation; in blighted areas, as we have seen, the inability of tenants to pay high rents

9. To ensure the comparability of our estimates with those of other chapters, we make them for a standard two-bedroom unit.
10. At the time the 1965 Housing and Urban Development Act was under consideration, the aggregate unemployment rate was approximately 4.3 percent, and 7.5 percent of the nation's rental housing inventory was vacant.
11. Housing investments create jobs at the construction site, in the industries that service or supply the construction materials, and in the local housing authority itself.
12. The conditions necessary for the leasing program to generate housing investments, particularly the physical upgrading of real properties, are examined in detail in Appendix B.

and the low quality of the schools and other public services limit the possible return on major capital improvements.[13]

Since the leased housing program accounts for little new construction, its major impact on employment comes when it is packaged with rehabilitation projects. To determine this employment effect, we must first allow for the wide range of housing improvements referred to as rehabilitation. Rehabilitation can designate activities that vary from the purely cosmetic (the spackling and repainting of a kitchen wall, for example) to the total reconstruction of an abandoned, multifamily apartment house. Since the work content, crew composition, and manpower requirements differ for each rehabilitation job, it is useful to classify these activities into some general categories:

Extensive Rehabilitation or Reconstruction.[14]—This level of rehabilitation involves the total gutting of a building, preserving only the envelope or exterior shell. The interior of the building is reconstructed by installing new partitions, plumbing, electrical systems, floors, and so on. The cost normally runs to over $10,000 per unit.

Moderate Rehabilitation or Modernization.—Essentially, this level of rehabilitation involves the modernization of some or all of the mechanical subsystems: heating, plumbing, and/or electrical. The exterior structure, floor layout, and interior walls are preserved. Costs can range from $2,000 to $10,000 per unit.

Minimal Repair, Renovation, or Maintenance.—This type of rehabilitation is limited to minor repairs; cleaning the cellar, hallway, and yards; and plastering, painting and repapering walls and ceilings to improve their appearance. Little, if any, structural or mechanical work is involved. Usually this type of property maintenance costs less than $2,000 per unit.

To analyze the employment effect of leased housing, we adopt the same methodology as was used for conventional public housing, with one refine-

13. For a detailed explication of the role of externalities in discouraging rehabilitation, see the example from the theory of games known as the prisoner's dilemma, Otto A. Davis and Andrew B. Whinston, "The Economics of Urban Renewal," in James Q. Wilson, ed., *Urban Renewal: The Record and the Controversy* (Cambridge, Mass.: MIT Press, 1967), pp. 54–58.

14. Most extensive and moderate rehabilitation has been confined to high-income prestigious areas. In fact, because of economic constraints, the only major exceptions have been projects induced by government incentives (either the negative compulsion of code enforcement or the positive attraction of grants and loans available in urban renewal areas). See Martin Meyerson, Barbara Terrett, and William L.C. Wheaton, *Housing, People and Cities* (New York: McGraw-Hill Book Co., 1962), p. 178.

Table 6.3 Level and Type of Housing Investment for Leased
Housing Program, Boston, 1970

Program Subcategory	No. of Units	Percent of Units
Existing units with minor repairs[a]	248	13
Existing units without repairs	1,462	77
Rehabilitated units[b]	140	7
New construction units	55	3
Total	1,905	100

Source: Compiled from the files of the Boston Housing Authority,
December 1970.
a. This level of housing investment is consistent with our "minimal repair, renovation, or maintenance" category. Also, according to HUD guidelines this level of repair is to be included with
the "existing, without rehabilitation" category. HUD Circular,
Guidelines for the Public Housing Leasing Program, March 6,
1969.
b. This level of housing investment includes two of our rehabilitation categories: extensive rehabilitation and moderate rehabilitation. Also, it is consistent with the revised HUD definition of
leased housing—with rehabilitation. HUD Circular, March 6, 1969.

ment—the leasing program's division into three new subcategories (newly
constructed, rehabilitated, and existing housing).[15] Whenever the government provides direct rental assistance rather than subsidizing capital construction, we must identify the final demand generated by rent receipts
before determining the primary labor requirements. This means that
ideally we should determine the allocation of rental revenue among maintenance, debt service, profit, and other operating requirements—in practice,
a difficult empirical task. We assume, instead, that labor requirements are
primarily a function of the level and type of construction or rehabilitation.
Table 6.3 sets forth the actual unit composition of the leased housing program.

As Table 6.3 indicates, 90 percent of Boston leased housing tenants have
been accommodated in existing structures. A fraction of these were below
local housing code standards at the time they were leased, necessitating the
owner to undertake some minor repairs as a condition for participating in
the program. From housing inspection reports, we were able to identify the

15. Because the employment effect varies with each of the program subcategories, this
division is necessary. However, since we measure the annual employment effect, it is
unnecessary to distinguish between the long-term Section 10 (c) and short-term Section 23
programs; for our purpose, the term of the lease is irrelevant.

most typical code violations, and then calculated their associated repair costs and labor requirements (as enumerated in Table 6.4).

The average repair cost for a leased unit, initially rejected because of code violations, was $265. Although some of the minor repairs were made by individual homeowners or maintenance men, most of the work was performed by small specialty contractors, thereby creating some additional on-site employment (26 man-hours as an average). If we assume the same ratio of off-site to on-site man-hours as given in the Bureau of Labor Statistics study of public housing construction, then an average of 33 additional off-site man-hours is created in the manufacture and delivery of building materials. However, since rehabilitation work is less labor-intensive than new construction, using this ratio probably causes us to understate the amount of off-site employment.

When, after signing a lease agreement with the local authority, a private owner or realtor chooses to undertake more substantial alterations, yet another level of job creation is involved. In fact, all of the units in the City of Boston classified as "leased housing—with rehabilitation" have been totally reconstructed, and the gross impact on employment has been substantial.[16] The actual manpower requirements vary, of course, with the type and size of structure, particularly since rehabilitation work seldom involves uniform dimensions, simple job layouts, or routine labor tasks.[17] These inconsistencies from job to job preclude economies of scale—above all, those associated with standardized production methods. In effect, the work must be customized to the idiosyncrasies of the individual building—its angles distorted by the stresses of age, its proportions and fixtures reflecting the architectural fashions of bygone days. Thus most extensive and moderate rehabilitation demands real craftsmanship and offers employment opportunities primarily for skilled labor.[18]

16. According to the revised definitions promulgated by the Department of Housing and Urban Development, a unit is classified as "leased housing—with rehabilitation" if it has undergone substantial alteration, involving a cost of at least 20 percent or more of the adjusted original fair market cost (or fair market value).

17. For an excellent review of rehabilitation construction, see Robert B. Whittlesey, *The South End Row House* (Boston: South End Community Development, 1969).

18. While there are few opportunities to substitute capital for labor, or to organize work crews more efficiently, unit cost economies can be achieved with large multidwelling developments. By rehabilitating several apartments within the same multifamily structure, the relatively fixed costs of masonry work, roofing, excavation, and heating can be allocated among a larger number of units, thereby reducing per-unit construction costs.

Table 6.4 Type of Renovation and Repairs Necessary to Correct Code Deficiencies for Leasing Existing Units, Boston, 1970

Code Violation[a]	Repair Cost[b]	On-Site Manpower Requirements[b]
1. Holes, cracks in hall walls	$ 50	4 hours, plasterer
2. No wire lath over furnace	60	2 hours, plasterer
3. No heat or hot water (boiler)	600	20 hours, plumber/pipefitter
4. Stains on bedroom ceiling	40	3 hours, painter
5. Exterminate roaches	40	3 hours, exterminator
6. Replace hall railing	300	12 hours, carpenter
7. Clean, paint dwelling (2 bedrooms)	275	40 hours, painter
8. Replace defective bathroom radiator	75	3 hours, plumber
9. Furnace miswired, change thermostat	150	16 hours, electrician
10. Molding defect in dining room	65	4 hours, carpenter
11. Cover bathroom pipes with asbestos	70	4 hours, asbestos worker
12. Paint door jambs, trip, facing	20	2 hours, painter
13. Another means of egress needed	95	8 hours, carpenter
14. Replace pull-type switch in bathroom	100	6 hours, electrician
15. Wallpaper peeling, repaper	85	4 hours, painter/paperhanger
16. Fix gutter on front of building	50	4 hours, carpenter
17. Repair front porch cement baluster	75	4 hours, mason
18. Electric outlets needed, dining room	85	5 hours, electrician
19. Repair radiator pipe leak, dining room	25	2 hours, plumber
20. Replace four broken windows	45	2 hours, glazier
21. Repair loose hallway floor boards	50	4 hours, carpenter
22. Install screens, storm windows	260	18 hours, carpenter

Source: Derived average costs and manpower requirements from the actual cost estimates and expenditures of BHA maintenance supervisors, private specialty subcontractors, and leased housing landlords.
a. All code violations are itemized on the housing inspector's report, which is made for each prospective leased housing unit.
b. The cost and labor required to correct each code violation were derived from a series of interviews with leased housing landlords, BHA maintenance supervisors, and private contractors.

The Bureau of Labor Statistics' studies of labor and material requirements for various sectors of the construction industry do not cover rehabilitation activity, so it was necessary to gather the requisite information by sampling the labor input of units rehabilitated in conjunction with the leasing program. This sample included seven structures and 65 units, accounting for $643,000 worth of rehabilitation work. If we assume a 25-year economic life (an appropriate estimate for rehabilitated units), the level annual principal payment on the improvements is $25,720 ($643,000 divided by 25) or $460 per unit. The average rehabilitation cost per unit is $9,892. The on-site manpower requirements per $1,000 of contract cost are presented in Table 6.5.

Table 6.5 Moderate to Extensive Rehabilitation On-Site Manpower Requirements for Leased Housing, Boston, 1970

Trade	Man-Hours/$1,000[a]
Floor layer	2.0
Tile setter	1.7
Plasterer	2.1
Tender	0.8
Lather	6.0
Painter	8.8
Roofer	1.0
Electrician	5.6
Plumber	3.8
Carpenter	23.2
Mason	2.1
Laborer	13.8
Apprentice/helper	2.2
Supervisor/administrator	5.0
Custodian	1.6
Truck driver	0.7
Total	80.4

Source: Boston Office, Federal Housing Administration, U.S. Department of Labor: Wage, Hour and Public Contract Division, payroll form.
a. The 1969–1970 contract construction costs were deflated so as to be comparable with the 1960 BLS study of labor requirements for new construction.

In order to make the labor requirements shown for these rehabilitated units comparable with those for new construction, we standardize the man-hours generated by a fixed dollar volume ($1,000). Moreover, we exclude the same types of employment omitted by the BLS public housing construction survey—that is, man-hours expended on preparation of plans and specifications, installation of public utilities, landscaping, and so on.[19] Otherwise, man-hour requirements are given for each construction trade. On this basis, we estimate that housing rehabilitation provides 80.4 man-hours of on-site employment per $1,000 of contract construction. This means that extensive remodeling, at least for our sample of garden apartments and row houses, is less labor-intensive than new construction of multistory reinforced-concrete structures (95.9 man-hours on-site employment per $1,000 of contract construction). Another important finding is that unskilled and semiskilled workers perform close to 33 percent of all on-site rehabilitation work compared to 23 percent for new construction. The significance of these findings is discussed in the concluding section of this chapter.

The final subcategory of the leased housing program refers to new housing constructed by agreement with the local housing authority, which then leases some portion of the units back from the private sponsor. We assume that the labor and material requirements per $1,000 of contract construction are comparable for private leased apartments and public housing built in the same city—a reasonable assumption since both activities produce multistory structures of reinforced concrete, rely on the same building contractors, and are covered by Davis-Bacon wage determinations.[20] In fact, this similarity has become more pronounced in recent years as the national government, through the turnkey option, has sought to increase the private sector's role in the construction of federally aided public housing; it allows us to apply the BLS estimate of on-site and off-site labor requirements to leased housing construction.

Leased housing expenditures also make a number of administrative jobs available within the local housing authority; for example, a staff is needed

19. See U.S., Department of Labor, Bureau of Labor Statistics, *Labor and Material Requirements for Public Housing Construction.*
20. Under the Davis-Bacon Act, the Secretary of the U.S. Department of Labor is empowered to determine prevailing wages for each community in which federally assisted construction projects are undertaken.

Table 6.6 Administrative, Management, and Clerical Staff for Leased Housing Program, Boston, 1970

Personnel	No. of Man-Years	Salary Rate	Annual Wage Bill
Director, leased housing	1	$17,225	$ 17,225
Management supervisor	1	15,660	15,660
Production supervisor	1	11,766	11,766
Leasing officer	4	10,926	43,704
Tenancy officer	1	11,766	11,766
Senior accountant	1	10,695	10,695
Tenant relations aide	1	9,030	9,030
Leased housing aide	2	6,165	12,330
Administrative assistant	2	8,037	16,074
Secretary	2	6,783	13,566
Clerk typist	2	5,815	11,630
Clerk stenographer	1	6,403	6,403
Superintendent of maintenance	1	12,020	12,020
Housing inspector	1	9,933	9,933
Legal counsel	1.5	13,243	19,865
Central office staffa	13	9,400 b	122,934
Total	35.5		$344,601

Source: Boston Housing Authority, Operating Budget for Fiscal 1970, "Schedule of All Positions and Salaries," HUD Form 52566.
a. The technical support of the tenant selection, accounting, and central office administrative staff has been prorated on the basis of the leased housing program's percentage of the total units under BHA administration.
b. This salary rate is the average for central office technical and professional personnel.

to inspect dwellings for compliance with minimum code standards, to negotiate leases with private owners, and to determine and recertify the eligibility of applicants. Table 6.6 lists the job categories associated with administration of the leased housing program, together with corresponding salary rates, annual man-year requirements, and yearly wage bills.

For the purpose of determining employment effects, the annual wage bill (aggregated for all administrative, management, and clerical personnel) is allocated among the leased housing program subcategories in proportion to their respective share of leased units. (See Table 6.7.)

Two steps are involved in calculating the dollar value of the first-round employment effect associated with each leased housing subprogram. First of all, as previously indicated, we compute the annual number of job opportunities attributable to capital construction (level principal payments) and

Table 6.7 Administrative, Management, and Clerical Staff by Leased Housing
Subcategories

Program Subcategory	No. of Units	Percent of Units	No. of Man-Years	Annual Wage Bill
Existing units	1,710	90	31.9	$310,140
Rehabilitated units	140	7	2.5	24,122
New construction units	55	3	1.1	10,338
Total	1,910	100	35.5	$344,600
Mean annual wage				$9,400

Source: Derived from Tables 6.3 and 6.6.

LHA operations, and, second we estimate their respective dollar value. A
full-employment economy with reasonably efficient labor markets is once
again assumed; in consequence, prevailing wages reflect social valuations.

Granted these assumptions, empirical findings can then be set forth for
each program subcategory. In the case of leased units in existing structures,
jobs are created through the need to remove code violations and to administer the program. Of the 1,710 existing units under lease in Boston,
248 required minor repairs, at an average cost of $265 per unit. We include
this cost in our per annum calculations of employment income, since minor
improvements of this kind are made on a continuing basis.[21] The $265
figure, added to the prorated administrative wage bill associated with existing units, gives us the first-round employment impact of leasing existing
units in 1970:

$$B^E_{L-E} = \sum_{n=1}^{248} (C_n + \overline{W}_3 M^E)$$

$$= (248 \times 265 + 9,400 \times 31.9)$$

$$= 65,720 + 299,860$$

$$= \$365,580$$

$$= \$214 \text{ per unit per annum or } \$18 \text{ per unit per month,} \tag{6.3}$$

21. Of course, the $265 includes repairs made by landlords as a condition for participation
in the leasing program. Thus, assuming a comparable expenditure on a continuing
basis (except where units are reinspected periodically and violations enforced) may be
somewhat overstating the employment impact of leased units in this subcategory.

where

$B^E_{L\text{-}E}$ = the employment benefit generated by the leasing of existing units,

C_n = the employment income generated by minor improvements,

$\overline{W}_3$ = the mean weighted salary rate associated with administrative, management, and maintenance labor requirements,

M^E = the administrative, management, and maintenance labor requirements associated with the leasing of existing units.

We compute the first-round employment impact of leased housing–rehabilitated units in a similar manner, assuming the same ratio of off-site to on-site man-hours as reported in the BLS study of public housing construction as well as the same per-hour wage rates. The latter assumption holds true especially during periods of high construction activity when the wage rates for nonunion workers approach those of union craftsmen and laborers. Then—taking the results of our study of on-site rehabilitation labor requirements, the per-unit level principal payment for moderate to extensive improvements ($184), and the prevailing wages in Boston during 1970[22] —we compute the employment effect resulting from the 140 rehabilitated units. Our calculations indicate that the annual employment income generated per unit is $329 ($27.50 per unit per month). For newly constructed leased housing units, the average income generated through construction (annualized through the use of the level principal payment), management, and maintenance activities was $673 per unit per annum.

Section 236 with Rent Supplements

Although the rent supplement program was enacted neither as a countercyclical measure nor as a means for relieving structural employment, Congress still recognized its potential impact on local manpower problems. In fact, subsequent housing legislation contained specific language referring to the distribution of employment opportunities: ". . . to the greatest extent

22. We estimate the prevailing wage for on-site construction workers as the weighted average, by man-hour, of the required construction tradesmen. The source of construction wage data for Boston was a publication by the Robert Snow Means Co., *Building Construction Cost Data, 1970* (Duxbury, Mass., 1970). For off-site labor, we estimate the weighted average wage of the requisite manufacturing, trade, service, and transportation occupations. The source of the wage data was a study by the U.S., Department of Labor, Bureau of Labor Statistics, *Area Wage Survey: Boston, Mass. Metropolitan Area*, Bulletin No. 1685-11 (August 1970).

feasible opportunities for training and employment arising in connection with the planning, construction, rehabilitation and operation of housing assisted under such programs are to be given to lower income persons in the area of such housing." [23]

As discussed earlier, Congress tied rent supplements to rehabilitation or new construction financed with FHA-insured mortgages. In effect, supplement funds are awarded as part of a development package. An important result of Congress's decision was to confer on the program a larger capacity for job creation than it would have possessed had it been legislated as simply a direct transfer payment.

The ability of rent supplement expenditures to stimulate private housing investment carries important social and economic implications. First of all, the availability of supplement funds—especially in conjunction with below-market-rate programs of rehabilitation and construction—lends some demand stability to the home-building industry. This industry comprises a key employment sector, drawing as it does upon a wide range of occupational skills; but it is acutely sensitive to national cyclical and monetary change.

Second, the usual location of most rent supplement projects within declining central-city areas improves the access of minorities to jobs in the building trades. Despite the highly organized nature of construction work, most decisions regarding hiring, training, compensation, and entry into the craft unions are made at the local rather than the national level; this makes the building trades somewhat responsive to community pressure. (Of course, this responsiveness can work both ways, with local interests successfully resisting strong federal pressure to open up union membership.) [24]

To measure the value of the rent supplement program as an employment generator, we must compute the manpower requirements and wage bill for both rehabilitation and new construction, including on- and off-site construction, management, and multiplier effects. However, to repeat a qualification made earlier with respect to the other housing programs, conven-

23. This commitment to hiring lower-income community residents on federally subsidized housing developments was contained in both the Housing and Urban Development Acts of 1965 and 1968.

24. Any review of the so-called Philadelphia plan and other hometown affirmative action programs will indicate the modest success of efforts to increase the proportion of minorities in the construction trades.

Table 6.8 Contract Construction Costs for Section 236–Rent Supplement Development, Boston

Program Subcategory	No. of Units	Construction Contract Costs, 1968	Construction Costs per Unit, 1968	Construction Contract Costs, 1970	Construction Costs per Unit, 1970[b]
Rehabilitation	731[a]	$5,484,906	$ 7,503	$6,149,384	$ 8,412
New construction	38	525,791	13,836	589,485	15,513

Source: FHA Insuring Office, Boston, Mass. Cost certifications of Grove Hall, Elm Hill, and Charlame 2 projects.
a. We include the total number of units in the rehabilitation projects, although only 724 units are under supplement contract.
b. We inflate the construction expenditures to the base year, 1970, to keep the real costs consistent with those used for the other low-income housing programs. For this purpose, we rely upon an updating of Robert J. Gordon's construction price index, *Final Price of Structures*.

tional economic welfare measures are precluded by a lack of suitable data, above all our inability to determine the conditions of unemployment by occupation, geographic location, and key occupational categories. Instead, as with the analysis of the conventional public housing and leased housing programs, we must rely on the first-round employment effect.

The Federal Housing Administration has contracted for three rent supplement projects in the city of Boston since the program was first authorized by the Housing and Urban Development Act of 1965: one a new development owned by a private nonprofit sponsor, and two rehabilitation projects undertaken by limited-dividend partnerships. All three are insured by the FHA under Section 221(d)(3), the predecessor of Section 236, and were constructed between mid-1967 and late 1968. The two rehabilitation projects were part of a large-scale effort called the Boston Urban Rehabilitation Program—at that time the largest rent supplement rehabilitation effort in the nation. Construction contract costs, adjusted to constant 1970 dollars, for the rehabilitated and newly constructed units are shown in Table 6.8.

Our calculation of the employment generated by FHA-insured projects with rent supplement units relies on the BLS study of public housing construction and our own survey of labor requirements for various levels of rehabilitation. Both surveys were designed to determine man-hour requirements for a fixed dollar volume ($1,000) of contract construction cost. For comparative purposes, these requirements have been expressed in constant 1970 construction prices. Consistent with our other calculations, we adjust the contract costs to reflect changes in productivity, profit margins, and material discounts but assume that man-hour requirements per $1,000 have remained fixed. The gross man-hour requirements for new construction and rehabilitation projects are computed separately. Regarding the latter, the level of work is taken to be "moderate" (as defined by the rehabilitation classification scheme outlined earlier in this chapter)—that is, some modernization of mechanical subsystems but retention of exterior and interior walls.

The rent supplement program also generates a variety of jobs for administrative, maintenance, and clerical personnel in the offices of both the FHA and the owner-managers of funded projects. The local FHA office routinely assigns one rent supplement specialist to approve tenant eligibility, review rent payment vouchers, and monitor program operations. Additional FHA staff, responsible for special tasks such as housing inspection, accounting, or clerical functions, is on call whenever necessary. The projects themselves, of course, are privately owned and managed. As part of the private sponsor's application for rent supplement funds, he must submit a management plan for preparing special monthly vouchers, certifying and recertifying tenants for eligibility, maintaining contact with the local welfare office and social service agencies. Table 6.9 presents the labor re-

Table 6.9 Management, Maintenance, and Clerical Personnel for Rent Supplement Program

Personnel	No. of Man-Years	Salary Rate[a]	Annual Wage Bill
FHA rent supplement specialist	1	$11,000	$11,000
Private owner-manager			
Property manager	0.5	15,000	7,500
Bookkeeper	0.5	6,500	3,250
Rent supplement liaison officer	1.5	7,500	11,250
Maintenance	4	9,000	36,000
Total	7.5		$69,000
Mean annual wage			$ 9,200

Source: FHA Insuring Office, Boston, Mass., and interviews with the respective sponsors (private).
a. Since the private sponsors would not provide specific salary rates, we relied on average figures for Boston realtors and management firms.

quirements, together with the salary rates used to compute the annual wage bill for personnel employed by both the FHA and the private owner-manager of a typical Boston-area project.

For the purpose of this analysis, we prorate the management, maintenance, and clerical man-years between the new construction and rehabilitation projects in accordance with their respective proportion of the total number of units—5 percent (0.375 man-years) to the former and 95 percent (7.125 man-years) to the latter. And to ensure comparability with our estimates for the other low-income programs, we calculate the labor requirements in each case on the basis of their respective annualized capital cost (that is, level principal payment). For newly constructed units, this annualized figure comes to $388 per unit. Thus the annual wage bill, in 1970 prices, for the 38 rent supplement–new construction dwellings in our Boston sample is $496 per unit per annum or $41 per unit per month.

The average annualized first-round wage bill of the rent supplement rehabilitated units is computed in the same manner. Using the prorated administrative and management manpower requirements and the on-site and off-site labor associated with the annual principal payments of $336 per unit, we find that the annual and monthly amounts of employment income generated are $384 and $32, respectively.

Comparative Employment Benefits

Our findings suggest that in areas of high unemployment, large-scale capital investments make the greatest contribution to aggregate growth (efficiency) objectives, other considerations being equal. The dollar value of the first-round employment wage bill for each of the federally assisted housing strategies is summarized in Table 6.10. New construction clearly provides

Table 6.10 First-Round Employment Wage Bill, Boston, 1970 (dollars per two-bedroom unit per month)

	Public Housing	Leased Housing	Section 236– Rent Supplements
New construction	$67.00[a]	$56.00	$41.00
Rehabilitation	—	27.50	32.00
Existing units	—	18.00	—

a. For turnkey public housing, the annual first-round gross wage bill, in 1970 prices, was $734 per unit per annum or $61 per unit per month.

the largest gross employment benefit, at least on the first round, while the leasing of existing units provides the smallest. Of course, under full-employment conditions, the *net* effect of each program will be close to zero as workers will merely be shifted among construction jobs.

Looking beyond the aggregate employment benefit, the federal government has expressed its desire that housing funds be expended in a way that enlarges job opportunities for disadvantaged community residents. With regard to this objective, it is instructive to compare new construction, rehabilitation, and housing management in terms of their labor intensity, the desirability of the careers made available, and the accessibility of these careers to unskilled low-income residents.

To obtain a measure of the labor requirements for rehabilitating as opposed to constructing a typical unit, we standardize the man-hours generated by a fixed dollar amount ($1,000) of construction cost in 1970 prices. As indicated in Table 6.5, extensive rehabilitation (complete gutting of dwellings) provides 80.4 man-hours of on-site employment per $1,000 of contract construction compared to 95.9 man-hours for public housing construction. Thus, contrary to general belief, the remodeling of garden apartments is less labor-intensive than the new construction of multistory, reinforced-concrete structures. This reversal of our intuitive expectations is explained by the fact that rehabilitation involves little or no work on the basic structure (especially when interior walls, plumbing, and electrical systems are preserved), while the more expensive finished materials such as doors, windows, and flooring are almost invariably replaced.

Our comparative findings on work force composition are equally important (see Table 6.11). Even though the rehabilitation mechanic himself must be a highly skilled craftsman, able to perform unusual tasks without supervision or drawings, many opportunities do exist for relatively unskilled labor to participate in rehabilitation projects (for example, by cleaning out debris, scraping and washing interior surfaces, unloading equipment). In fact, close to a third of all on-site rehabilitation work, and a quarter of new construction work, is performed by unskilled and semiskilled workers. In the case of most moderate rehabilitation, crews of carpenters and laborers can accomplish almost half the on-site work. Furthermore, close to 50 percent of the operating jobs in public housing (cashier, clerk, laborer, some maintenance crafts) have relatively minimal skill re-

Table 6.11 Comparison of On-Site Manpower Requirements by Craft for Extensive Rehabilitation and New Construction per $1,000 Construction Contract Cost, Boston, 1970

Trade	Man-Hours Rehabilitation[a]	Man-Hours New Construction[b]
Laborers/helpers/tenders	25.4	22.9
Bricklayers	5.2	6.6
Carpenters	19.2	13.0
Ironworkers (ornamental, structural, reinforcing)	1.4	3.6
Sheetmetal workers	—	0.6
Lathers	1.9	6.0
Tile setters	—	0.1
Plasterers	3.7	4.4
Roofers	1.4	0.5
Operation engineers	—	2.5
Painters	5.4	3.4
Floor layers	—	0.2
Plumbers	7.9	11.3
Electricians	3.7	5.1
Asbestos workers	—	0.6
Cement finishers	—	4.0
Elevator mechanics	—	0.8
Glaziers	—	0.4
Field supervisor	2.3	2.2
Professional, technical, clerical	1.4	2.1
Truck drivers	0.6	0.6
Custodial workers	—	2.6
Other	0.9	2.4
Total	80.4	95.9

a. Source: Computations made from FHA Weekly Payroll Data, Boston Area Office.
b. Source: U.S., Department of Labor, Bureau of Labor Statistics: *Labor and Material Requirements for Public Housing Construction,* Bulletin No. 1402, 1964. We relied on the estimate for high-rise reinforced-concrete structures in the Northeast.

quirements and, as such, represent additional employment opportunities for tenants and low-income community residents.

Manpower officials and minority spokesmen are concerned with the quality as well as the number of jobs made available for the poor. Both construction and administrative-maintenance work represent primary job opportunities with reasonable compensation, prospects for advancement, fringe benefits, grievance procedures, and union representation.[25] However, they vary in several important respects. In construction work, the proportion of skilled workers is much higher than in housing management; moreover, seasonal and geographic variations contribute a degree of insecurity. Under the circumstances, it is curious that government job quotas and affirmative action programs focus exclusively on the construction trades in spite of the fact that public housing operations offer a larger number of opportunities, less risk of layoffs, and better working conditions.

With regard to national economic growth and stability, our computation of the employment benefit confirms our bias in favor of monetary and tax policies as more effective means for accomplishing these objectives. The countercyclical contribution of housing expenditures is severely limited, first, by the long period elapsing between the authorization of any given residential development and its occupancy and, second, by the frequent lack of congruence between the location of high unemployment and the areas of greatest housing need. Insofar as low-income housing programs have a useful role in national and local employment policy, it is in helping to redistribute job opportunities to low-income residents within their own communities.

25. This applies only to large-scale construction, however; few of the laborers working for small contractors (and this includes most firms specializing in rehabilitation) enjoy union protection. In these cases, fringe benefits (such as medical and pension plans) and job security are minimal or nonexistent.

CHAPTER 7

The Costs of Subsidized Housing

What cannot be costed out are the myriad returns in dollars and cents as well as intangibles to a city that is relatively free of slums, that does not wall up its minority citizens in a ghetto, that has the economic health to be able to respond to the needs of its residents. We have to approach it from the other side, and count the costs of present inaction.

Report of the National Commission on Urban Problems

The costs of subsidized housing are as varied as the differing assistance schemes used by the federal government to house the urban poor. In part, these cost variations can be attributed to the many guidelines, procedures, and requirements of each program. However, to a large extent, they reflect the differentials in cost inherent in the major strategy options with which we have been concerned throughout this book—in particular, new construction as opposed to use of the existing stock, and production incentives as opposed to income supplementation.

In this chapter we examine the costs of providing federally assisted low-income housing from the point of view of both the federal government and the welfare economist. We begin the analysis by calculating the full economic costs of the major program alternatives (conventional and turnkey public housing, leased housing, and rent supplements) and then allocate these cost totals among the tenants, the municipal government, and the federal government. Finally, we consider how comparative costs vary over time.

Costs, Criteria, and Public Expenditure Models
We can measure the cost effectiveness of a given program in closing the housing gap by estimating the number of families moved from substandard to standard housing for a given expenditure. The first step in such an analysis is to calculate the full costs to the economy of providing shelter under each subsidy alternative, that is, the overall value of its resource inputs—land, labor, and capital. We accomplish this by summing the capital, operating, and administrative costs for a standardized two-bedroom dwelling unit under each program to derive a comparative set of total annual or monthly costs per unit.[1] Because the welfare of private individuals is our

1. Since some costs of low-rent housing are contracted at one particular time, while others vary continuously over the life of the program, ideal cost estimates would be based on discounted present worth. However, because of the uncertainty involved in making cost

ultimate concern, it is appropriate, conceptually, to express these costs in terms of the individuals who, through their tax payments, actually provide the revenue for housing payments:

$$C = \sum_{i=1}^{n} C_i^F + C_i^A, \tag{7.1}$$

where

C = the total annual economic cost of a federal housing program,

C_i^F = the annual economic cost of federal expenditures that accrue to individual i,

C_i^A = the annual economic cost of associated expenditures that accrue to individual i.

As noted in Chapter 2, the annual federal project cost consists of capital and operating expenditures, which can be represented as follows:

$$C^F = \sum_{i=1}^{n} O_i^F + K_i^F, \tag{7.2}$$

where

O_i^F = the annual federal operation and maintenance cost for individual i,

K_i^F = the annual federal capital cost (level debt service) for individual i.

The associated cost includes necessary expenditures by state and local governments as well as private costs, and is written as

$$C^A = \sum_{i=1}^{n} (O_i^P + K_i^P + O_i^L + K_i^L + T_i^F + T_i^L), \tag{7.3}$$

where

O_i^P = the annual private operating and maintenance cost for individual i,

---

projections (estimating future rent assistance, maintenance costs, or modernization expenditures), the cost of providing standard housing will actually be estimated for one typical year (1970). In order to compare costs with benefits calculated in earlier chapters, results will be converted to monthly figures.

$K_i^P =$ the annual private capital cost for individual i,

$O_i^L =$ the annual state and local government operating and maintenance cost for individual i,

$K_i^L =$ the annual state and local government capital cost for individual i,

$T_i^F =$ the annual federal forgone tax revenue—due to exemptions, accelerated depreciation provisions, and abatements—which result in real costs for individual i,[2]

$T_i^L =$ the annual local forgone tax revenue for individual i.

Contrasting Cost Calculations of Welfare Economists and Federal Officials

In the analysis that follows, the cost estimates differ from the ideal welfare economics model in two respects. First, because of the extreme difficulty of determining the alternative use for any given resource, contractual rather than opportunity costs will be used. Second, resource inputs will be treated in terms of their gross rather than their net cost to the economy. Normally, the welfare economist estimates the net or real welfare cost of any program input as the difference in value between its new use and its previous use.[3]

2. In the existing federal budget, forgone revenue from tax exemptions is not treated as the equivalent of federal expenditures. In this analysis, treating forgone revenue as the functional equivalent of direct expenditures is desirable, however, since it allows a true estimate of the total impact of the housing program on the national budget. Several have suggested this type of full accounting. See, for example, Otto Eckstein, "A Survey of the Theory of Public Investment Criteria," in James M. Buchanan, ed., *Public Finances: Needs, Sources and Utilization* (Princeton, N.J.: Princeton University Press, 1961), p. 244; Stanley Surrey, "The U.S. Income Tax System: The Need for a Full Accounting," remarks before the Money Marketeers, New York City, November 15, 1967, and Boris L. Bittker, "Accounting for Federal Tax Subsidies in the National Budget," *National Tax Journal*, June 1969.
3. When productive resources are fully employed and markets operate efficiently, the real cost is zero since the value of the additional units of housing produced and the value of the resources released from other industries are equivalent. Where markets do not operate efficiently, however, real costs are not zero. In the case of low-income housing, for example, the government's provision of tax concessions makes housing artificially inexpensive relative to other goods and services. This means that consumers are faced with prices that do not reflect the real marginal cost of producing different goods. Because the tax concessions distort the price system, and thereby consumer choice, the appropriate welfare measure is the real loss to the economy resulting from the price distortion. Economic inefficiencies attributable to tax-induced distortions of consumer choice are known as the "excess burden of taxation." For a detailed explication of this concept, see, for example, Richard Musgrave, *The Theory of Public Finance* (New York: McGraw-Hill Book Co., 1959), pp. 140–154.

Therefore, for the purposes of this study, we do not deduct the value of
released resources from the value of program inputs. This is consistent
with our earlier measurement of program benefits in terms of gross values,
and thereby allows us to calculate cost-benefit ratios.

Calculating Resource and Budgetary Costs

Conventional and Turnkey Public Housing Construction

We begin by estimating the average monthly cost for a two-bedroom unit of
conventional public housing constructed in Boston in 1970. This estimate
consists of two major cost categories: first, the *capital cost* for the development of the unit, converted to a monthly basis, and, second, the unit's
monthly *operating cost*.

Computing the real capital cost necessitates two separate adjustments to
the Boston Housing Authority's historical data on development costs. The
data are first standardized in terms of the prices for a single base year (1970)
by applying Robert J. Gordon's Final Price of Structures Index.[4] This adjustment eliminates any price differentials attributable to inflation. The
adjusted mean development cost per unit, in 1970 dollars, is $17,070. Sec-
ond, the physical quality of the developments themselves must be made
comparable, since public housing construction requirements have become
more stringent over the years with respect to the quality of construction,
site improvements, utilities, and equipment. To attain this comparability,
we use the average of two different estimates: the adjusted mean development cost (just derived above) and the development cost of a two-bedroom
public housing unit in a metropolitan area having average construction
costs. The estimate for the first is $17,070, and for the second, $18,200,[5]
giving an average of $17,635.

This average development (or capital) cost is then converted to a
monthly payment ($123) by using the prevailing market rate (8 percent
for our 1970 base year) and the 40-year amortization period that is normal

4. A detailed explanation of the composition of the index is set forth in Robert J. Gordon,
"A New View of Real Investment in Structures, 1919–1968," *Review of Economics and
Statistics,* Vol. 50 (November 1968).
5. For the source of this $18,200 estimate, see Frank de Leeuw, *The Cost of Leased
Public Housing* (Washington, D.C.: Urban Institute, December 22, 1970), p. 26 and
Appendix C.

Table 7.1 Gross Economic Cost of Conventional and Turnkey Public Housing per Unit per Month, Boston, 1970

Costs	Conventional Public Housing[a]	Turnkey Public Housing
Capital Costs		
Capital cost	$123.00	$110.00
Forgone federal revenue	—	—
Operating and Administrative Costs		
Operating cost	69.50 [b]	69.50
Local administrative cost	—	—
Forgone local revenue	15.00	15.00
Federal administrative cost	8.00	8.00
Total per unit per month	$215.50	$202.50

a. The per-unit per-month costs are computed on the basis of average costs for 10,155 units.

b. Boston Housing Authority Annual Budget, Fiscal Year 1970. Our estimate of public housing operating costs in Boston for 1970 is $69.50 per dwelling unit per month. This is consistent with de Leeuw's estimate of $58.36 for 23 sample cities in 1968. If an annual average inflationary increase of 4.0 percent is used, the 1970 operating cost per unit per month for the sample cities would have been approximately $66.50. See Frank de Leeuw, *Operating Costs in Public Housing: A Financial Crisis* (Washington, D.C.: Urban Institute, 1971), p. 28.

for public housing bonds. We cannot apply the actual interest rate on these bonds because, thanks to their tax-exempt status, they are issued at below-market rates. These low rates, if used in our calculation, would artificially reduce the figure obtained for capital costs.

In recent years some public housing units have been constructed by private firms and then sold to local housing authorities under the Turnkey public housing program. As a result of efficiencies attributable to private sponsorship, the BHA Planning and Development staff estimates that the turnkey approach achieves a 10 percent saving in development costs.[6] Table 7.1 summarizes the figures for both conventional and turnkey public housing.

Next we turn from capital to operating and administrative costs, again using data for a typical two-bedroom public housing unit in Boston. Accord-

6. Interview with Andrew Olins and Daniel Smith, former Director and Special Assistant, respectively, of the Boston Housing Authority Planning and Development Division, November 11, 1970.

ing to BHA records, the average operating cost for 1970 was $69.50 per unit per month. However, because these records are for property-tax-exempt projects, they underestimate real operating costs. Instead of paying full property taxes, as do the private owners of short-term leased housing and Section 236 rent supplement units, the local housing authority makes a payment in lieu of taxes (PILOT) on its holdings. The PILOT for 1970, computed as 10 percent of shelter rent receipts (gross tenant rental payments minus utility costs), was $64.80, or $5.40 per month. Forgone property taxes are equal to the difference between the full tax ($20.00 per unit per month in 1970) and the PILOT, that is, approximately $15.00 per unit per month for that year.[7] The value of this forgone local revenue is then added to the operating costs. Finally, we include a direct expenditure for federal administrative costs. In 1967 the average federal administrative cost was $7.10 per dwelling unit per month for all public housing projects,[8] or assuming an average increase in personnel and material costs of 4 percent per annum, approximately $8.00 per unit per month in 1970 prices.

Leased Housing: Using the Existing Stock

For leased housing, as for conventional public housing, we estimate the monthly economic cost for a two-bedroom unit, using 1970 Boston data. The local housing authority incurs operating and administrative costs whenever it leases existing private units, but capital costs are minimal.[9] However, when private developers and real estate owners respond to program incentives by constructing or rehabilitating standard units, their capital outlays are substantial. Moreover, because of Internal Revenue Service allowances for accelerated depreciation, this form of private participation imposes a revenue loss on the federal treasury. Because the magnitude of these private capital costs and tax losses varies with the amount of construction or rehabilitation involved, cost calculations for leased housing must be

7. The estimated full property taxes are computed first by capitalizing the adjusted rent receipts from the public housing units (tenant rents plus the implied value of the rent subsidy) to determine the aggregate property value and then applying the prevailing property tax rate to the full assessed value of the property. See Chapter 5.

8. See B. T. Fitzpatrick, "FHA and FNMA Assistance for Multifamily Housing," *Law and Contemporary Problems*, Vol. 32 (Summer 1967), p. 457.

9. The maximum amount of annual contribution is determined by estimating the development cost of a newly constructed public housing project for comparable occupancy and then establishing the level debt service needed to retire a 40-year tax-exempt LHA serial bond.

divided into three program subcategories: leasing with existing, rehabilitated, and newly constructed units. The federal and local administrative costs are prorated among these three subcategories in proportion to their respective shares of the total units in the Boston program.[10]

The cost of leasing an existing dwelling under Section 23 consists of expenses for management and maintenance, for the government's administrative overhead, and for the capital payments on outstanding mortgages as well as on any debt incurred while removing code violations. Since private owners pay full property taxes, we have no need to make an adjustment for property tax exemptions as we did in the case of conventional public housing. When marginally substandard units are leased, some minimal expenditure is required to bring the property up to code requirements. Thus, after incorporating the official estimate of overhead cost per unit as one-third that for administering public housing, we obtain a figure of $137 as the average monthly cost for Section 23 leased housing with existing units. (See Table 7.2.)

The average capital cost for the substantial rehabilitation of multifamily housing undertaken as a consequence of an agreement with the local housing authority was $8,412 per unit, in 1970 prices. Assuming a 25-year, 8 percent mortgage, this translates into a monthly capital cost of $65 per unit. The average capital cost of new construction under BHA long-term leasing was $15,512 per unit, in 1970 prices, or $108 per unit per month at an interest rate of 8 percent with a 40-year term.

Since the 1969 Tax Reform Act provides a special five-year write-off for expenditures incurred in rehabilitating rental housing for low-income occupancy (reducing the investor's capital cost), the value of this tax subsidy must be included in our cost estimate. We compute this value by establishing the depreciation schedules for both the accelerated (five-year) and conventional straight-line (25-year) depreciation methods, calculating the annual differential, and then multiplying this differential by the marginal

10. Congress allocates federal administrative funds for low-rent public housing but does not prorate the funds among conventional public housing, turnkey, and leased housing. However, the Budget Office in the Office of the Secretary, U.S. Department of Housing and Urban Development, estimates that the federal administrative cost for leased housing is approximately one-third that of conventional public housing. Telephone interview with William Rhodes, HUD, March 1971.

Table 7.2 Gross Economic Cost of Leased Housing per Unit per Month,[a] Boston, 1970

Costs	Existing Units	Rehabilitation	New Construction
Capital Costs			
Capital cost[b]	$ 42.00[c]	$ 65.00	$108.00
Forgone federal revenue[d]	—	7.50	4.50
Operating and Administrative Costs			
Operating cost	82.00	89.00	65.00
Forgone local revenue	—	—	16.50
Local administrative cost	10.50	10.50	10.50
Federal administrative cost	2.50	2.50	2.50
Total per unit per month	$137.00	$174.50	$207.00

a. The per-unit per-month costs are computed separately for the 1,710 existing units, 55 newly constructed units, and 140 rehabilitated units.
b. The monthly capital costs are paid out of tenant rent payments and federal rent assistance.
c. This figure includes both the average monthly capital cost on outstanding mortgages and the additional capital cost incurred in removing code violations.
d. For the computation of the average monthly forgone federal revenue from accelerated depreciation, see Appendix C, Table C.2.

tax rate of real estate investors.[11] By this method we compute the average monthly value of federal revenue forgone with the leasing of rehabilitated units (using a 10 percent discount rate) as approximately $7.50. If the operating and administrative costs are added to the sum of the capital costs and the forgone federal revenue calculated above, the monthly per unit cost of leasing with rehabilitation is $174.50.

In the case of the leased public housing program with new construction, we must allow for both a federal and a local tax subsidy. The cost of the federal subsidy is lower than for rehabilitation, however, since new construction projects are not allowed a special five-year write-off, having to be depreciated instead by the double declining balance method. Offsetting

11. We assume that the marginal tax rate for real estate investors is 50 percent. Moreover, the amount of the deductible depreciation is valued more highly in the early years; thus, to avoid the bias entailed in using the value of the tax loss for any single year, the average of the annualized discounted present values is employed. In calculating the present value of the tax shelter (or forgone federal revenue), the deductions for interest payments, real estate taxes, and other expenses incurred during the construction period are also included. It is assumed that these deductions are equal to 10 percent of the total construction cost. Also, tax revenue from the sale of the property offsets some of the earlier tax losses. To calculate this offset, it is assumed that the sale occurs at the end of the twentieth year.

this, however, the city extends a property tax exemption for the long-term (40-year) leasing of newly constructed units but makes no such exception for rehabilitated properties. The value of this local property tax subsidy ($16.50 per unit) must be added to operating expenses in order to determine the full economic cost of the new construction program.

Section 236 with Rent Supplements

We assume that the construction or rehabilitation costs associated with rent supplement units are equivalent to those already derived for the leasing program, since there is no a priori reason why they should differ. Moreover, given the small number of newly constructed rent supplement units in Boston, the use of their actual development costs might distort our comparison with the other programs. These few projects might well have had idiosyncratic histories, with their building costs skewed either unusually high or low. By assuming the same capital costs as for leasing, we can compare the administrative efficiency with which each program delivers essentially the same physical structure.

The leasing program has higher local administrative costs since housing authority staff has responsibility for locating and inspecting individual dwelling units, determining market rents, negotiating lease arrangements, and monitoring landlord-tenant relations. By contrast, the FHA office in Boston, responsible for administering the rent supplement program at the local level, assigns only one staff specialist to approve tenant eligibility and oversee program operations. Conversely, the rent supplement units experience higher on-site operating costs. In part, this results from their superior physical and environmental qualities, located, as they are, in FHA-insured moderate-income developments. These developments are generally found in neighborhoods with better public services and amenities than those enjoyed by public housing projects. The differential in operating cost can also be attributed, in part, to program structure; a program, like rent supplements, that pays an owner the difference between a fixed percentage of tenant income and the fair market rent of the occupied unit encourages participating households to occupy the most expensive housing made available.

With regard to federal administrative costs at the area or national level, we assume that those for rent supplements approximate those for leased housing, since the subsidies go toward the rental of units bearing FHA-

Table 7.3 Gross Economic Cost of Section 236 Developments[a] per Unit per Month, Boston, 1970

Costs	Rehabilitation per Unit per Month	New Construction per Unit per Month
Capital Costs [b]		
Capital cost	$ 65.00	$108.00
Forgone federal revenue	7.50	4.50
Operating and Administrative Costs		
Operating cost	102.00	72.00
Forgone local revenue	—c	—c
Local administrative cost	3.00	3.00
Federal administrative cost	2.50	2.50
Total per unit per month	$180.00	$190.00

a. The per-unit per-month operating and administrative costs are computed on the basis of average costs for 731 rehabilitated units and 38 newly constructed units.
b. For the purpose of this analysis, it is assumed that capital costs and forgone federal revenues of rehabilitated rent supplement units and newly constructed rent supplement units are equivalent to those of rehabilitated leased housing units and newly constructed leased housing units, respectively.
c. In those municipalities which provide a property tax exemption for FHA mortgage-insured developments in which rent supplement units are located, there will be an additional cost in the form of forgone local revenue. In most instances the value of this local property tax subsidy, however, is less than the public housing exemption.

insured mortgages. Unlike the HUD officials who oversee public housing development, administrators for the rent supplement and leased housing programs do not have to review architectural drawings, development plans, and participate in other construction-related activities.[12] Moreover, under both programs, responsibility for ownership and development is shifted from the public to the private sector, with resultant cost savings for federal administration. We can compute the monthly cost of rent supplement–rehabilitated units as $180, assuming the same capital costs and forgone tax revenue as with leased housing, and adding these to operating and administrative cost figures supplied by the local FHA. The monthly per-unit cost of providing newly constructed residences with rent supplements is computed in the same manner, but is higher than for rehabilitated units because of differences in development costs. These higher capital costs are sufficient to offset the lower cost associated with the less accelerated depreciation schedule. (See Table 7.3.)

12. Since the rent supplements are linked to FHA-insured newly constructed or rehabilitated dwellings, there is an additional federal administrative cost associated with the review, monitoring, and inspection of the FHA-sponsored developments.

Allocating the Costs

Having estimated the total monthly cost of providing a two-bedroom unit of standard housing under alternative housing strategies, we now consider how these costs are allocated among the tenants, the federal government, and the local government. This analysis provides answers to some important questions regarding program effectiveness and equity: How much of the total cost of housing the urban poor through federal programs is actually borne by the poor themselves? What is the difference between the economic costs and the full accounting costs? [13] What is the cost of the tax concessions received by high-income investors purchasing tax shelters? In sum, who ends up paying for subsidized housing?

Conventional Public Housing

The cost of providing a newly constructed two-bedroom conventional public housing unit in Boston during 1970 ($215.50 per month) can be allocated among the tenants, the federal government, and the local government, as shown in Table 7.4. The federal government pays the full capital cost of both conventional and turnkey developments through its retirement of the local housing authority (LHA) 40-year serial bonds. For those local authorities suffering operating deficits, the federal government makes an additional direct payment of $120 per annum for each family that is elderly, displaced by public action, extra large, or unusually poor. Moreover, in recent years Congress has authorized annual contributions to modernize substandard projects and to relieve the burden of excessive rents. This latter provision (the so-called Brooke Amendment) obligates the federal government to pay the LHA an amount equal to the difference between 25 percent of a household's net income and their project rent, whenever the latter exceeds the former. Finally, the Department of Housing and Urban Development expends a certain amount to cover its own administrative costs. In Boston, these direct federal outlays, taken together, account for 56 percent of the total cost of conventional public housing. In addition, the tax loss or forgone federal revenue from the tax exemption on housing authority bonds represents an indirect federal cost amounting to 5 percent of the total.[14]

13. The full accounting costs include both the direct federal expenditures and the value of forgone revenue resulting from preferential tax treatment.
14. For the computation of the average monthly forgone federal revenue from the tax exemption on the housing authority bonds see the technical note at the end of this chapter.

Table 7.4 Cost Allocations for Public Housing, Leased Housing, and Section 236–Rent Supplements per Unit per Month, Boston, 1970

| Program | Total Cost | Full Accounting Federal Budgetary Cost | | | Tenant Payment |
		Federal Expenditure	Forgone Federal Revenue	Forgone Local Government Revenue	
New Construction					
Conventional public housing	$215.50	$120.50	$11.00	$15.00	$69.00
Turnkey public housing	202.50	107.50	11.00	15.00	69.00
Leased housing	207.00	110.50	4.50	23.00	69.00
Section 236 – rent supplements	190.00	112.50	4.50	—b	73.00
Existing Housing Stock					
Leased housing with existing units	137.00	68.00	—	—	69.00
Leased housing with rehabilitation	174.50	98.00	7.50	—	69.00
Section 236–rent supplements with rehabilitationa	180.00	99.50	7.50	—b	73.00

a. Under the Section 236 program the federal government subsidizes the interest payment on the mortgage, thereby increasing the direct federal expenditure and lowering the tenant rental payments. The federal government pays the annual difference between the debt service on the mortgage at the market rate plus the mortgage insurance premium and the debt service at a 1 percent interest rate. However, when a Section 236 development contains rent supplement units—as in our analyses—the interest rate subsidy reduces the fair market rent rather than the tenant payment since the latter is based on tenant income. In effect, there is a reduction in the government's rent supplement payment equivalent to the interest rate subsidy. This means that the total federal expenditure per unit remains the same as under the rent supplement 221(d)(3) market rate program.
b. Although some municipalities provide a property tax exemption for Section 236 projects, we do not make this assumption in our study. In those instances where preferential tax treatment does occur, the city assumes the cost, while the landlords pass some fraction of their property tax savings on to the tenants.

The public housing tenants in each project finance most of the day-to-day operations through their rental payments, even though these payments are set at a fixed proportion of net income (22.8 percent in Boston). The tenant payments account for 32 percent of the cost of conventional public housing.

The local government provides the remaining 7 percent of the operating cost subsidy through its property tax abatement; instead of paying full property taxes, the housing authority, as discussed earlier, makes a payment in lieu of taxes. In effect, the difference between full property taxes and the PILOT constitutes a local subsidy contributed by the municipal government.

Leasing Existing Housing
In allocating costs for the leased housing program, we must once again distinguish among the leasing of existing, rehabilitated, and newly constructed units. Table 7.4 shows how the monthly costs for providing a two-bedroom unit under each of these program subcategories ($137.00, $174.50, and $207.00, respectively) are allocated among the tenants, the federal government, and the local municipality.

When used private housing is leased, no federal capital costs are incurred. Instead, the contribution from Washington (50 percent of the total) helps to cover the LHA's operating expenses, to subsidize the rents of leased housing tenants, and to support the federal government's own administrative and technical assistance activities. Rent payments from the subsidized tenants meet the remaining balance of operating and capital costs. Newly constructed and rehabilitated units involve additional private outlays when individual landlords make investments in their properties pursuant to a lease agreement. A related federal cost (in the form of a tax loss) results from the accelerated depreciation taken on these same investments.

Section 236 with Rent Supplements
The total monthly costs of newly constructed and rehabilitated two-bedroom units were $190 and $180, respectively, for dwellings subsidized through the rent supplement program. These costs, based on 1970 data, are allocated between the federal government (about 60 percent of the total) and the tenants (roughly 40 percent), as shown in Table 7.4. In some other municipalities, however, the local government assumes certain of the costs when it provides a property tax abatement to rent supplement units

located in Section 236 rental housing. With this one exception, the program involves no cost to the local treasury.

All direct capital costs of Section 236 developments are borne by the private sponsor. Direct federal expenditures are made to supplement the rents of poor households (the program's raison d'être) and to support the government's administrative activity. (Of course, a portion of these rent supplements as well as the tenant's own rent payments is ultimately used by the private owner to service his debt, but this has no bearing on the cost allocations). When the FHA's participation takes the form of a Section 236 subsidized mortgage rather than a 221(d)(3) market rate mortgage, the federal government must pay an interest subsidy to the mortgagee (generally a savings bank) and, hence, assumes a larger share of the monthly mortgage payments. Yet, there is no increase in the total federal government cost since the amount of the rent supplement is reduced by an amount equivalent to the interest rate subsidy. Finally, we must here again count the tax loss from accelerated depreciation allowances as a cost against the federal treasury.

Summarizing the Cost Allocations

Having allocated the direct and indirect costs associated with each form of housing subsidy, we can now compare these results with respect to the comparative cost of new construction strategies and alternative approaches for using the existing stock (for example, rehabilitation and leasing used housing). Even though the federal budget makes no acknowledgment of forgone tax revenue, each special tax concession reduces the government revenue available for program activities, just as do increases in direct government expenditures. Therefore, in order to represent more accurately the total impact of the housing programs on the national treasury, we include both federal tax subsidies and direct federal expenditures in our analysis. Local tax subsidies, in the form of property tax exemptions, are also incorporated.

The cost allocations, as summarized in Table 7.4, have several implications. First, our findings indicate that, although tenants in the respective subsidy programs contribute approximately the same dollar amount for their units, the quality of the housing and neighborhood environment differs substantially, with those living in newly constructed units enjoying disproportionately higher consumption benefits than those in rehabilitated or existing units. This is clearly inequitable since households with equivalent needs receive differential benefits. A second finding concerns the relative costliness of conventional public housing as a means for sheltering the poor, when the full magnitude of indirect subsidies is considered. The federal government assumes responsibility for retiring the LHA bonds and, at the same time, extends a tax exemption to the interest payments received by bondholders. The local municipality provides an additional subsidy by allowing the LHA to make payments in lieu of taxes rather than pay full property taxes. This negative impact on the local tax base acts as a disincentive against a municipality's choosing to participate in the program. In the other production programs as well, the federal government uses inefficient subsidy approaches. In the Section 236–rent supplement program, for example, the federal government could raise the development capital through the sale of bonds rather than encourage high-income investors through the sale of tax shelters created by favorable depreciation laws. A direct subsidy to developers would be more efficient and less costly to the government since the purchasers of tax shelters demand a higher after-tax return on investment than real estate developers do. And using the existing stock under the leased housing program costs the government less than half the amount of the production subsidies.

Cost of Alternative Housing Strategies
By assuming that families residing in conventional public, leased public, and rent supplement housing units have been moved from substandard to standard housing, we can use the estimated resource cost of each program to measure their respective cost effectiveness in "closing the housing gap." The total number of households currently living in substandard housing constitutes the housing gap. To close the housing gap is to move these households into standard housing. This type of gross performance measure, analogous to a poverty gap measure, assumes that standard and substandard housing are dichotomous bundles. Thus an implicit assumption is made that a significant improvement in living conditions results from moving into standard housing. Obviously, the limitation of the housing gap measure is its failure to make any distinction between differential housing conditions above or below the minimum standard level, as well as its emphasis on structural conditions rather than neighborhoods or municipal services. But since data are generally available in dichotomous form, the programs are

Table 7.5 Closing the Housing Gap in Federally Assisted Rental Housing per Two-Bedroom Unit per Annum, Boston, 1970

Program	Annual Resource Cost	Number of Families Moved from Substandard to Standard per $1 Million Resource Cost	Rank
New Construction			
Conventional public housing	$2,586	387	7
Turnkey public housing	2,425	412	5
Leased housing	2,484	403	4
Section 236–rent supplements	2,280	439	3
Existing Housing Stock			
Leased housing with existing units	1,644	608	6
Leased housing with rehabilitation	2,094	478	1
Section 236–rent supplements with rehabilitation	2,060	485	2

compared on this basis. This comparison is made by dividing a fixed amount of resource expenditure by the resource cost per unit per month for each program. The results are summarized in Table 7.5.

These figures clearly argue that the leasing of existing units is substantially more cost-effective than any strategy centered on rehabilitation or new construction. Although the specific costs for other cities might well vary with different factor prices (land, labor, and capital) and market conditions (such as vacancy rate), the basic result is conclusive: the leasing of existing units provides the highest number of families with standard housing per dollar of resource expenditure.

Of the many variables that contribute to these findings, two seem most significant: differences in housing condition and in construction costs. With respect to the first, many of the leased housing–existing units are marginally above minimum code standards. In fact, a large percentage receive minor repairs in order to remove code deficiencies. By contrast, the substantially rehabilitated and newly constructed leased housing and rent supplement units provide residential services exceeding those required by minimum code standards (for example, more generous space, newer mechanical systems, and special amenities). In the case of conventional public housing, inefficient development and operating procedures also contribute to low cost effectiveness, as evidenced by the cost savings associated with turnkey construction as opposed to publicly developed projects.

The second explanation for the cost differentials lies in the rapidly rising prices of construction materials, labor, urban land, and interest rates. While this cost inflation has a serious impact on the financing of new development, the capital cost of existing units reflects the historically lower interest rates and construction costs that prevailed at an earlier time. Thus used housing generally carries smaller mortgages and lower monthly amortization costs. However, it should be remembered that these units are leased for only ten years or less. As a result, over the long term, either their leases will be re-negotiated periodically, or lease arrangements will be made for other units instead—in both cases, at a future, and most likely higher, market rate. On the other hand, capital costs for public housing and FHA rent supple-ment projects remain constant over their 40-year economic lives.[15] Thus one can speculate as to how the cost differential will fluctuate over time, in all probability narrowing as price indexes continue to rise.

Living as we do in a stochastic world, where uncertainty and imperfect information are the order of the day, we cannot estimate future costs with any certainty. Yet on the basis of past experience, we can comment on how cost differentials should tend to behave over time. First, there is no a priori reason to believe that the operating costs of leasing existing units will in-crease at a faster rate in the future. Indeed, as government administrators gain more familiarity with leasing procedures and more units are added to the program's inventory, economies of scale may lower the per-unit admin-istrative costs. Second, although the capital costs of leasing existing units can be expected to increase over time (while the level monthly amortiza-tion payments for new developments remain fixed at the time of construc-tion), the present cost differentials between new construction and using the existing stock are too substantial for future changes to alter the results for an average year. Moreover, since the future cost differentials must be discounted to determine their present worth, we value existing differentials more highly than those anticipated in the years ahead. For all these reasons,

15. As mentioned earlier, public housing construction is financed with 40-year serial bonds; FHA mortgages for low- to moderate-income development also provide for a 40-year payback period.

then, we can assume that to house poor families in existing units will remain the most cost-effective strategy over the long as well as the short term.

Technical Note: The Federal Tax Loss on Public Housing Bonds
In the public housing program one major source of federal tax loss (forgone federal revenue) is the income tax exemption on local housing authority bonds. This tax exemption has two separate effects on the federal budget. First, since the interest payments on the bonds are exempt from federal income taxes, there is a loss of federal revenue. Second, since the interest rate on tax-exempt housing authority bonds is lower than the rate for fully taxable bonds, there is an interest cost saving to the federal government, which is responsible for retiring the bonds. Thus, to estimate the *net* effect of issuing tax-exempt housing authority bonds on the Treasury, we deduct the federal government's interest cost saving from its forgone revenue:

$$T^F = F - I, \tag{7.4}$$

where

T^F = the net effect per annum on the U.S. Treasury from issuing tax-exempt bonds on BHA family developments,

F = the federal revenue forgone per annum from bonds issued for BHA family developments,

I = the federal interest cost savings per annum from retiring BHA family development bonds.

In order to determine the magnitude of the interest cost saving, we have to determine the probable interest rate (or yield) on tax-exempt housing authority bonds without the exemption feature. It is the differential interest cost on tax-exempt and fully taxable housing authority bonds which provides an estimate of the federal government's interest cost saving. In an extensive survey of capital market experts on the probable yield of tax-exempt municipal obligations, without the exemption feature, there was a general consensus that the yield would approximate that of corporate bonds, of the same credit category and maturity.[16] Therefore, as a first ap-

16. See David J. Ott and Allan H. Meltzer, *Federal Income Tax Treatment of State and Local Government Securities* (Washington, D.C.: Brookings Institution, 1962), p. 49.

proximation of the yield or interest rate on housing authority bonds, without the exemption, we shall use Aaa-rated corporate bonds. To compute the annual interest cost saving, therefore, we find the yield differential between public housing and Aaa corporate bonds, assuming that the total issue was sold in 1970:

$$I \ = \ \sum_{j=1}^{15} B_j \, (a_c - a_{PH}), \tag{7.5}$$

where

I = the value of federal interest cost saving from the tax-exempt housing authority bonds issued for BHA family developments in 1970,

B_j = the value of the BHA bond issue, adjusted to 1970 development costs, for family development j,

a_c = the level monthly payment necessary to amortize a loan of \$1.00 on a 0.0703 interest rate 40-year Aaa corporate bond,

a_{PH} = the level monthly payment necessary to amortize a loan of \$1.00 on a 0.0554 interest rate 40-year public housing authority bond.

The magnitude of the forgone revenue, on the other hand, depends upon the amount of the housing authority issue, the distribution of the bond sales,[17] the yield on alternative investment opportunities,[18] and the average

---

Capital market experts believe, moreover, that the yields would actually rise by more than the current differential between new issues on tax-exempt municipals and comparable quality corporate bonds, but it is felt that the differential is less for housing authority bonds since the secondary market and overall marketability is better than that for most other municipal bonds.

17. Since there is no statistical series on the distribution of local housing authority bonds, we assume the same distribution of bond holdings as for all other tax-exempt municipal bonds. All such bonds are generally comparable, but the existence of a more active secondary market for housing authority bonds means that they are more liquid and easier to sell.

18. For investors, especially institutional investors, who purchase tax-exempt municipal bonds, the most probable fully taxable alternative investment is corporate bonds (Aaa). See Roland I. Robinson, *The Postwar Market for State and Local Government Securities* (Princeton: Princeton University Press, 1960). The relative comparability of corporate bonds was corroborated, in telephone interviews, with Professors James Duesenberry and Stanley Surrey, Harvard University, September 1970.

marginal tax rate of institutional and individual municipal bondholders,[19] If the tax-exempt feature of municipal bonds, including housing authority bonds, were eliminated, then the distribution of new taxable issues among investors would be altered. We assume, therefore, that these investors would purchase corporate bonds (Aaa) as their most comparable taxable investment alternative.[20] Assuming, then, that all of the Boston Housing Authority bonds for federally aided family developments were issued in 1970, we compute the federal tax forgone by multiplying the amount of the bond issue by the average yield (Aaa corporate bonds) and the average marginal tax rates of the investor groups. Symbolically, we estimate the revenue loss by multiplying the annual income from the interest payments by the respective average marginal tax rates:

$$F = \sum_{j=1}^{15} (B_j \bar{y} \bar{r}), \tag{7.6}$$

where

F = the annual value of forgone federal revenue from the tax-exempt housing authority bonds issued for BHA family development,

B_j = the value of the bond issue, adjusted to 1970 development costs, for BHA family development j in thousands of dollars,

$\bar{y}$ = the average annual interest payment on Aaa corporate bonds per $1,000,[21]

$\bar{r}$ = the weighted average marginal tax rate in 1970 for household and institutional investor groups.

19. Our estimate of the average marginal tax rate of the respective investor groups is based on a modification of the estimate developed by Susan Ackerman and David Ott. See Susan Ackerman and David Ott, "An Analysis of the Revenue Effects of Proposed Substitutes for the Tax Exemption of State and Local Bonds," *National Tax Journal*, Vol. 23 (1970).
20. This assumption introduces an upward bias to our estimate, since many investors would otherwise purchase tax sheltered bonds, real estate, or cattle. Therefore, we can consider our estimate of the net dollar effect of issuing tax-exempt bonds on public housing to be an upper ceiling.
21. We compute the average annual interest payment on Aaa corporate bonds per $1,000 as $\bar{y} = (a_c n) - 1,000$, where a_c = the level monthly payment necessary to amortize a loan of $1,000 on a 7.03 percent 40-year Aaa corporate bond, and $n - a$ is constant twelve months per year.

Our empirical analysis indicates that the exemption of public housing bonds reduces revenue to the federal treasury (see Equation 7.7). This means that the forgone revenue exceeds the interest cost savings. The federal government's annual interest cost savings from retiring the 40-year housing authority serial bonds[22] has been computed by comparing the interest cost with and without the exemption feature. Our empirical estimate of the forgone federal revenue, however, is more complex. For example, since the distribution of bond purchases varies with monetary conditions, the average distribution of municipal bond purchases for a range of years rather than for a single year is used.[23] We estimate the forgone federal revenue, then, using the present distribution of new issues purchased during 1963–1967 and the average marginal tax rates for 1969 (without the surtax).

Combining the results reported in Table 7.6 with our findings on interest cost savings, we compute the net annual effect of issuing tax-exempt bonds, for BHA family developments, on the federal Treasury in 1970 as follows:[24]

$$T = F - I \tag{7.7}$$

$$= \sum_{j=1}^{15} (B_j \overline{yr}) - B_j(a_c - a_{PH})$$

$$= \sum_{j=1}^{15} (10{,}693 \times 49.6 \times 0.47) - 10{,}693 \times 12(16.214 - 5.157)$$

$$= \sum_{j=1}^{15} (249{,}275 - 135{,}630)$$

$$= (3{,}739{,}125 - 2{,}034{,}450)$$

$$= \$1{,}704{,}675 \text{ per annum}$$

$$= \$113{,}645 \text{ per development per annum}$$

$$= \$11 \text{ per unit per month.}$$

22. Normally, public housing authority bonds are 40-year serial bonds that are amortized in a manner similar to that of housing mortgages.
23. In years of easy-money policy, commercial banks purchase almost all new municipal issues, while in tight money conditions non-life-insurance companies and high-tax-bracket households purchase a larger share of such issues. See Ackerman and Ott, "Revenue Effects of Proposed Substitutes for the Tax Exemption of State and Local Bonds," pp. 3–6.
24. We compute $\overline{Y} = (a_c n) - 1{,}000 = (6.214 \times 12) - 1{,}000 = 49.6$.

Table 7.6 Forgone Federal Revenue from Tax-Exempt Housing Authority Bonds

Investor Group	Percent of Purchases[a] Municipal Bond Issues (1963–1967)	Amount[b] of Investment in BHA Bonds	Average Percent[c] Yield Aaa Corporate Bonds	Annual Interest Payment	Averaged[d] Marginal Tax Rate	Forgone Federal Taxes
Households	19	$ 30,476,000	7.03	$2,142,463	$42.8	$ 916,974
Nonfinancial corporations	2	3,208,000	7.03	225,522	48.0	108,251
Commercial banks	67	107,468,000	7.03	7,555,000	48.0	3,626,400
Non-life-insurance companies	12	19,248,000	7.03	1,353,134	48.0	649,504
	100	$160,400,000e				$5,301,629

a. Source: Federal Reserve Board of Governors, Federal Reserve System, *Federal Reserve Bulletin* (May 1968).
b. The total bond issue, adjusted to 1970 development costs, for Boston's fifteen federally aided family developments would be $160,400,000.
c. Source: U.S. Board of Governors, *Federal Reserve Bulletin* (August 1970), p. A-34.
d. Source: An adjusted version of the average marginal tax rates estimated by Ackerman and Ott, "Revenue Effects of Proposed Substitutes for Tax Exemption of State and Local Bonds." While the authors estimated the respective tax rates on the basis of 1969 tax rates including the 10 percent surtax, we modified their results by computing the average marginal tax rates *without* the surtax (multiplying their results by 10/11 or 0.91).
e. The total development cost includes the two projects that were deeded to the BHA by the federal government.

CHAPTER 8
Evaluating Social and Environmental Effects

When households consume 'housing', they purchase or rent more than the dwelling unit and its characteristics. They are also concerned with such diverse factors as health, security, privacy, neighborhood and social relations, status, community facilities and services, access to jobs, and control over the environment. Being "ill-housed" can mean deprivation along any or all of these dimensions, and relative deprivations can lead to widespread discontent and suffering.

Jon Pynoos, Robert Schafer, and Chester Hartman, eds.,
Housing Urban America, Introduction

Over the years, national housing policy has pursued a shifting set of objectives: to upgrade and enlarge the nation's housing stock, to ensure fair housing opportunities, to create better living environments, to facilitate relocation of persons displaced by public action, to improve locational mobility and housing conditions for the urban and rural poor. With respect to many of these objectives, program performance can be evaluated in monetary, or at least rigorously quantitative, terms. The preceding chapters have presented methodologies for attaching market values or money prices to housing consumption, municipal revenue, employment benefits, and resource costs, respectively. This type of formal analysis employs essentially a single criterion to compare housing strategies: the difference between the dollar value of benefits and costs. However, the same housing programs have a variety of important social and environmental effects that do not lend themselves to monetary valuation but that nonetheless should be given full consideration in any weighting of program alternatives. The use of efficiency criteria alone can be deceptive if it leads policy makers to assign only secondary importance to the non-dollar-valued effects of housing assistance.

This chapter is intended to complement Chapters 3–7, first, by discussing the importance of non-dollar-valued benefits in any assessment of multiple-objective programs; second, by treating the qualitative effects of public housing, leased housing, and interest subsidy programs with rent supplements (like Sections 236 and 221(d)(3)) in as much detail as possible, with an emphasis on the contrast between new construction strategies and those using the existing stock. Finally, on the basis of this evaluation, the relative effectiveness of each strategy is ranked on an ordinal scale.

Housing Policy Analysis and Multiple Objectives
The investment model of traditional welfare economics, as described in the
technical note in Chapter 2, ranks programs in terms of their economic
efficiency or their contribution to aggregate national income while excluding those social and environmental factors not amenable to quantification.
This omission results in part from the historical preoccupation of policy
analysts with the economic effects of public expenditures but also in part
from the conceptual and empirical problems inherent in obtaining significant measures of social and environmental impacts. Many of these effects
can be neither divided into discrete units nor measured in numerical terms;
others exhibit a confusing array of externalities. For example, causal relationships between a tenant's physical or mental well-being and his housing
condition are hard to establish, and, even where such causality appears
self-evident, the precise relation between inputs and outputs may still remain immeasurable.

Trade-offs for Decision Makers
Despite these difficulties, however, it is important to consider non-dollar-
valued effects for two reasons. First, recent studies suggest that housing
conditions significantly influence the health, attitudes, and behavior of
tenants. Second, in the last two decades, the consciousness of social and
environmental issues has risen among consumers and policy makers, thus
bringing with it a policy imperative to make social, environmental, and economic trade-offs as explicit as possible.

Let us consider, first, the relationship between housing and health. There
is some evidence linking seriously deficient housing with a heightened sus-
ceptibility to certain illnesses and reduced life expectancy. In a careful study
made in Baltimore, for example, Daniel Wilner and his associates found that
the incidence of acute respiratory ailments, infectious childhood diseases
(measles, chickenpox, and whooping cough), skin diseases, digestive ailments, and enteritis (typhoid, dysentery, and diarrhea) were correlated with
inadequate heating or ventilation, crowded sleeping arrangements, shared
use of toilet, water, and washing facilities, and inadequate space for cold
food storage. Wilner also documented that injuries resulting from fire and
home accidents were clearly related to crowded or inadequate kitchens,
poor electrical connections, and poorly lighted and unstable stairs.[1] Other

1. Daniel M. Wilner, Rosabelle Price Walkley, Thomas C. Pinkerton, and Matthew

studies link poor housing and overcrowding with pneumonia, tuberculosis, lead poisoning, and poor mental health and suggest that an improved living environment tends to reduce the incidence of illness and disease.[2]

Turning to the relationship between housing improvements and indicators of antisocial behavior, we enter an area of greater uncertainty. It is difficult, for example, to demonstrate that a particular architectural configuration results in increased crime or any other disruptive activities. Nonetheless, some indicators do suggest that inadequate housing (particularly overcrowded units), the lack of outdoor recreational space, and blighted neighborhood conditions have adverse effects on social behavior. Poorly designed and dreary buildings, run-down neighborhoods, and cramped quarters can result in dysfunctional housekeeping habits and child-rearing practices.[3] Slum living erodes aspirations, self-respect, and morale. When a family rents or purchases a home, it obtains not only a physical structure but also a particular location, neighborhood environment, and combination of municipal services (schooling, policing, public transportation, and so on); thus housing choices that are constrained have an effect on a family's access to educational, social, and employment opportunities as well as on the quality of the public services received by a family.

These effects derive from factors such as high residential densities in low-income neighborhoods, negative externalities, inequities in the delivery of municipal services, the increased suburbanization of job opportunities and imperfections in the housing market. Financial disabilities, lack of

Taybeck, *The Housing Environment and Family Life* (Baltimore: Johns Hopkins Press, 1962).

2. See A. Pond, "The Influence of Housing on Health," *Marriage and Family Living,* Vol. 19, No. 2 (1957), pp. 154–159; New York Academy of Medicine, Report of the Sub-Committee on Housing of the Committee on Public Health Relations, *Bulletin of the New York Academy of Medicine,* June 1954; D. Wilner and R. Walkley, "The Effects of Housing on Health, Social Adjustment and School Performance," presented at the 39th Annual Meeting of the American Orthopsychiatric Association, Los Angeles, California, March 23, 1962.

3. See Alvin L. Schorr, *Slums and Social Insecurity*, U.S., Department of Health, Education and Welfare, Social Security Administration, Division of Research and Statistics, Research Report No. 1, 1966. See also Harold N. Proshansky, Willliam H. Nelson, and Leanne G. Rivlin, eds., *Environmental Psychology: Man and His Physical Setting* (New York: Holt, Rinehart & Winston, 1970).

information, discriminatory land-use regulation and real estate practices (such as snob zoning, large lot requirements, and selective screening devices used by real estate brokers) act to limit housing choice and to reinforce patterns of economic, racial, and ethnic segregation. The interdependence of property values affects the upkeep of structures within a given area and consequently may contribute to neighborhood instability and blight.[4]

Consumer advocates, tenant organizations, and civil rights leaders have become increasingly vocal in proclaiming the ill effects associated with inadequate housing; scholars and journalists have helped to publicize and document these claims. Today, as a result, policy makers at both the local and national level are more conscious of these deleterious effects and have some understanding of their causes. And federal courts have acted to enforce free choice of housing and to offset some of the negative spillover effects from concentrating subsidized housing in ghetto areas.[5] Despite this widespread acknowledgment that housing has important noneconomic effects, few studies other than the Wilner analysis have actually attempted to treat them systematically.

No single housing program can claim superior performance with respect to the entire range of qualitative objectives. In fact, program objectives may often conflict; for example, a mayor confronted by severe fluctuations in the local housing market may have to choose between a program's adaptability, on the one hand, and its market efficiency or benefit-cost ranking, on the other. Thus, in making a fully rational choice among program alternatives, it would be necessary to provide relative weights or values for each program output. This poses an operational problem, of course, since

---

4. As discussed in Chapter 2, decisions that are economically rational for individual property holders (failure to upgrade their properties in declining areas, for example) may accelerate the spread and severity of neighborhood blight. See Otto R. Davis and Andrew B. Whinston, "The Economics of Urban Renewal," in James Q. Wilson, ed., *Urban Renewal: The Record and the Controversy*.

5. Acting to neutralize political pressures on the design and location of public housing, Federal District Judge Richard B. Austin ordered the Chicago Housing Authority in 1969 "to build 75 percent of all new public housing projects in predominantly white communities and at least one mile from the edge of the nearest black ghetto; to limit future projects to no more than three stories, and to avoid the selection of project sites with the alderman of the wards involved." See citation in Leonard Freedman, *Public Housing: The Politics of Poverty* (New York: Holt, Rinehart & Winston, 1969), pp. x-xi.

policy makers can hardly value outputs that are incommensurable.[6] For example, how much racial integration can be traded for each additional dollar of housing consumption? How much value should be assigned to neighborhood amenities?

To obtain an explicit base for evaluating and comparing the noneconomic effects of alternative housing strategies, we use an ordinal ranking system to measure the performance of each program output. However, before these rankings are established, some general discussion of the alternative strategies is warranted.

Qualitative Assessment of Program Effectiveness

For the most part, criticisms of federal housing programs center on economic and management issues—unjustified per-unit and aggregate costs,[7] inefficiency and lack of responsiveness in the delivery system, inequities in the distribution of benefits, wastefulness, and lack of quality control. However, other voices, more concerned with social and environmental effects, have addressed the lack of related social services (like health care, job counseling, day care, and recreation), the failure to reduce racial segregation, the infringements on consumer sovereignty, the concentration of problem families in particular areas, the weakening of neighborhood stability, and the creation of instant slums. Several of these criticisms apply in some measure to all major subsidy programs, while others may pertain to only a single program. For this reason, it is useful to examine each program separately in terms of its social and environmental impact. Since conventional public housing and Section 236 (and 221(d)(3)) rely on newly constructed developments while the leased housing program relies primarily on the existing

6. For a succinct summary of various approaches to the problem of combining incommensurable benefits, see A. Myrick Freeman III, "Public Design and Evaluation with Multiple Objectives," in the *Analysis and Evaluation of Public Expenditures: The PPB System*, Vol. 1 (1969), p. 565, Joint Economic Committee, 91st Congress, 1st Session (Washington, D.C.: U.S. Government Printing Office, 1969).
7. The runaway costs of subsidy programs were reported in the *Third Annual Report on National Housing Goals*, 1969, as follows: ". . . for the three years 1970 to 1972 we have already obligated the federal government to subsidy payments of perhaps $30 billion over the next 30 to 40 years. . . . By 1978 present estimates suggest that the federal government will be paying out at least $7.5 billion in subsidies. . . . Over the life of the mortgage this could amount to the staggering total of more than $200 billion." Message from the President of the United States, *Third Annual Report on National Housing Goals* (Washington, D.C.: U.S. Government Printing Office, 1971), p. 22.

stock scattered over various sites, our comparison illustrates the relative performance of two important policy options.

Conventional Public Housing

Ever since its enactment, the public housing program has been the subject of national and local controversy. The criticism emanates from a disconcerting variety of sources, including the home-building industry, private property owners, neighborhood organizations, social scientists, and public housing tenants themselves. Even though each of these groups tends to couch its grosser prejudices in seemingly neutral terms (inefficiency, preservation of neighborhood values, local control), such phraseology rarely conceals the self-interest in which their respective critiques are rooted.[8] For example, as a matter of ideology and economic self-interest, home builders, through their industry associations, oppose conventional public housing as unfair competition with private developers and as a threatening precedent for socialized housing production. Local property owners and neighborhood groups resist public housing construction in their communities because they anticipate a decline in neighborhood character and property values, a possible deterioration in public safety, added burdens on municipal services, not to mention racial or ethnic integration. Tenants often regard public housing projects as institutions rather than homes, as "prisons without walls," which carry a social stigma, fail to provide security of person and property, and isolate residents from normal community life. Housing administrators complain that many tenants are hostile and irresponsible, that vandalism renders self-defeating any investment in grounds and exteriors, that federal paper work adds needlessly to administrative overhead, and that operating budgets are inadequate to cover rising costs.

Many of these critiques retain their validity despite the narrow self-interest of the parties giving them voice. Institutional rigidities, neighborhood spillover effects, architectural sterility, shoddy construction, and inadequate financing deserve consideration in any disinterested appraisal of the conventional public housing program. Unfortunately, most of the literature treats these issues in too cursory and inconclusive a manner to be of help in adjusting program regulations or forming policy decisions. Furthermore, in many instances social scientists, city planners, and architects

8. The following discussion of housing interest groups, their positions and ideology, relies in large part on the study of public housing politics by Freedman, *Public Housing*.

impose their own values on program evaluations—values that reflect neither the preference of tenants, administrators, and builders nor the intent of Congress.

With these caveats in mind, it is still useful to examine what literature is available on social and environmental impacts. The late Catherine Bauer Wurster, an early public housing advocate, articulated a common view among the housing professionals in her observations on the limbolike state of the program after two decades of operation—continuously controversial, not dead, but never more than half alive.[9] Most social scientists and housing specialists agree, for example, that public housing has failed to provide decent housing, that it has segregated tenants by income and race, and that it has isolated residents from the larger community. Meyerson and Banfield's study of the Chicago Housing Authority portrays a classic case of how local politics ensure segregated patterns of tenant and site selections.[10] Social scientists and reformers have also criticized the institutional rigidities, infringements on consumer choice, and depressing project design characteristic of many large-scale public housing projects; they have documented the custodial attitude of many project administrators, which tends to perpetuate paternalistic regulations.[11] Still other commentators have emphasized how the physical design of housing projects visually reinforces their institutional character, pointing to such features as high-rise towers, concrete play areas, the absence of landscaping and inviting common spaces, poor lighting, and general anonymity.[12]

Some housing specialists, dismayed by the extent and persuasiveness of

9. Catherine Bauer Wurster, "The Dreary Deadlock of Public Housing," *Architectural Forum*, Vol. 106, No. 5 (May 1957).

10. Many studies of public housing have pointed out the isolation of public housing tenants from the larger community. The Meyerson and Banfield study is particularly useful because it analyzes the political process underlying this phenomenon. See Martin Meyerson and Edward Banfield, *Politics, Planning and the Public Interest* (New York: Free Press, 1955).

11. See, for example, J. Mulvihill, "Problems in the Management of Public Housing," *Temple Law Quarterly*, Vol. 163 (1962), and Robert Moore Fisher, *Twenty Years of Public Housing* (New York: Harper & Row, 1959).

12. As one architect long associated with the housing movement has commented, the projects are unimaginative, monotonous, ugly blocks of cement that fail to blend with or complement the existing neighborhood. See Albert Mayer, "Public Housing Architecture," *Journal of Housing*, Vol. 19 (1962), and Albert Mayer, "Public Housing Design," *Journal of Housing*, Vol. 20 (1963).

such criticisms, acknowledge the program's deficiencies but still argue the possibility of reform, taking heart from some relatively successful innovations in both the development and management of public housing over the past decade. These improvements include the encouragement of better-quality design, the provision of limited on-site social services and community facilities, the wider use of scattered site development instead of large-scale projects, greater tenant participation in administrative, security, and maintenance functions, and more use of private contractors in both project development and management. Still other students of government housing policy contend that public housing may have performed better than its critics concede.[13] Lawrence Friedman, in his legal-historical evaluation of government and slum housing, argues that a large part of the literature is preoccupied with the most notorious situations (San Francisco's Hunter Point Project, St. Louis's Pruitt-Igoe, and Boston's Columbia Point), where racial polarization and social breakdown largely reflect conditions that already prevail in the surrounding neighborhoods as well. He points to many relatively successful projects in smaller cities and towns, contending, moreover, that in purely physical terms, public housing does offer its tenants genuine improvement in their living conditions. Like-minded spokesmen maintain that public housing has offered many low-income families their first opportunity to live in a decent environment and, in the process, has helped reduce the social and economic costs of slums.[14] A few statistical studies document that, with respect to several measures of health and social conditions, families transplanted from the slums to public housing experience a beneficial change in their circumstances.[15] As the foregoing discussion indicates, however, the literature is inconclusive, while public housing continues to limp along, and its critics continue to call for new directions.

13. Lawrence M. Friedman, *Government and Slum Housing* (Chicago: Rand McNally, 1968), pp. 144–146.
14. See, for example, Fisher, *Twenty Years of Public Housing*.
15. John Dean, "The Myths of Housing Reform," in William L. Wheaton, Martin Meyerson, and G. Milgram, eds., *Urban Housing* (New York: Free Press, 1966), pp. 257–258. In a footnote Dean makes reference to the statistical studies by Naomi Barer, "Deliquency Before, After Admission to New Haven Housing Developments," *Journal of Housing*, December 1945, and Stuart Chapin, "An Experiment on the Social Effects of Good Housing," *American Sociological Review*, Vol. 5, December 1940.

Leased Housing: Using the Existing Stock

The leased-housing program, enacted in 1965, has had a brief history; nevertheless, sufficient information is available (national data, case studies of certain cities) for an evaluation of its effectiveness. Acceptance of the program has been rapid and widespread, as evidenced by congressional testimony and general community interest [16] and confirmed by national statistics (over 35 percent of the units added to the national inventory of low-rent public housing during fiscal 1970 were leased under Section 23; a total of over 150,000 leased units either under contract or in process by the end of the same year).[17] Moreover, several medium-sized and small communities that have refused conventional public housing funds over the 35 years since they first became available have, nonetheless, been willing to participate in the leased housing program.

Local housing authorities are attracted to the flexibility of leasing as compared to the large-scale and long-term commitment to conventional public housing development. For example, the leased housing program has been used to house the elderly in Chicago, low-income but upwardly mobile families in Oakland, extra-large families in Omaha, and families relocated as the result of government activities in Oklahoma City.[18] In housing markets with low vacancy rates, such as Washington, D.C., and Worcester, Massachusetts, the availability of leased housing funds has induced owners of substandard dwellings to upgrade their properties.[19] In fact, the Urban Institute study of the Section 23 leasing program indicates that half of the local authorities in their nation-wide sample reported that 60 percent or more of the units under lease had undergone significant upgrading, more than routine painting and redecoration, in order to meet local code standards.[20] In an earlier statistical study it was determined that close to 30 percent of the leased housing units in the country were either

16. See, for example, Edward Aronov and Hamilton Smith, "Large Families, Low Incomes and Leasing," *Journal of Housing*, Vol. 9 (October 1965), pp. 486–487.
17. U.S., Department of Housing and Urban Development, Housing Assistance Administration, *Report on Low-Income Housing Programs as of December 31, 1969.*
18. Lawrence Friedman and James Krier, "A New Lease on Life: Section 23, Housing and the Poor," *University of Pennsylvania Law Review*, Vol. 116 (1968), pp. 640–641.
19. Aronov and Smith, "Large Families, Low Incomes and Leasing," p. 482.
20. Frank de Leeuw and Sam H. Leaman, "The Section 23 Leasing Program: Progress Report," Urban Institute, Washington, D.C., Working Paper 112–35, 1972.

newly constructed or substantially rehabilitated.[21] Both reports indicate the potential of the leasing program (as well as other programs using the existing stock) to conserve and upgrade housing in low- and moderate-rent neighborhoods.

Equally important, leasing enables subsidized units to be obtained anywhere within the metropolitan housing market, subject, of course, to certain price and discriminatory constraints. As a result, families can be dispersed into small structures in stable neighborhoods rather than shepherded into large complexes, thus substituting a more or less normal tenant-landlord relation for the stigmatization and official scrutiny endured by many public housing occupants. This holds especially true for communities like Boston, where the tenant himself may negotiate the lease agreement with the private owner while the housing authority remains a relatively unobtrusive third party; here, in effect, the subsidized family may seek out any unit available in the local market that satisfies its preferences with respect to housing type and location, as long as its condition is standard and its price within the allowable limits.

On the whole, the leased housing program has not only succeeded in freeing recipients from the project syndrome but also widened locational choices as well. Relying primarily on existing housing, the leasing program uses scattered sites far more than any other federal housing program. In the most comprehensive study to date of the leased housing program (39 housing authorities), the Urban Institute found that the neighborhoods in which leased units are located are areas where moderate- rather than low-income housing is concentrated.[22] Moreover, the great majority of local authorities prefer to place nonelderly families in single-family houses or duplexes, on sites scattered around the city. Although leased units are not evenly distributed throughout the cities and counties served by local authorities, there has been a clear preference for neighborhoods with adequate personal safety and well-maintained properties.

Criticisms of the leasing program include its alleged inability to add units

21. Sam H. Leaman, "The Leased Housing Program: A Statistical Review," Urban Institute, Washington, D.C., Working Paper 112–30, March 1971.
22. De Leeuw and Leaman, "The Section 23 Leasing Program."

to the existing stock[23] and its limited usefulness under tight market conditions. Indeed, there is a general presumption that leasing, as a major strategy option, proves most advantageous in times of housing surplus, when an ample supply of modest vacant units exist, or when the market is reasonably competitive and landlords are eager to stabilize their rent-roll through a government-supported lease agreement. Even when vacancy rates are low, however, the ability of the local housing market to absorb the increased demand for standard units without unacceptable price increases will depend upon competition among landlords and the consequent degree to which modest units are made available, substandard dwellings are repaired and upgraded, larger units are subdivided, and higher-priced dwellings filter down to a lower price level. When short-run price increases are accompanied by these landlord responses, the leased housing program serves as an important deterrent to neighborhood decline.

Section 236 with Rent Supplements

Rent supplements, like leased housing, received a legislative authorization in 1965, but because Congress refused to appropriate any operational funds for the first year of the program's enactment, experience with it dates only from 1966. Despite this abbreviated history, the availability of extensive congressional hearings, statutory and administrative guidelines, and some feedback from operational experience allows us to make a preliminary assessment.

On a conceptual level, the rent supplement program is attractive because of its recognition that the urban housing problem is, above all, one of limited incomes: the inability of poor families to compete for decent housing on the open market or, in other words, to pay the price necessary to ensure the private investor a reasonable profit. By supplementing the rent-paying ability of low-income families, the government enhances their effective demand on the private housing market. The amount of rent subsidy varies in accordance with the tenant's need, his share of the market rent being

23. Under certain circumstances, the leased housing program does generate new construction and substantial rehabilitation. While the federal contributions can be committed only for existing units, most state statutes allow housing authorities to contract for the leasing of dwellings to be constructed or rehabilitated. Thus, the LHAs have been able to commit leased units to prospective developers through "letters of intent" which, in turn, have assured mortgage financing for rehabilitation or new construction. For a more extensive discussion of the leased housing program as a stimulus to housing production, see Appendix B.

set at 25 percent of his adjusted income. If income increases after initial occupancy, the amount of the rent supplement is reduced, and it is ultimately discontinued once earnings reach a self-sufficient level. This sliding rent scale has two virtues. First, since the marginal rent increase on additional income is only 25 percent, the qualified tenant still has an incentive to earn as much as possible; even if his income increases beyond the program's maximum limit (as set for the purposes of initial acceptance), he can remain in the same unit simply by paying the full market rent. Second, since the federal payments are keyed to individual needs, rather than fixed-interest or level annuity payments on assisted structures, program costs reflect actual subsidy requirements. Moreover, as with leased units, participating landlords can maintain normal relations with their tenants, as opposed to the inherent custodianship of public housing management.

The rent supplement program, when tied to FHA mortgage-insured developments, stimulates an increase in low-rent housing starts. By guaranteeing in advance a large proportion of a new development's rent-roll, the government dangles an alluring bait for private investment. In effect, the combination of a rent supplement plus the interest subsidy on the mortgage assures *both* a market for the completed apartments and a lower cost for the tenants. The availability of an FHA-insured mortgage, moreover, is particularly enticing when conditions in the national economy curtail the supply of debt capital for housing investments.

Despite the program's conceptual strengths, restrictive statutory and administrative provisions have kept it from realizing anything near its full potential.[24] Consumer choice is severely restricted by guidelines tying rent supplements to specific buildings under contract with the FHA. The possibility of a normal landlord-tenant relationship is undermined by provisions that transfer the subsidy payments directly to the private owner, on behalf of the qualified tenants, instead of to the beneficiaries themselves.

With respect to residential integration, the rent supplement program has also fallen far short of its expectations. As originally conceived, the program would encourage economic as well as racial integration by reserving

24. Walter L. Smith, "The Implementation of the Rent Supplement Program: A Staff View," *Law and Contemporary Problems,* Vol. 32, No. 3 (Summer 1967), pp. 483–485. Many of the limitations of the rent supplement program were first set forth in Smith's article.

for poor families a certain percentage of the units in FHA moderate-income developments (especially Section 221(d)(3) and Section 236 rental housing). In practice, however, inflated construction costs, low rent ceilings,[25] and government design standards have prevented the inclusion of attractive architectural features and amenities in rent supplement projects and consequently have limited the appeal to nonsubsidized tenants. Nevertheless, in some cities rent supplements have been used successfully as a means of mixing low- and moderate-income families. Normally, this is accomplished when a specific percentage of the units in FHA projects are set aside for low-income households. But any expectation of achieving widespread economically and racially integrated developments has been frustrated by a congressional provision requiring the consent of the local governing body prior to construction activity; suburban governments have used this provision to exclude subsidized projects proposed for their communities.[26] Even after Congress removed this requirement, local communities were able to exercise an effective veto with regard to federally subsidized developments because of their control over the provision of streets, water and sewer lines, rights-of-way, and municipal services. In those instances when FHA mortgage-insured projects are built in declining areas, with poor schools and unattractive environments, moderate-income families choose not to live there. In more attractive suburbs, FHA-sponsored projects with rent supplements face serious community resistance.

An Ordinal Ranking of Program Effectiveness

The brief qualitative review of federal housing programs completed in the preceding section suggests a number of specific output objectives against which social and environmental impacts can be measured. These objectives are to enhance consumer sovereignty, encourage racial and economic integration, stabilize the demand in low-rent housing markets, offer programs adaptable to changing local market conditions, and provide an "acceptable"

25. Guidelines impose a maximum rental limit of $175 per month, including utilities, for a unit with three or more bedrooms. The establishment of these rent limits suggests that the rent supplement program was intended primarily for medium and small cities, with its greatest usefulness in lower-cost regions such as the Southeast and Southwest.
26. In at least one state, Massachusetts, the state housing finance agency (MHFA) has used rent supplements creatively as a means of mixing low- and moderate-income families with those able to pay prevailing market rents, in a three-way income mix.

residential environment. Though this list is by no means exhaustive, it does provide the basis for a preliminary evaluation of some of the non-dollar-valued benefits associated with subsidized housing. To compare the effectiveness of each housing program with respect to specified qualitative outputs, we apply an ordinal scale ranging from zero (lowest benefit) to five (highest benefit). However, we deliberately make no effort to weight the importance of each output measure in relation to the others, since a subjective judgment along such lines would be unlikely to correspond with the value systems of every decision maker.

The ordinal rankings are based on Boston data as well as a review of the literature, and since the social and environmental effects being measured are largely inherent in the new construction, rehabilitation, and used-housing approaches, our findings should have general applicability, providing decision makers with a more explicit basis for making policy trade-offs. The following review of social and environmental effects provides the basis for the ordinal rankings.

Enhancing Consumer Sovereignty

Our culture places a high value on consumer sovereignty, and most of our national housing legislation implicitly assumes that free residential mobility contributes to individual well-being. In determining an ordinal rank for each major housing program with respect to consumer sovereignty, we consider three components of housing choice: the initial housing package (neighborhood, type of structure, and location), the opportunity to remain in the same apartment unit once family income has risen above the program limit, and the chance to achieve a normal tenant-landlord relationship free of public supervision.

Conventional public housing receives a low ranking in terms of all three criteria for several reasons: prospective tenants have a circumscribed choice of physical design and location, families whose incomes rise above prescribed limits are usually evicted, and tenant-management relations are institutionalized. Therefore conventional public housing, as judged by the record in most cities, is assigned a value of one with respect to its consumer sovereignty effect.

The FHA mortgage-insured projects with rent supplements score somewhat better, largely because subsidized families may retain their units if, with changed personal circumstances, their income rises above the limit used to screen new applicants. However, supplement payments, rather than being entrusted to the tenants themselves, go directly to private owners. More important, consumer choice is severely constricted under the program by regulations confining subsidies to specific buildings under contract with FHA, by workable program requirements that initially barred rent supplement tenants from the suburbs, and by construction cost ceilings that limit the quality of structures and preclude location in areas of high land costs.

Rehabilitation, as we saw in Chapter 7, costs less than new construction; thus, within a given cost range, improving old units offers the consumer a greater variety of choice than developing new units. Given this contrast, our rankings assign rent supplements with new construction a value of two and rent supplements with rehabilitation a value of three.

In theory, at least, all of the privately owned and managed leased housing units—with the exception of those in newly constructed developments— offer a larger degree of consumer sovereignty than either conventional public housing or Section 236 with rent supplements. If a tenant's income rises above the allowable maximum, he may continue to live in the unit, paying market rents and receiving no subsidy. Leases are drawn up between tenants and landlord, allowing a fairly normal landlord-tenant relationship. The program makes available a relatively broad selection of structure types, locations, and neighborhoods, although, as indicated earlier, political realities have somewhat limited the leasing of units in more affluent suburban communities. On balance, the program's relative flexibility dictates a high ranking (a value of four) when used to secure existing or rehabilitated units.

Encouraging Economic and Racial Integration

In recent years many commentators, including some spokesmen for minority groups, have come to question the value of complete residential integration —pointing to the incredible difficulties of breaking segregated housing patterns and to the apparent desire of many ethnic and racial minorities to remain in their own communities, even when given other options, and in some cases, also asserting the positive values (political, psychological, and cultural) of group cohesiveness in a racially and economically stratified society. Nonetheless, few would deny the right of an individual to live in the neighborhood and community of his choice or the inequity of his having to pay an extra premium for a home of any given quality simply because of his skin color or ethnic background. Thus, even if one remains skeptical of proposals for thoroughgoing integration, any assessment of publicly subsidized housing should consider the extent to which each approach helps modify segregated living patterns.

Concentrating the poorest families in the worst housing creates negative spillover effects—above all, neighborhood environments characterized by vandalism, broken families, vagrancy, and other social pathologies. Also, there is an assumption, but little empirical evidence, that mingling households from different income levels not only provides the disadvantaged with better access to educational and employment opportunities and a better home environment but also helps moderate antisocial behavior attributable to enforced ghettoization.[27]

Like most cities, the record of Boston's housing programs with respect to residential and economic integration has been one of frustrated intentions or, sometimes, hostile resistance. Public housing projects are either located in the most blighted, least desirable neighborhoods or, as in the notorious case of Columbia Point (the largest public housing project in New England), placed on desolate sites, entirely cut off from the rest of the city. The tenant population is increasingly composed of nonwhite families, and close to half of the families are without a male head or wage earner. The initial commitment of political and housing officials in Boston to promote racial and economic dispersion in the rent supplement program was frustrated by tight housing market conditions, by the need to relocate families displaced by the FHA-sponsored Boston Rehabilitation Program (BURP), and, above all, by neighborhood hostility. Residents from several white neighborhoods managed to frustrate the city's "in-fill" program—an innovative scheme for combining scattered-site construction with rent assistance. In other cities the record seems little better.

In contrast, the leased housing program has relied on the existing stock of housing, using scattered sites rather than individual projects. Although the allowable rent levels prevent the leasing of units in upper-middle-income neighborhoods, the leased units are dispersed throughout the rest of

27. As one of the limited number of empirical studies on the effects of income and racial mixing, see U.S., Department of Health, Education, and Welfare, Office of Education, *Equality of Educational Opportunity* (Washington, D.C.: U.S. Government Printing Office, 1966). This report is better known by the name of its principal investigator, the (James) Coleman Report.

the city. This is especially true for units that are from the existing stock rather than either newly constructed or substantially rehabilitated. Thus, with respect to promoting economic and racial integration, all three federal housing programs have been assigned a low ordinal ranking, with the leasing of existing units the only exception.

Stabilizing Low-Rent Housing Markets

For methodological reasons, our analysis has essentially limited the formal measurement of benefits and costs to an average year. However, in evaluating alternative housing strategies, we are also interested in their long-term effects on the stability of low-income housing markets. Both the stability and length of the government's commitment carry important implications not only for the security of the subsidized families themselves but also for the investment psychology of private property owners—that is, their assessment of the risks associated with participating in any given program, particularly their willingness to improve their properties.

If the ability of a given program to stabilize housing demand over time varies with the duration and credibility of the federal commitment, then legislative authorizations, by themselves, contribute little in the way of assurance. Enabling acts, it is true, may authorize expenditures over several decades, but appropriations are made on an annual basis and, as such, are vulnerable to congressional and political whim.[28]

Far more pertinent to this analysis are the various contractual arrangements among the federal government, local housing agencies, private landlords (builders, developers, management companies), and the recipient families. Analyzing the policy alternatives in these terms, we find that new construction programs offer a long-term commitment to a single structure, but not necessarily a stabilizing effect on the low-rent housing market. Under current procedures, a 40-year commitment is made in the form of retiring serial bonds for public housing and mortgage interest rate subsidies for Section 221(d)(3) and 236 new construction projects. In contrast, the re-

---

28. Several examples from recent history illustrate the uncertainty associated with federal funding. As this book goes to press, a presidential moratorium imposed early in 1973 on federally sponsored low- and moderate-income housing programs still remains in effect. In the interest of countering inflation, the President has also declared his intention to impound funds for several programs of social action and pollution control, even if appropriated by Congress over his veto.

habilitation and direct consumer subsidies (for example, the leasing of private dwellings) provide a guaranteed rent-roll over a short time period, enough of an inducement for a modest upgrading of the existing stock. Rather than construct a small number of large-scale developments, the modest rehabilitation of many dwelling units is a more appropriate activity for stabilizing declining neighborhoods.

Adaptability to Local Market Conditions

A program's adaptability to housing market conditions comprises its ability to meet distinct local needs and to adjust its scale to fluctuations in demand. This aspect of program performance may have important environmental consequences, since a large number of vacancies in public housing or serious underutilization of the existing private stock can contribute to the spread of neighborhood blight.

New construction programs take supply and demand factors into account in the initial decision to proceed with any given development proposal. However, once constructed, the housing is there, an immovable fact, no matter how market conditions may vary;[29] for this reason, and because new developments are financed through long-term bond or mortgage commitments, programs of new construction receive a low ordinal ranking with respect to their market flexibility.[30] Section 236 projects with rent supplements are a shade more flexible than public housing since, in the FHA projects, the proportion of subsidized to nonsubsidized occupants can be changed over time. In contrast, the short-term leasing of used housing is extremely versatile. It can be used to house extra-large families, households displaced by public work projects, or blue-collar families suffering temporary economic hardship. Leased housing funds, when spent for older units (whether rehabilitated or unimproved), permit more intensive use of the

29. Some demonstration proposals have been made to liquidate all or part of the federal investment on specific public housing projects, by converting them to tenant-owned cooperatives or condominiums. Critics fear that these efforts will merely victimize the tenants, saddling families having no experience with homeownership with buildings that have been poorly designed and maintained and have little resale value on the private market.

30. Here we see how a program feature (such as the 40-year mortgage granted FHA-insured buildings with rent supplements) can constitute both a virtue with respect to one performance measure (long-term stability of demand) and a liability with respect to another (adaptability to market conditions).

existing stock.[31] Under tight market conditions, such expenditures might generate some inflationary pressures on rental prices—a result LHAs try to avoid at such times by leasing only units that would otherwise be unavailable (for example, units already vacant). With a return to slack housing demand, the LHA can once again search for its units more freely, without fear of harmful side effects on rent levels.

An "Acceptable" Home Environment

Good housing, as technically defined, meets local building, housing, and health codes; contains hot running water and private toilet and bath; is not dilapidated, deteriorated, or overcrowded. However, experience demonstrates that, by itself, a sound physical structure does not constitute a suitable living environment. Clean surroundings, playing space for children, personal safety and security, and access to work and shopping areas represent only a few of the many prerequisites for an acceptable home and neighborhood.

A tour of Boston's or any other large older city's public housing projects (Mission Hill, Charlestown, Columbia Point) reveals the bleakest of cityscapes: faceless buildings with an asphalt expanse for open space. Litter, broken glass, graffiti-splattered walls, vandalized benches, and at night the glare of floodlights, all testify to the dispirited population living within. Of course, such extreme desolation is by no means inherent in the idea of subsidized construction itself but rather reflects the attitudes of public officials during the years in which most public housing was built—above all, the belief that providing any accommodations beyond a sanitary but spartan minimum would be overindulging the poor and would perhaps act as a disincentive for their ever becoming self-sufficient in the future.

Today virtually all housing officials would oppose duplication of the mammoth institutional structures that comprise the popular image of a public housing project; instead, they generally favor the dispersal of subsidized units in smaller concentrations and the introduction of more variety and amenity in their design. In recent years, the environmental qualities of

31. There is some evidence, for instance, that the leased housing program accelerates the downward filtering of dwellings from moderate- to low-income families. Such a result would not be surprising, since the leasing program, through the rental assistance it provides, increases the rent-paying ability of the poor vis-à-vis moderate-income families. Unfortunately, our limited knowledge of housing market dynamics precludes a more extensive theoretical or empirical analysis of this filtering phenomenon.

most subsidized construction (conventional public housing, as well as FHA-sponsored multifamily rental units) represents a distinct improvement over the past; however, because of cost constraints, and, in some instances, continued design restrictions, commonplace, if not sterile, architecture is still the frequent result. By contrast, the use of rehabilitated units or of the existing stock at least ensures that the subsidized housing is situated in a more or less normal neighborhood environment. The quality of that environment is, of course, a function of circumstances such as the age and condition of the buildings, the degree of social homogeneity and stability, the level of public services, the character of accessible commercial areas, the presence of special amenities, if any (parks, recreational facilities, landscaping), and location within the overall constellation of urban activity.

Table 8.1 summarizes the ordinal rankings assigned each of the five non-dollar-valued effects discussed in this chapter. The results indicate the differential environmental and social impacts associated with the major subsidy programs, and with new construction, as opposed to use of the existing stock. Our knowledge about how these factors affect a particular household's social relationships or psychological health is limited, and we cannot determine how any individual policy maker will weight these variables. However, as indicated earlier, systematic comparison should help to clarify necessary trade-offs and policy options. The rankings presented here represent a preliminary attempt to compare alternative housing strategies in terms of their ability to foster consumer sovereignty, to promote racial and economic integration, to stabilize low-income housing demand, to adapt to local housing market conditions, and to provide a decent living environment.

Table 8.1 Ordinal Rankings of Non-Dollar-Valued Benefits for Public Housing, Leased Housing, and Section 236a

Program	Consumer Sovereignty	Racial and Economic Dispersal	Stabilization of Demand for Low-Rent Housing Markets	Adaptability to Housing Market Conditions	Provision of an Acceptable Environment
New Construction					
Conventional public housing	1	0	2	1	2
Leased housing	3	1	2	2	3
Section 236–rent supplements	2	0	2	2	4
Existing Housing Stock					
Leased housing with existing units	4	3	3	5	4
Leased housing with rehabilitation	3	1	3	3	4
Section 236–rent supplements with rehabilitation	3	1	3	3	4

a. The range of this ordinal system is from 0 to 5, with 0 the least positive and 5 the most positive; for example a ranking of 5 means the program fosters complete economic integration, while a ranking of 0 means complete segregation.

CHAPTER 9

Redirecting National Housing Policy

Future housing subsidy programs must be based on modest upgrading of
the standing stock, not new construction; unless what we really want is
abandonment of the cities themselves with the inevitable degradation of
the quality of life for those left behind in the rubble.
Annette K. Altschuler,
Home Owners Association of Philadelphia,
New York Times, Letter to the Editor,
November 28, 1972

Criticism is notoriously easier than prescription. To actually bring into
being new and effective programs that are at once equitable, efficient, politically feasible, and financially sound demands wisdom, patience, imagina-
tion, and a shrewd eye for timely intervention. With regard to housing
policy, anyone venturing a "new solution" has particular reason to proceed
with humility. Housing markets are extremely complex, and our knowledge of their dynamics is still primitive. Thus no one can predict with
absolute confidence how the multitude of actors whose behavior determines
the market response—the builders, developers, landlords, craft unions,
realtors, materials suppliers, mortgage bankers, insurance executives, state
and local officials, as well as the millions of individual renters and homeowners themselves—will react to any new form of government intervention.

Moreover, one cannot help being impressed by the amount of ingenuity
and energy that has gone into housing legislation already on the books and
by the almost uniformly disappointing results. Programs launched with
the greatest of hopes have floundered because of political and economic obstacles, many of them totally unanticipated. Nevertheless, past frustrations
cannot excuse our present inertia as long as millions are still living in physically unsound or overcrowded units or unhealthy neighborhoods or paying
an excessive proportion of their income for shelter—with existing federal
subsidy programs incapable of offering genuine relief.

It is with these caveats before us that this final chapter proposes what
appear to be the most promising directions for federal housing policy.
These recommendations are supported in the empirical findings that have
emerged from this study and from many years' experience with state and
local housing agencies. One theme predominates over all others: the need
to end our official obsession with housing production subsidies and to rely,

instead, on a set of strategies for utilizing the existing housing stock.

As has been reiterated throughout the text, we have relied for too long, as a nation, on a single approach—new construction—to achieve both our social objective of better housing for the poor and our aggregate economic objective of an equilibrium between housing supply and demand. Aggregate economic growth and cyclical stability are best achieved by expanding the supply of middle- and upper-income housing; such a policy has already proved itself capable of satisfying the demand generated by population increases, family formation, and dwelling unit losses, while promoting a filtering process through the rest of the housing stock. *But social objectives are better served by direct subsidy of housing consumption, particularly in a manner that encourages more efficient use of the existing stock, and by the coordination of shelter improvements with broader community development efforts.* New construction for occupancy by the poor should be limited to special circumstances in which vital public interests cannot be advanced in any other way. The justification for reorienting subsidies along these lines and the implications for national policy are spelled out in the pages that follow.

Challenging the Conventional Wisdom: The Need to Redirect National Housing Policy

We are deluding ourselves if we continue to think that providing new units for 5 percent of those eligible for federal subsidies will have any substantial or durable impact on inadequate housing and neighborhood conditions. Among the programs already in operation, the one that relies on the existing stock and most resembles a direct consumer subsidy—the leased housing program—is, at once, the most effective and the least utilized. The relative success of this approach, despite its modest application to date, testifies to the promise of similar but more ambitious proposals, such as income-maintenance and housing allowances.

There are at least six compelling arguments for shifting federal policy from a production- to a consumer-oriented strategy:

1. Twice as many families can be moved into decent standard housing for any given federal dollar commitment.
2. Short of bulldozing and rebuilding (which has already proved itself politically, morally, and financially unacceptable), it is the only strategy

designed to stabilize and modestly upgrade declining inner-city neighborhoods.

3. Tying the subsidy to the family rather than the dwelling permits a flexible response to changing local market conditions and programmatic needs.
4. Direct subsidies to consumers offer the most practical means for dispersing low-income households outside impacted, blighted areas.
5. Using the existing supply of older housing minimizes vertical and horizontal inequities.
6. The choice of housing type, structure, and location is placed in the hands of the tenants themselves rather than the government.

Resource limitations, as reflected in the annual budgetary appropriations, are an unavoidable fact of life for any area of public policy. For decision makers trying to achieve an optimum result within a given dollar appropriation, a cost-effectiveness analysis is useful in determining the most efficient means of attaining specified objectives. The method is appropriate for comparing alternative housing programs since the national housing goal, "to provide every American with decent shelter and a suitable living environment," offers a relatively unambiguous standard against which performance can be measured. As Table 9.1 indicates, the leasing of private dwellings for the poor compares favorably with other programs with respect to two measures of cost effectiveness: first, the monthly resource cost of providing a two-bedroom unit; and, second, the number of households that can be moved from substandard to standard housing for a $1 million expenditure.[1] This second measure also illustrates the horizontal inequity of production programs since it highlights the fact that deep subsidies for a few mean no subsidies for the many. In addition, the leasing of existing units and other approaches relying on the existing stock rank highest with regard to social and environmental effects as well. In fact, the only performance measure which yields a higher rank for any production program is that of economic efficiency. This finding is noteworthy since the economic efficiency or benefit-cost criterion is the only measure traditionally included

1. Although the actual cost of new construction, rehabilitation, or leasing existing dwellings in other cities may vary because of differences in the price of land, labor, and construction materials, as well as local market conditions, the cost advantage of using the existing housing stock remains considerable. See, for example, Frank de Leeuw, *The Cost of Leased Public Housing* (Washington, D.C.: Urban Institute, December 22, 1970).

Table 9.1 Comparative Analysis of Alternative Housing Strategies[a]

Program	Cost Effectiveness[b]	Number of Households Moved from Substandard to Standard Housing per $1 Million (Horizontal Equity)	Economic and Racial Dispersal[c]	Consumer Sovereignty	Benefit-Cost Efficiency Ratio[d]	Tenant Share of Total Benefits (Vertical Equity)
New Construction Programs						
Conventional public housing	$215	387	0	1	−0.16	64%
Leased housing with new construction	207	403	1	3	+0.14	79
Section 236 with rent supplements	190	439	0	2	+0.60	81[e]
Existing Housing Stock						
Leased housing with existing units	137	608	3	4	+0.35	81
Leased housing with rehabilitation	174	478	1	3	+0.28	79
Section 236– rent supplements with rehabilitation	180	485	1	3	+0.51	83[e]

a. The estimates are based on data for a two-bedroom unit located in Boston in 1970.

b. Cost effectiveness is measured in terms of resource costs per two-bedroom unit per month.

c. The range of the ordinal ranking system is from 0 to 5, with 0 the least and 5 the most positive; for example, 5 means program fosters complete economic and racial integration, while 0 means it promotes complete segregation.

d. The welfare efficiency measure, or benefit-cost ratio, was derived by subtracting the gross resource costs of each housing program from its gross benefits (housing consumption, municipal services consumption, and employment earnings) to obtain the numerator, and using the constrained federal budgetary outlays as the denominator. This provided a measure of net benefit per dollar of scarce federal budgetary expenditure. Using the equity weight estimated in Chapter 4 does not alter the benefit-cost rankings. See "Technical Note," Chapter 2.

e. Previous published estimates of the percentage of subsidy dollars diverted to government intermediaries did not include the cost of the negotiations, monitoring, and inspection of FHA-sponsored newly constructed and rehabilitated units. See Arthur P. Solomon, "Housing and Public Policy Analysis," *Public Policy*, Vol. 20 (Summer 1972).

in welfare economics studies. Another implication of our analysis, then, is that the traditional benefit-cost criterion offers too limited a basis for policy analysis. Once social and environmental impacts are included in the evaluation, the trade-offs become more explicit, and, in this case, the ranking of programs changes. Moreover, as discussed in Chapter 3, our measure of the housing consumption benefit for newly constructed units may overstate their social value anyway, which means that even the economic efficiency of production programs may fall short of strategies which rely on rehabilitation, direct consumer transfers, or other programs for using the existing housing stock.

Our experience confirms the findings of numerous other observers that, for the inner city, housing improvement is inseparable from the overall problems of neighborhood decline (for example, nonresidential facilities and infrastructure) and inadequate municipal services.[2] The unfortunate preoccupation of national housing policy with new housing starts leaves the far more elusive but critical problems of neighborhood decay largely unaffected. While direct consumer subsidies, as well as other strategies relying on the existing housing stock, cannot hope to revitalize the so-called "crisis ghettos"—where residents hesitate to walk in the streets, garbage accumulates uncollected, storefronts remain barricaded like defense installations, and despair pervades the atmosphere—they promise to counteract the existing physical decline of more viable low- and moderate-income neighborhoods. In the latter areas, though the quality of individual structures is little better and the residents are just as poor, the market remains active. These neighborhoods, unlike the crisis ghettos, retain their basic strength because of ethnic cohesiveness, locational advantages, distinctive structural characteristics, proximity to public transportation, substantial owner occupancy, or other stabilizing factors.

It is in these viable low- and moderate-income neighborhoods that the additional purchasing power provided by government-assisted leasing arrangements (housing allowances or income maintenance) promises to counteract existing physical decay by helping to stabilize demand and thereby creating an investment climate in which owners will be more disposed to conserve

2. See, for example, George Sternlieb and Robert W. Burchell, *Residential Abandonment: The Tenement Landlord Revisited* (New Brunswick, N.J.: Transaction Books, 1973), and Michael A. Stegman, *Housing Investment in the Inner City* (Cambridge, Mass.: MIT Press, 1972).

and even enlarge the supply of decent housing at moderate prices.[3] With a higher level of rental income, along with a reasonably stable residential environment, landlords should find it worthwhile to marginally upgrade their properties, invest more money in maintenance and repairs, and respond more readily to building service requirements and utility disruptions. Positive experiences with the public housing leasing program in this country and with housing allowances in other countries suggests that demand-side subsidies will stimulate a modest upgrading of the existing private housing stock.[4] When the increase in purchasing power is accompanied by a reduction in landlord risks, stemming from direct government payments to landlords or guaranteed lease agreements, the likelihood of improved housing services is even greater.

In many low- and moderate-rent neighborhoods, then, the combined incentives of the 1969 Tax Act provisions for accelerated depreciation (and the accompanying tax shelters), the availability of rent assistance, and a reduction in landlord risks can provide an adequate stimulus for modest private investment. Of course, the availability of rehabilitation loans and grants, as in urban renewal and code enforcement areas, can facilitate the response of housing suppliers. *Thus, if direct consumer subsidies were to be provided on a more generous scale—while still supplemented by present insurance, loan, and grant programs—we could, for the first time, create a more stable and effective demand for inner-city housing.* This is *central* to any policy that is to avoid the same disappointments encountered by the community development reforms of the 1950s and 1960s.

Consumer subsidies not only lend themselves to stabilizing the rental

3. Appendix B presents a more detailed discussion of the leased housing program's ability to generate modest upgrading of the existing stock, even in blighted neighborhoods. Although federal subsidies can be committed only for existing units, most state statutes allow local housing authorities to contract for the leasing of dwellings about to be constructed or rehabilitated. Thus, as legal offspring of their respective states, the LHAs have been able to commit leased units to prospective developers through "letters of intent," which, in turn, have assured mortgage financing for private investments. The extent to which these letters of intent and other program inducements have stimulated housing investments is explored in the appendix. This effect is noteworthy since the potential of the leasing program (or any demand subsidy) as a stimulus of housing investment has received little attention.

4. See, for example, Lawrence Friedman and James Krier, "A New Lease on Life: Section 23 Housing and the Poor," *University of Pennsylvania Law Review*, Vol. 116 (1968), p. 632, and Frank de Leeuw and Samuel Leaman, "Section 23 Leasing Program: Progress Report," Urban Institute, Washington, D.C., 1972, Working Paper 112-35.

market in the inner city but should also facilitate some modest dispersal of low-income families into areas from which they have been previously excluded because of insufficient income or discrimination. While, for obvious reasons, government programs cannot eliminate deep-rooted prejudices, it is still much easier for an individual household to rent a single unit in a middle-income central-city neighborhood or suburb than it is for the government to locate a large-scale federally subsidized development outside an impacted poverty area. Because of federal cost ceilings and site constraints, most newly constructed low- and moderate-income housing has assumed the form of huge multistory projects. Even small-scale developments generally arouse hostile resistance from middle-income residents, who mobilize over issues such as incompatible land uses, overcrowding of schools, added traffic congestion, and increased crime. At times the objections raised are legitimate but often are merely thin disguises for class fears and racial biases. Moreover, once a new development has sparked controversy, it is particularly vulnerable to political defeat since it must run the gamut of public hearings and reviews (for site selection, zoning variances, building permits, subdivision approvals, and so forth). Thus we can conclude that demand-side strategies—under which the recipient household, with its income augmented by some form of income subsidy, need only negotiate a lease with a single landlord—are a far less cumbersome means for advancing residential integration.

In Chapter 4, we evaluated the major housing programs in terms of their ability to promote a more equitable distribution of wealth. With regard to vertical inequity—that is, the diversion of subsidy dollars to the nonpoor —we found little difference among alternative production and consumer strategies, the only exception being the conventional public housing program, which diverts a significant portion of funds to governmental intermediaries and to high-income purchasers of tax-exempt 40-year serial bonds. Horizontal inequities emerge as far more serious. Instead of aiding the maximum number of poor households possible for a given federal appropriation, new construction programs allow a few families to occupy housing far in excess of minimum code standards, while leaving the vast majority of the poor without any relief whatsoever. An even more explosive aspect of the equity issue is that some poor families are provided with new housing of a quality beyond the financial means of many blue-collar workers (whose earning power is only moderately higher but sufficient to disqualify them from participation in subsidy programs). Even if demand-oriented subsidies enacted in the future fail to provide universal coverage, at least resentment should be less when the assisted households occupy modest older housing rather than brand-new units.

A further virtue of demand-side strategies is that they offer tenants far more discretion than do production programs: the subsidy recipient, rather than the government, chooses a home from among a wide range of neighborhoods, structural types, and locations;[5] he may remain in the same apartment unit at full market rent should his income rise above program ceilings; he enjoys a greater opportunity to achieve a normal landlord-tenant relationship, independent of public supervision and scrutiny. Moreover, by relying on the existing stock, leased housing and other proposed consumer subsidies avoid the physical isolation and depressing uniformity characteristic of many new multiunit developments. Since the subsidized family moves anonymously into a private dwelling unit, it is less conspicuous and hence less stigmatized and segregated than the tenants of public projects.

In designing the leased housing program (the precursor, as we have seen, for other direct consumer subsidies), Congress provided local governments with a flexible housing instrument for responding to changing market conditions and maintaining the liquidity of the public's investment. Short-term leasing agreements with private landlords allow for the poor to be housed without making a 40-year commitment to construct and manage a particular development. The possible abandonment of the $30 million Pruitt-Igoe project in St. Louis, after only fifteen years, dramatizes the risk inherent in tying up large sums in brick and mortar in a fixed location.

A Policy for the Bad Housing Problem
Housing conditions, like other surface aspects of city life, are determined in part by more profound shifts in the underlying structure of urban growth and development. The postwar era has witnessed a dramatic slackening in

5. Eligible families already occupying standard housing but paying a disproportionate share of their income for rent (over 25 percent) can obtain financial assistance while remaining in their present quarters.

the demand for older high-density housing—particularly in those neighborhoods lacking "quaintness," "charm," or some other distinguishing amenities. An absolute loss of population, accompanied by a higher concentration of the poor, has seriously weakened the market for central-city properties. It is this loss of an effective and stable demand, rather than the exploitative practices of a few pernicious slum landlords, which lies at the heart of our urban housing problem. A new strategy is clearly needed if we are to improve the housing conditions of the poor, to restore the confidence of private investors and lenders in aging neighborhoods, and to dispel, or at least reduce, the serious dichotomy between suburbs that are lily-white and affluent and inner cities that are increasingly black and destitute. Such a strategy should contain the following three components:

1. A national program of direct consumer subsidies;
2. The elimination of existing housing and capital market barriers that inhibit a positive landlord response to increases in consumer demand;
3. The coordination of direct consumer subsidies with programs of community development.

Subsidizing Housing Consumers

For the foreseeable future, any such strategy must accept, as given, a high concentration of poor families in the urban core. Any policy attempting to offer these families general relief must both increase their ability to pay for better housing and give them options besides enforced ghettoization. The most direct and least costly means to this end is the replacement of the present system of welfare assistance and housing subsidies with an adequate program of income maintenance. While some housing professionals may argue that an earmarked income transfer, such as housing allowances, would stimulate a larger increase in housing expenditures, it is more consistent with democratic concepts of consumer sovereignty and human dignity (and less likely to cause rent inflation) to give the individual discretion to budget his own expenditures in accordance with his needs and preferences, however he perceives them.[6] On the other hand, expenditures for

6. Most of the poor have a pressing need for better food and clothing, as well as improved shelter. In any case, most studies of consumer spending have indicated that the average household will continue to spend the same proportion of its income on housing, especially if the increase in income is permanent rather than temporary. For an excellent review of this literature, see Frank de Leeuw, "The Demand for Housing: A Review of Cross Section Evidence," *Review of Economics and Statistics,* Vol. 53, No. 1 (February 1971).

housing, unlike other items of consumption, can have positive spillover effects on other individuals (by containing the spread of blight, reducing the probability of contagious fires, and so on). This is the major argument for earmarking the transfer payments. Whether the primary goal of reforming the federal housing (and welfare) system should be the elimination of poverty—through income transfers—or the enhancement of the living environment—through housing allowances—seems less important than the compelling need to replace our current production strategy with a national program of direct consumer subsidies. Whether the consumer subsidies are earmarked or not remains more of a political/philosophical than a technical issue.

The federal government, in any event, need not await the enactment of an income maintenance program before beginning the transition to direct consumer subsidies. Within the framework of the programs already in existence, much can still be done to tie subsidies to the family rather than to items of consumption, to place more reliance on the (corrected) functioning of the marketplace, to relate assistance to the level of need, to provide support adequate for obtaining standard housing in the private market, and to allow recipients maximum discretion in the use of their funds. These principles can be advanced through reforms, such as the following:
—Shift public housing funds from conventional and turnkey construction to the leasing of private dwellings.
—Designate suburban sponsors of the leased housing program to supplement the activities of local housing authorities whose jurisdictions are usually confined to central cities.
—Increase the availability of long-term, low-interest loans and grants for rehabilitation.
—Allow rent supplement funds to be used for existing non-FHA-sponsored housing.
—Expand the use of existing and rehabilitated housing in the Sections 235 and 236 interest subsidy programs.
—Expand the number of cities in the experimental housing allowance program authorized by the Housing and Urban Development Act of 1970.
—Increase the level of welfare assistance for shelter payments.[7]

7. The serious inadequacy of the prevailing welfare allotment for housing in most states is given graphic documentation in a recent study of Baltimore, Maryland. In 1968 the

Eliminating Housing and Capital Market Barriers

Since demand strategies rely on the functioning of the private housing and capital markets, they must be accompanied by efforts to remove the barriers that discourage landlords from upgrading their properties in response to an increase in rent-paying ability among the potential tenant population. In order for the direct consumer subsidies to have an optimal effect, all levels of government must make a genuine attempt to eliminate restrictive zoning, collusive real estate practices, and other discriminatory activities that distort housing market allocations. Public officials can demonstrate their commitment to these ends by the aggressive enforcement of federal and state fair housing laws, the funding of additional poverty lawyers and housing technicians, and the provision of better housing market information and counseling services.

An adequate flow of funds, at competitive interest rates, also is essential if private landlords (and homeowners) are to upgrade their housing stock in response to the infusion of demand subsidies. In transitional and declining neighborhoods, conventional loans are obtainable, if at all, for only short periods at high rates of interest; lenders tend to shy away from the high risk of default and other uncertainties inherent in real estate investment in such areas. Where housing markets are weak, money for improvements is all but impossible to obtain. The provision of direct consumer subsidies, however, would increase the effective demand for modest older housing, while the supportive community development programs (discussed later in this chapter) would improve public facilities, the quality of municipal services, and other environmental features. In the early stages of neighborhood renewal, however, even these measures may not convince more cautious institutional lenders that the commitment by the public sector is genuine and durable. To induce private lenders to make conventional loans in the neighborhoods where they previously experienced high rates of mortgage defaults and foreclosures will undoubtedly require more

---

maximum rent for families of seven or more persons was $61, and for two-person families the maximum shelter rent was only $47. The level of welfare assistance is a critical factor in low-rent housing markets since, according to the authors, the welfare program represents the largest single housing subsidy in Baltimore, exceeding $20 million per year out of a total housing assistance budget of $33 million in 1968. See William Grigsby, Louis Rosenburg, Michael Stegman, and James Taylor, "Housing and Poverty" (Philadelphia: Institute for Environmental Studies, University of Pennsylvania, 1972), mimeographed.

direct government assurances such as direct public loans or incentives for the pooling of mortgage risks. An additional impact of improved financing and mortgage-recasting mechanisms is the facilitation of property transfers between "trapped" investors who want to get out and community owners or outside professionals who have more management and community relation skills. At the same time, in areas where conventional lenders still refuse to make loans, a need will remain for more government regulation and monitoring of the unscrupulous practices often associated with land installment contracts, purchase money mortgages, and other unconventional lending activities.

With so many advantages associated with subsidizing the use of the existing stock, one might well ask why the federal government continues to rely on production subsidies as the dominant theme of national housing and why leased housing—the most cost-effective and flexible among current programs—is not utilized more extensively. Many of the reasons are discussed in Chapter 1: historical precedent, a strong home-building lobby, a confusion among national housing objectives, and so on. Yet another factor is a fear of rent inflation. Subsidies for existing units increase the demand for available standard housing on the private market but do not create an instantaneous increase in the housing supply—hence the anxiety that, while subsidized families are being better housed, the increase in demand will serve primarily to drive up rents.

In trying to assess this criticism, we find remarkably little empirical information. To be sure, there is a great deal of rhetoric and undocumented assertion by proponents and detractors alike but practically no evidence. And the little evidence that exists indicates that the dangers of inflation under a demand-oriented strategy may be exaggerated. In a paper written for the House of Representatives, for example, de Leeuw tentatively concluded, from statistical studies at the Urban Institute, that about 70 percent of the increased demand from a comprehensive system of housing allowances would lead to better housing.[8] The other 30 percent would go into higher rents. Similarly, none of the more qualitative evaluations of the leased housing program or the small-scale housing allowance demonstra-

8. See Frank de Leeuw, "The Housing Allowance Approach" in papers submitted to Subcommittee on Housing Panels, Committee on Banking and Currency, House of Representatives, 92nd Congress, 1st Session, June 1971.

tions in Kansas City, Missouri,[9] and in the state of Hawaii have indicated any excessive pressures on rents and prices.

Support for the view that demand subsidies would improve housing conditions far more than they would inflate rents comes from the underlying structure and condition of urban housing markets as well. Despite the popular view of a few large slum landlords owning most of the inner-city housing stock, case studies of Baltimore, Newark, and Providence[10] indicate that these submarkets are quite competitive. The existing fragmentation of ownership in such areas suggests that, rather than raising rents, landlords are likely to compete for tenants with higher rent-paying ability by increasing building services and maintenance expenditures. Moreover, high vacancy rates in the low-rent housing submarkets of many cities indicates that even short-run inflationary effects may be negligible. For many central cities, the 1970 vacancy rate was close to 10.0 percent[11] for units renting at less than $100 per month. For rational landlords, operating in these loose housing markets, serious undermaintenance would be counterproductive, as it would result in lower rental income, increased vacancies and arrearages, and cost increases stemming from less desirable tenants.

Largely because of the thinning out of central-city populations, substantial numbers of essentially sound housing units are underutilized. Under these market conditions, subsidies for existing housing would encourage more effective use of the older standing stock, preserving one of the central and older suburban communities' most valuable assets. In addition, over the long run, the flow of consumer subsidies should help ensure the housing market stability that landlords require if they are to venture further investments in their properties with some confidence in the economic returns.

With respect to the rent inflation issue, there are two other facts that must be considered as well. First, the effect of demand-side subsidies on price and housing stock changes depends, to a large extent, on the scale of

9. See Arthur P. Solomon and Chester G. Fenton, "The Nation's First Experience with Housing Allowances: the Kansas City Demonstration," Cambridge, Mass., MIT-Harvard Joint Center for Urban Studies, Working Paper No. 23, September 1973.
10. See Stegman, *Inner City Housing Investment;* George Sternlieb, *The Tenement Landlord* (New Brunswick, N.J.: Center for Urban Studies, Rutgers University, 1966); and George E. Peterson, Arthur P. Solomon, William Apgar, Jr., and Hadi Madjid, *Property Taxes, Housing and the Cities* (Lexington, Mass.: D. C. Heath, 1973).
11. Figures for a small number of these cities were presented in Table 1.1.

the program, the amount of the assistance per household, the phase-in period, the program design, and the ability of the local market to absorb the incremental demand. Obviously, the pressure on housing prices would be less severe in a program with strict eligibility requirements and low assistance payments, a gradual phasing-in period, and partial earmarking (that is, only a small fraction of the subsidy must be spent on housing). Also, if vacancy rates are high, the demand subsidy is less likely to have severe rent effects, even in the short run.

Second, granting the fact that there is some inflationary effect with consumer-oriented subsidies, policy makers should also recognize that new construction subsidies are not without their own inflationary effects as well. Increases in federally assisted housing activity have contributed to the dramatic rise in the cost of construction labor and building material supplies over recent years. And some question still remains as to whether subsidized production has any net effect on housing starts at all or merely shifts resources away from privately financed development that would have occurred in its absence. Given these uncertainties, any final verdict on contributions to aggregate housing starts or to rent inflation must await further empirical research. In any case, as a more stable and effective demand for housing is created, and more opportunities for dispersal become available, owners of low-quality housing will experience a capital loss since the demand for modest standard units will replace current demand for substandard dwellings. A modest short-term increase in rent, then, seems a small price to pay for a genuine long-run improvement in living conditions for the urban poor.

Coordination with Community Development
All too often financially starved municipal governments neglect their older residential areas, thereby reinforcing rather than offsetting private disinvestments. Central to any national housing policy, therefore, is the formulation of comprehensive "environmental management plans" at the local level which coordinate the delivery of housing assistance with municipal services, public works, and other related community development activities.

At the very least, these environmental management plans have to provide for the minimum standard of personal safety, public services, and supportive facilities essential to inspiring the confidence of private and institutional investors, as well as community residents themselves. Whether the financial support for these plans comes from special revenue sharing, property tax relief, or other proposed federal and state community development assistance is beyond the scope of this study, but *the principle of coordinating housing and community development is essential to the attainment of our social housing objectives.*

What are the prospects for the success of the strategy outlined here when urban renewal, Model Cities, Project Rehab, and existing federal housing subsidies have largely failed? What are the advantages, if any, of an approach embracing direct consumer subsidies, the elimination of housing and capital market barriers, and the coordination of housing and community development activities within a local environmental management plan? First of all, earlier slum clearance efforts merely reduced the supply of low-rent housing in the worst neighborhoods and, in the process, shifted the demand for inexpensive dwellings to other areas without dealing with the basic fact of urban poverty as it affects housing conditions: the cost of decent shelter and the ability of the poor to pay. By failing either to increase incomes or lower housing costs, programs such as urban renewal ended up treating superficial symptoms rather than root causes. However, the eradication of poverty, by itself, will not eliminate slums. It is a necessary but not a sufficient condition, since the existence of market and institutional barriers as well as neighborhood externalities makes the solution of the urban housing problem exceedingly complex. For this reason, above all others, housing assistance must be provided as part of a well-orchestrated community renewal effort.

The failure to recognize that housing is part of a larger neighborhood fabric doomed the Project Rehab program as well.[12] Envisioned as a major breakthrough in upgrading the existing stock, it was hoped that Project Rehab would demonstrate the feasibility of economies of scale and effective management through volume rehabilitation. This effort floundered, however, for a number of reasons. Not only were sponsors asked to carry out the complex task of planning, organizing, and managing a large-scale rehabilitation project, but any chance of success was undermined, from the start,

12. Much of the discussion of the Project Rehab program is based on an eighteen-month monitoring report carried out by the Arthur D. Little company. See Arthur D. Little, *Project Rehab Monitoring Report Overview*, report to the U.S. Department of Housing and Urban Development, May 1971.

by government requirements to ensure employment and subcontracts for community residents, to negotiate with myriad grass-root organizations, and to gain endless approvals from local, state, and federal agencies. Probably most important, however, was the failure to select neighborhoods most suitable for rehabilitation. Instead, the majority of sponsors attempted to acquire individual buildings, especially vacant ones, that were financially feasible for rehabilitation. Such a strategy is appropriate if the surrounding area is sound or in the process of being upgraded. But in declining or blighted neighborhoods, without a general neighborhood renewal of residential properties, community facilities, and municipal services, single-building or small-scale rehabilitation projects are soon engulfed by the surrounding poverty and forces of decay.

If urban renewal, Project Rehab, and housing production subsidies were too narrowly conceived, certainly this was not true of Model Cities—the opposite, in fact, was true. In its conception, the Model Cities program recognized the complex interrelationship of the social, economic, and physical environment, but, in practice, its efforts at coordination and flexibility were more rhetorical than operational.[13] Bureaucratic entanglements, political rivalry among federal agencies, and resistance to changing categorical program priorities obstructed the attempts of local officials to achieve significant results. Also, the uncertainty surrounding the Model Cities program, almost from its inception, strengthened the position of the entrenched bureaucracies against the more innovative social reformers.

The strategy proposed here should overcome many of these economic, institutional, and political obstacles through a combination of the following policies:

—Locally initiated "environmental management plans" to coordinate the activities of all municipal agencies in designated areas;

—Community development bloc grants, which eliminate the artificial fragmentation of local bureaucracies and intergovernmental friction encouraged by the categorical grant system;

—Direct consumer subsidies, which can create the necessary demand for

13. For an excellent analysis of the Model Cities program, see Bernard Frieden, Marshall Kaplan, and Charles Haar, "The Federal Role in Model Cities," MIT-Harvard Joint Center for Urban Studies, manuscript in process.

central-city properties that was missing in earlier programs;
—Elimination of housing and capital market barriers, which frustrate both
the dispersal necessary to relieve impacted areas and the availability of financing necessary for property upgrading.

The provision of direct consumer subsidies—through income transfers,
housing allowances, or leased housing—will enhance and stabilize the demand of subsidized families for a modest level of housing services. This
increase in purchasing power will enable low- and moderate-income consumers to search the housing market for a wider range of structural types,
locations, and neighborhoods. Obviously, some families will choose to move
into higher-quality neighborhoods in suburban communities as units become available through the natural turnover of the existing housing stock.
But experience with the national leased housing program as well as the
Kansas City housing allowance demonstration indicates that the vast majority of recipients will try to improve their housing conditions within the
boundaries of the central city itself.

While one would be naïve to assume that deep-rooted exclusionary practices will yield to this strategy, opportunities for consumers to select their
own residential environments will be enlarged. Most recipients will probably reject those areas where there is no longer any institutional or social
fabric and where public and private disinvestment is occurring. Additional
municipal or private investments in such areas is unwise from both an
economic and a social perspective, since such investments cannot sustain
themselves over time. Yet, the families trapped in these areas should be
given the necessary assistance to relocate in more healthy surroundings.
And in the more viable low- and moderate-income neighborhoods, where
most subsidized tenants will choose to move, government should provide
improved public facilities and services to support and sustain the increased
demand for residential properties. It is only through the coordination of
direct consumer subsidies with community development activities that any
long-term improvement in the living conditions of the urban poor is possible.

A Residual Role for Production Subsidies

While a shift to a consumer-oriented strategy has been advocated throughout this study, inevitably special housing needs will remain which justify

the continuation of production subsidies in some form. For example, such subsidies may be needed for the following:

—Groups with special shelter requirements not ordinarily served through the working of the filtering process, for example, the handicapped, extra-large families, Indians;

—Rural communities, small towns, and special urban areas with chronic housing shortages;

—Special unpredictable circumstances, such as natural disasters, hurricanes, floods;

—Suburbs, rapid-growth fringe areas, and new towns where income and racial mixing would not otherwise occur.

New construction for the special groups, communities, and situations identified here serves social objectives that otherwise would remain unattended. The physically handicapped, for example, require special design features that are easier to incorporate into newly constructed units than in the conversion of existing structures: extra-wide doorways, ramps, and elevators are essential for interior mobility; hygiene and therapy may necessitate special plumbing, wiring, and equipment. Poor families living in areas with a chronic housing shortage simply cannot depend upon the existing stock to meet their minimal shelter needs. The filtering mechanism does not operate effectively in such areas. Finally, because of the political controversies attending the location of federally subsidized housing, most newly constructed units will continue to be restricted to less desirable central-city and older suburban areas. Should opportunities arise where it appears politically feasible to obtain class and racial mixing in newer suburbs, production subsidies should be available to take advantage of them. It must be remembered, however, that the foregoing circumstances are exceptions and that the long-run goal of improving the housing of the urban poor must be met through a national program of direct consumer subsidies.

Housing Subsidies and the Social Welfare System
If a national program of direct housing subsidies is enacted, it is likely that it will have to be integrated, at least in the short run, into the existing system of cash and in-kind transfer programs. The need for integration, or at

least coordination, is inevitable unless all earmarked transfer programs—for food, health care, clothing, day care, and so forth—are replaced by a single unconditional income transfer. This type of wholesale reform of the social welfare system in the United States is not a realistic possibility in the immediate future. Instead, it seems reasonable to assume that the Aid to Families with Dependent Children (AFDC) and General Assistance programs will remain relatively unchanged for the next several years, while the Old Age and Disability Assistance programs may be placed under federal administration, as provided for by the Nixon Administration's Family Assistance Plan (FAP). The purpose of this section, then, is to identify the major policy issues involved in integrating a national housing transfer into the existing social welfare system.

Many families already receiving public assistance, Medicaid, food stamps, and Old Age Survivors and Disability Insurance (OASDI) would be eligible for a housing allowance (or other direct housing subsidy). How would housing allowance benefits, then, relate to these programs, and vice versa? How would the level of housing assistance be adjusted or taxed with changes in earnings? How can we preserve work incentives in a system of multiple transfers? How equitable would be the effects vis-à-vis the working poor? Who will administer the direct housing transfers?

As these questions indicate, the coordination of the nation's social welfare programs will involve a number of complex administrative and economic issues; and the manner in which these issues are resolved will have a significant effect on the adequacy of the transfer payments, their work incentive effects, their horizontal and vertical equity, and their cost to the American taxpayer. Clearly, the enactment of yet another earmarked transfer program, for housing, makes all the more compelling the need to rationalize the nation's social welfare system.[14]

14. A recent survey of program beneficiaries conducted by the Joint Economic Committee of Congress, for example, indicated that a significant number of families already receive multiple benefits. Sixty-eight per cent of the urban families in the survey received benefits from at least two transfer programs, and 45 percent received benefits from at least three programs. There were fewer multiple recipients in rural areas, but there were still many households receiving assistance from more than one transfer program. See U.S. Congress, Joint Economic Committee, Subcommittee on Fiscal Policy, *Studies in Public Welfare: How Public Welfare Benefits are Distributed in Low-Income Areas*, Paper No. 6 (Washington, D.C.: U.S. Government Printing Office, March 1973).

All of the foregoing issues fall into two categories. The first derives from the substantial overlap and inconsistencies in administrative functions under the various transfer programs. Each agency administering such a program makes an independent determination of eligibility. Incomes are calculated, certified, and recertified. Administrative staff and records are maintained. A multiplicity of rules and regulations are promulgated, monitored, and acted upon. Not only does the foregoing imply an administrative morass, but it has significant effects on program outcomes as well. For example, even the choice of the period of time over which income is considered in computing benefit entitlements (the income accounting period) has a profound effect on recipients. A comparison of the AFDC and rent supplement programs will illustrate the point. In the AFDC program, income for the preceding month is used in determining the benefit level for the current month. In the rent supplement program, however, income for the whole preceding year is considered in computing a family's monthly housing assistance. Given two comparable families with the same annual income but differences in their respective monthly distributions of income, the one whose earnings are concentrated in the first six months will receive more AFDC assistance (but the same level of housing subsidy) than the family whose earnings are distributed evenly throughout the year. Not only are the consequences inequitable, but the existence of duplicate administrative structures is wasteful and inefficient. The same point can be made for other administrative and social service activities as well.

The second set of issues involves the fiscal and economic effects. Presumably, housing transfers will be available to low-income workers and non-earners alike. For nonearners, or at least those receiving other transfer payments, one of the key needs is to rationalize the relationship of transfer programs to one another. If a housing allowance or other earmarked housing transfer was enacted, all other programs would have to decide whether to include housing allowances in their income calculations and, if included, how to adjust their own benefits to this new source of income. The same dilemma, of course, will have to be faced by housing allowance authorities. In the case of the Food Stamp program, for example, the enabling legislation specifically states that other transfer programs may not count the value of food stamps as income in their determination of benefit levels. Yet the

Food Stamp program regulations themselves take into account income from other income transfer programs. How and in what order the various programs define income and calculate benefits has an impact upon vertical equity, horizontal equity, work incentives, and the cost to the respective government agencies.[15]

Vertical equity refers to the effect of programs in reducing poverty (the proportion of the transfer which actually reaches the target population). Transfer programs that tax the payments made by other such programs result in lower levels of assistance than ones that mutually exclude such other payments. Questions of horizontal equity come into play when the programs result in unequal treatment of families in comparable situations. For example, programs that reduce their benefit levels only for earned income, and not for other transfer payments, are inequitable in their treatment of the working poor—in contrast to transfer programs that take into account the specific difference between earned and transfer income (by taxing transfer income and/or providing work-related expense deductions).

Of all the fiscal and economic issues involved in coordinating the various transfer programs, probably the most politically explosive concerns the cumulative tax rate on earnings, that is, the overall amount by which government transfers are reduced as earnings increase. Earnings and other sources of income must be treated in some explicit manner in determining net benefits under a direct housing transfer program. The amount by which government transfers are reduced must be examined closely for its effect on the labor supply. If every dollar of earnings results in a dollar loss to the family in transfer payments, there is little incentive to work. Lower tax rates on earnings preserve work incentives while providing more adequate levels of support for recipient families. If each transfer program ignores the tax on earnings employed by other programs, the cumulative tax rate will be high, in some instances possibly exceeding 100 percent. Alternatively, if the social welfare system requires each program to take into ac-

15. There are four major approaches to program integration, identified by economists as independent addition, full benefit offset, sequencing, and mutual exclusion. For an excellent analysis of the fiscal and economic effects of these alternative approaches, see Barry L. Friedman and Leonard J. Hausman, "Integrating Housing Allowances with AFDC, FAP, and Other Transfer Programs," MIT-Harvard Joint Center for Urban Studies, Working Paper No. 25, October 1973.

count the tax rates of other programs, the effective cumulative tax rate will be lower and should mean higher benefit levels and more work incentives —although at greater government costs.

The foregoing issues are complex and challenging, both technically and politically. Yet, it is clear that creation of an adequate, unified, and equitable social welfare system is one of the most compelling problems facing the nation as we enter the last quarter of the twentieth century.

The Evolution of Housing Strategies for the Urban Poor

The first national low-income housing program was established in the Housing Act of 1937. Its aim was to stimulate a depressed economy and to provide accommodations for those temporarily unable to afford private housing. The sponsors of the program championed public housing as an instrument of national economic stabilization as well as a strategy for slum clearance. Originally, it was designed to serve the submerged working class, the "deserving poor" of the depression. For these families public housing was supposed to provide temporary quarters until economic conditions improved. Once the families' incomes exceeded the maximum limits for continued occupancy, they were expected to find private housing. The concept of a continuous turnover was a key feature of the program, since with temporary occupants it was anticipated that a large number of units would regularly become available for other low-income families.[1]

As with other social legislation, however, the operation of the program has differed significantly from its original conception and intended function. Instead of supplying a small stock of public housing, with a steady turnover and a continuous supply of available units, the program has offered something quite different. Stimulated by wartime housing needs for defense workers and returning veterans, the requirements of those displaced by urban renewal and highway programs, and the recent interest in accommodating the elderly, the program has grown far beyond the expectations of its sponsors. In 1970 there were 2.7 million people—over 1 percent of the nation's population—living in federally aided public housing. Nationally, there are over 800,000 dwelling units under public management and another 300,000 either authorized, in a preconstruction phase, or under construction.[2] The program has spread throughout the nation, as every state legislature has passed the requisite enabling legislation. Yet, local participation is highly correlated with city size; while only 8 percent

1. For a more detailed discussion of the importance of the turnover concept in public housing, see Commonwealth of Massachusetts, Special Commission on Low-Income Housing, *A Program for Low-Income Housing in the Commonwealth* (Boston: Wright & Potter Co., 1965), pp. 15–16.
2. National housing statistics for all federally aided programs are available in the U.S. Department of Housing and Urban Development's *Statistics Yearbooks* and *Annual Reports*.

of the jurisdictions with populations of less than 2,500 have public housing, every city with a population over 250,000, with the exception of San Diego, has an active program.[3]

Just as the magnitude and dispersion of the public housing stock was unanticipated, so was its role in providing a permanent residence for many of the dependent poor. As previously noted, public housing was originally intended to provide temporary homes for victims of the depression, but a number of circumstances changed this function. First, the initial turnover of public housing occupants coincided with the mass migration of rural Southern agricultural workers to the major cities of the North and Midwest. Many of these migrant families eventually became public housing tenants. Second, the age, skill, race, and educational level of many second- or third-generation public housing occupants made them particularly vulnerable to conditions of structural unemployment, and therefore they were in no position to leave subsidized housing. Since the end of World War II, an increasing proportion of public housing families have been without any wage earners, relying on welfare benefits and social security payments for their entire income.

In 1968 the President's Committee on Urban Housing (the Kaiser Committee) could report that one-half of all public housing units were occupied by blacks and one-third by elderly tenants. Since most of the present tenants are economically immobile, the public housing developments have relatively low turnover rates.[4] This helps to account for low vacancy rates and long waiting lists.

Under these circumstances, both the Administration and Congress have turned to the private sector. As former Senator Paul Douglas, a long-time proponent of public housing, observed, "we can no longer rely on the public housing program to provide an adequate volume of housing for the poor, we need to harness the private profit motive for the public good." [5] Thus,

3. National Institute for Education in Law and Poverty, Northwestern University, "Programs for Public Housing" (mimeographed, 1970), Chapter 4.
4. According to data available from the Boston Housing Authority, close to 60 percent of the tenants have occupied public housing units for six or more years, 30 percent for eleven or more years. See Richard Scobie, "Selective Social and Economic Statistics of Tenants" (Boston Housing Authority, mimeographed, November 1970).
5. Paul Douglas, "Rent Supplement Program," *Journal of Housing*, Vol. 9 (October 1965), p. 473.

early in 1965—following the election of a more "liberal" Congress (the Eighty-Seventh), the achievement of an overwhelming mandate for the Johnson Administration, and the first rioting in several large American cities—the conditions were at last ripe for passage of the first major low-income housing legislation since the depression. The design of the new federal programs was influenced in part by the growing disparity between the cost of decent shelter and the financial ability of the poor. However, the actual form the federal subsidies would take was determined largely by the widespread disenchantment with conventional public housing and the need for an increased supply of standard low-rent dwellings. The Eighty-Seventh Congress created two strategies: leased housing and rent supplements, both relying more on the private sector.

By enacting Section 23 and amending Section 10(c) of the 1937 Housing Act, Congress authorized local housing authorities to provide accommodation for the poor in dwellings leased from private owners. Unlike the conventional public housing program, leased housing was not established as an anticyclical or slum clearance device. Instead, the leading provisions were designed to provide housing for the poor by taking advantage of vacancies or potential vacancies in the private housing market. The local authorities would be able to supplement the units already available in the housing projects by making better use of the existing private stock.

Through the Housing and Urban Development Act of 1965, the rent supplement program was created as well. The aim of this program was to encourage the private sector to increase the stock of low-rent housing. Under one of the Federal Housing Administration (FHA) mortgage-insurance programs, a private sponsor would be able to substantially rehabilitate or to build new housing. The rents of these dwellings were to be brought within the reach of the poor through direct governmental subsidies to the owners on behalf of qualified tenants. Under the rent supplement approach, therefore, the responsibility for ownership, construction, and management of assisted housing was shifted from the local housing authorities to private entrepreneurs.

Of the two programs, leased housing was passed with the least controversy. While the leased housing program sailed through Congress, the Administration's rent supplement proposal was under considerable fire from legislative conservatives and private housing interests from the start. It was not that rent supplements were a new concept;[6] rather, the source of the controversy was a basic philosophical difference over who should benefit, and how much. As one housing official has noted, the fundamental clash was between the need to fulfill the pledge of a decent home for the poor and the need to encourage individual initiative and equitable treatment for the overwhelming majority of nonrecipients.[7] The Administration introduced the program as a substitute for the Section 221(d)(3) below-market interest rate (BMIR) program for moderate-income families, but Congress restricted eligibility to the poor. The imposition of this restriction, coupled with the emphasis on new construction, was what generated the opposition. The possibility that the poor, at subsidized rents, would live in better housing than many "hardworking" families was unacceptable to a number of legislators.

The clash of values was graphically illustrated in the statements of President Johnson and key congressional committees. In presenting his legislative message on the "Problems and Future of the Central City and Its Suburbs," the President heralded the promise of his new program: "The proposed rent supplement is the most crucial instrument in our effort to improve the American City." [8] Such inflated rhetoric is not uncommon for our political leaders, but the sharpness of the ideological conflict expressed in the majority and minority reports of the House Committee on Banking and Currency was unusual. The majority report stated this view:

. . . your committee believes that the rent supplement program would enable many people of low and moderate income to translate their needs into effective demand and thus lend support to the homebuilding component of the economy.

The minority report, reflecting a vastly different perspective, stated its position as follows:

. . . The Administration's rent supplement proposal is foreign to American concepts [because]

6. Programs similar to rent supplements were tried in England as early as 1934; a rent certificate program has operated in Canada; and rent subsidies of various forms have been proposed to Congress over the years.
7. See Irving Welfeld, "Toward a New Federal Housing Policy," *The Public Interest,* No. 19 (Spring 1970), p. 466.
8. Lyndon B. Johnson, "The Problems and Future of the Central City and Its Suburbs," The President's Message to the Congress on Urban Problems, March 2, 1965.

—it kills the incentive of the American family to improve its living accommodations by its own effort;
—it kills the incentive for home ownership, it makes renters wards of the government;
—it fosters a system of economic integration . . . through government subsidy;
—it is the way of the socialistic state.

Despite this controversy, the rent supplement program was ultimately enacted, but its operation was seriously restricted by its congressional opponents. After it passed the House of Representatives by a margin of six votes, the House-Senate Conference denied any operating funds—although $450,000 was appropriated for the preparation of plans and procedures. And in 1966 the President's request for $30 million was cut to $12 million. (These funds were increased modestly to $20 million in 1967 and to $50 million in 1970.) In addition to these financial restrictions, many of the program's objectives were also compromised. Under congressional pressure, for example, the Department of Housing and Urban Development was forced to impose crippling limitations on construction costs and maximum market rents, which inhibited housing production and minimized project amenities. These restrictions have reduced the opportunities for new construction in high-cost central cities and have limited the program's appeal to nonsubsidized tenants. Consequently, the vast majority of tenants in rent supplement projects are those receiving rent assistance, undermining the Administration's original goal of mixing economic groups. On top of all this, a subsequent rider on the 1966 appropriations bill restricted the location of rent supplement projects to localities that have either "workable programs" or official local approval.

As this brief description of the evolution of housing strategies suggests, the programs differ considerably in approach. These differences reflect, essentially, different perceptions of both the urban housing problem and how local housing markets are likely to respond to various forms of intervention.

Leased Housing and Neighborhood Renewal

The leased housing program allows for the commitment of leases for units to be privately constructed or rehabilitated, but it does not offer any direct financial support for these investments. Nevertheless, there is considerable evidence, in Boston as well as other cities, that the agreement to lease private dwellings for a specified number of years actually encourages the modest rehabilitation of vacant dwellings and promotes the physical upgrading of units containing code deficiencies. Since such investments have the potential of stabilizing decaying inner-city areas without involving substantial federal or local government expenditures beyond those necessary to lease existing units, it is essential that we understand the inherent attributes of the leasing program which provide for this possibility.

In our analysis of leased housing we have identified four major characteristics of the program which explain its ability to serve as a critical factor in neighborhood renewal:

—The long-term lease commitment, through the LHA's letter of intent, is a sufficient guarantee for banks to commit mortgage loans for central-city rehabilitation.

—The government's direct rental assistance creates an effective market for modestly improved units at postrehabilitation rent levels.

—The lease agreement assures larger and more stable rental receipts over the term of the lease.

—The lease agreement assures lower operating costs.

While the cause and effect of the first two characteristics are obvious, the last two require some explanation.

It appears that the amount of private investment generated by the leasing program is a matter of local policies and private economic incentives. In some communities, such as Washington, D.C., the physical improvement of the leased unit is a requirement for participation in the program. The results of this policy have been impressive, as most of the original properties under lease in the Washington program have been rehabilitated, reconverted, or restored.[1] However, local requirements for physical upgrading are meaningless unless the economic incentive for the private landlord is

---

1. Lawrence Friedman and James Krier, "A New Lease on Life: Section 23 Housing and the Poor," *University of Pennsylvania Law Review,* Vol. 116 (1968), p. 632.

sufficient. Neither the large realty company nor the individual owner of a three-family row house will undertake a housing investment unless the anticipated increase in revenue exceeds the proposed expenditures.[2]

For the economically rational private landlord, we assume that profitability is the predominant criterion in making investment decisions. Therefore, in determining whether to purchase and reconstruct a high-vacancy structure or to eliminate code violations so as to qualify for the leasing program, the private landlord calculates the economic return from his capital improvement and compares the return with alternative investment possibilities. The extent of rehabilitation that an owner is willing to undertake, therefore, depends upon the increase in rental income or the reduction of carrying charges resulting from the leasing agreement. The private realtor or landlord will make an investment in the physical condition of a property only if the discounted present value of the additional net rental income exceeds or equals the discounted value of the additional amortization costs:

$$O \leqslant \sum_{t=1}^{n} \frac{(R'_t - R_t) - (O'_t - O_t)}{(1 + i)^t} - \sum_{t=1}^{n} \frac{A_t}{(1 + i)^t} \, , \qquad (\text{B.1})$$

where

A_t = the total amortization cost (principal and interest) at time t,

R_t = the expected rent receipts at time t without rehabilitation,

R'_t = the rent receipts at time t after rehabilitation,

O_t = the expected operating costs at time t without rehabilitation,

O'_t = the operating costs at time t after rehabilitation,

n = the length of the mortgage,

i = the landlord's rate of return on alternative investment opportunities of the same risk and liquidity.

The leased housing program indirectly subsidizes the rehabilitation investment through its effects on rental receipts (ΔR_t) and operating costs

2. There are exceptions to this economically rational investment calculation, of course, whenever a legal compulsion exists—as with code violations—or when a landlord is motivated by noneconomic considerations.

ΔO_t). Whether the leased housing incentives justify the rehabilitation of a particular structure depends upon the economic cash flow as well as a number of other factors, including expectations about the future of the neighborhood, the investment activity of other property owners, and the availability of private loans. A large-scale leasing program can improve the overall investment climate of a neighborhood, thereby affecting future expectations as well as the investment activity of property owners not directly participating in the subsidy program. Still, for the individual investor, the marginal revenue from upgrading his property would have to exceed the marginal costs, discounted to their present value. As Table B.1 indicates, the leasing program provides several economic incentives for property upgrading.

Table B.1 The Incentives for Rehabilitation Offered by the Leased Housing Program

Increase in Rental Receipts (ΔR_t)	Reduction in Operating Costs (ΔO_t)	Other Incentives
Postrehabilitation rents higher	Reduces vacancies and turnover	Letter of intent assures financing
Guarantees rent-roll during lease	Eliminates bad debts and collection losses	Accelerated depreciation[a]
Stabilizes demand for central-city rehabilitation	Lowers maintenance costs	Sale of tax shelter[a]

a. While these consequences are not part of the leased housing program, they are additional federal incentives that can be taken advantage of.

The leased housing program affects an investor's cash flow on both the revenue and the expenditure side of the ledger. There is a positive effect on rent receipts created by the availability of the government's rent assistance and the elimination of rent arrearages and collection losses over the period of the lease. This increases the level as well as the certainty of rent payments. The rent subsidy creates a market for units whose post-rehabilitation rents would otherwise be prohibitive for poor families. And the assurance of guaranteed rental income over the period of the lease, without the risk of collection loss or vacancies, creates the stability necessary to induce private investors to upgrade their properties.

Over the period of the lease there is a reduction in operating costs as well, since the federal government, through the local housing authority, guarantees landlords against high collection costs, extraordinary maintenance expenditures, and so forth. Families considered poor credit risks become acceptable credit risks, thereby reducing the management and legal costs associated with rent arrearage, bad debts, and evictions. Moreover, the maintenance costs created by turnovers and vacancies are reduced since the tenants lose their subsidy, which is tied to the dwelling, once they move. With the exposure of vacant units to vandals and others, the theft of plumbing fixtures and the cost of security often exceed the value of the loss in the rent-roll. Thus the creation of an effective and stable demand for inner-city properties should, in concert with other community development activities, serve as a significant factor in neighborhood renewal.

APPENDIX C

Development Costs, Depreciation Schedules, and Tax Shelters

This appendix includes tables on the developmental cost of the conventional public housing, leased housing, and rent supplement programs. In Table C.1, the initial and adjusted costs (1970) for the new construction and modernization of all federally assisted public housing developments in Boston is set forth. In Tables C.2 and C.3, the value of the tax shelter or forgone tax revenue from the accelerated depreciation of the leased housing and rent supplement new construction and rehabilitation projects is estimated.

Table C.1 Public Housing Development Costs, Modernization, and Level Annuity Payments, Boston Housing Authority

Project	Effective Date	Initial Fiscal Year	Original Development Costs	1968 Funds for Modernization	Adjusted [a] Development Costs, 1970	Adjusted [a] Modernization Costs, 1970
Charlestown	7-17-43	1943	$ 6,159,642	$1,612,110	$ 15,660,000	$ 1,805,000
Mission Hill	7-17-43	1943	5,458,335	1,212,546	13,863,000	1,357,000
Lenox Street	7-17-43	1943	1,739,023	357,490	4,417,000	400,000
Orchard Park	8-31-50	1950	4,450,565	856,463	7,743,000	959,000
South End	8-31-50	1950	6,851,490	594,474	11,920,000	665,000
Heath Street	8-31-50	1950	2,388,244	499,021	4,155,000	559,000
East Boston	8-31-50	1950	2,555,308	485,860	4,446,000	544,000
Franklin Hill	8-31-50	1950	4,912,514	308,331	8,547,000	345,000
Whittier Street	8-31-50	1950	2,628,006	253,527	4,573,000	283,000
Washington and Beech	8-31-50	1950	3,291,787	275,331	5,728,000	308,000
Mission Extension	8-31-50	1950	7,494,109	630,520	13,040,000	706,000
Bromley Park	9-15-55	1955	9,757,633	892,230	14,636,000	999,000
Columbia Point	9-15-55	1955	20,191,514	1,672,152	30,286,000	1,873,000
Mary Ellen McCormack[b]	10-13-69	—	—	1,672,152	—	1,268,000
Old Colony[b]	10-13-69	—	—	1,182,082	—	—
				Total	139,014,000 [c]	12,071,000
				Average	10,693,385 [d]	862,214 [e]
				per Unit	$ 15,796	$ 1,274

a. We use Robert J. Gordon's Final Price of Structures Index to adjust the development and modernization costs on the tax-exempt bonds.

b. Both developments were deeded over by the federal government.

c. If we assume that the development costs of Mary Ellen McCormack and Old Colony were the same as the average for the other thirteen projects, the total development cost for all fifteen projects would be $160,400,000.

d. The level debt service payments would be based on a 40-year mortgage, beginning in 1970, with an interest rate of 6 percent.

e. The level annuity payments for modernization would be based on the average number of years of economic life remaining for the family developments, eighteen years, and a 6 percent interest rate on the loans.

Table C.2 Rehabilitation with Leased Housing or Rent Supplements:[a] Accelerated Depreciation and Forgone Federal Revenue, Boston

Year	60-Month Straight-Line Depreciation[b]	60-Month per Unit[b]	Normal Straight-Line Depreciation[b]	Normal per Unit
	$ 614,917[c]	$ 841	—	—
1	1,229,834	1,682	$245,967	$336
2	1,229,834	1,682	245,967	336
3	1,229,834	1,682	245,967	336
4	1,229,834	1,682	245,967	336
5	1,229,834	1,682	245,967	336
6			245,967	336
7			245,967	336
8			245,967	336
9			245,967	336
10			245,967	336
11			245,967	336
12				
13				
14				
15				
16				
17				
18				
19				
20				
21				
Average Annual Discounted Present Value	($1,839/21)			

a. The total number of leased housing and rent supplement–rehabilitation units in Boston is 871. Their average rehabilitation cost, in 1970 construction prices, is $8,412 per unit. We assume that the normal economic life for the rehabilitation expenditures is 25 years.
b. When a developer syndicates limited partnership interests to investors for a syndication price in excess of the implied equity, the investors will be able to add this excess equity to the depreciable base. The net syndication proceeds received by the developer and by the syndication broker are taxable. It has been assumed that the cost of the increased depreciation to the Treasury is balanced by the taxes collected on the syndication proceeds.

Table C.2 (continued)

Depreciation Deduction Differential	Tax Savings 50% Bracket	Tax Savings Present Value Total at 10%	Per Unit at 10%
$614,917	$307,450	$307,500	$ 421
983,867	491,934	447,100	612
983,867	491,934	406,400	556
983,867	491,934	369,400	505
983,867	491,934	335,800	459
983,867	491,934	305,200	417
(245,967)	(122,984)	(69,400)	(95)
(245,967)	(122,984)	(63,100)	(86)
(245,967)	(122,984)	(57,500)	(77)
(245,967)	(122,984)	(52,100)	(71)
(245,967)	(122,984)	(47,500)	(65)
(245,967)	(122,984)	(43,000)	(59)
		(39,200)	(54)
		(35,500)	(49)
		(32,400)	(44)
		(29,400)	(40)
		(26,800)	(37)
		(24,400)	(33)
		(22,200)	(30)
		(20,200)	(28)
		(18,300)	(25)
		(246,500) [d]	(338)
		$1,343,900	$1,888

c. It has been assumed that the items deductible during the construction period, such as interest and real estate taxes, are equal to 10 percent of the total construction cost.
d. Sales price = outstanding mortgage = $4,730,000; the tax on sale = (sales price less adjusted basis) times capital gains rate = (4,730,000 — 0) × 0.35 = $1,656,000.

Table C.3 New Construction with Leased Housing or Rent Supplements:a Accelerated Depreciation and Forgone Federal Revenue, Boston

Year	200% Declining Balance Depreciationb	Per Unit	Straight-Line Depreciation	Per Unit
	$58,947c	$1,551	—	—
1	29,472	776	$14,736	$388
2	27,999	737	14,736	388
3	26,599	700	14,736	388
4	25,269	655	14,736	388
5	24,006	632	14,736	388
6	22,806	600	14,736	388
7	21,665	570	14,736	388
8	20,582	542	14,736	388
9	19,553	515	14,736	388
10	18,575	489	14,736	388
11	17,645	465	14,736	388
12	16,765	442	14,736	388
13	15,926	419	14,736	388
14	15,130	399	14,736	388
15	14,374	378	14,736	388
16	13,655	359	14,736	388
17	12,972	341	14,736	388
18	12,324	322	14,736	388
19	11,707	308	14,736	388
20	11,122	292	14,736	388
21				

a. The total number of Section 10(c) leased housing and rent supplement–new construction units in Boston is 93. Their average construction cost, in 1970 construction prices, is $15,512 per unit. A depreciable life of 40 years has been assumed. Separating out various components by their own depreciable lives, for example, depreciating the roof over 10 years, would yield a composite useful life of as little as 33 years. The difference in the net accelerated depreciation is reasonably insignificant, however.

b. When a developer syndicates limited partnership interests to investors for a syndication price in excess of the implied equity, the investors will be able to add this excess to the depreciable basis. The net syndication proceeds received by the developer and the syndication broker are taxable. It has been assumed that the cost of the increased depreciation to the Treasury is balanced by the taxes collected on the syndication proceeds.

Table C.3 (continued)

Differences in Depreciation Deductions	Tax Savings 50% Bracket	Tax Savings Present Worth at 10%	Tax Savings Present Worth per Unit
$58,947	$9,473	$29,500	$776
14,736	7,368	6,200	163
13,263	6,632	5,480	144
11,863	5,932	4,460	117
10,533	5,267	3,600	95
9,270	4,635	2,880	76
8,070	4,035	2,280	60
6,929	3,465	1,780	47
5,846	2,923	1,370	36
4,817	2,409	1,020	27
3,839	1,919	740	19
2,909	1,458	510	13
2,035	1,017	320	8
1,190	595	170	4
394	197	50	1
(362)	(181)	(40)	(1)
(1,081)	(540)	(120)	(3)
(1,764)	(882)	(170)	(4)
(2,412)	(1,206)	(220)	(6)
(2,929)	(1,464)	(240)	(6)
(3,614)	(1,807)	(270)	(7)
		(13,130)d	(346)
		$46,170	$1,216

c. It has been assumed that the items deductible during the construction period are equal to 10 percent of the total construction cost.

d. Tax on sale = (sales price — adjusted basis) × capital gains rate
= (463,000 — 211,200) 0.35 = $88,130

Index

Publications of the Joint Center for Urban Studies

The Joint Center for Urban Studies, a cooperative venture of the Massachusetts Institute of Technology and Harvard University, was founded in 1959 to organize and encourage research on urban and regional problems. Participants have included scholars from the fields of anthropology, architecture, business, city planning, economics, education, engineering, history, law, philosophy, political science, and sociology.

The findings and conclusions of this book are, as with all Joint Center publications, solely the responsibility of the author.

Published by Harvard University Press

The Intellectual versus the City: From Thomas Jefferson to Frank Lloyd Wright, by Morton and Lucia White, 1962

Streetcar Suburbs: The Process of Growth in Boston, 1870–1900, by Sam B. Warner, Jr., 1962

City Politics, by Edward C. Banfield and James Q. Wilson, 1963

Law and Land: Anglo-American Planning Practice, edited by Charles M. Haar, 1964

Location and Land Use: Toward a General Theory of Land Rent, by William Alonso, 1964

Poverty and Progress: Social Mobility in a Nineteenth Century City, by Stephan Thernstrom, 1964

Boston: The Job Ahead, by Martin Meyerson and Edward C. Banfield, 1966

The Myth and Reality of Our Urban Problems, by Raymond Vernon, 1966

Muslim Cities in the Later Middle Ages, by Ira Marvin Lapidus, 1967

The Fragmented Metropolis: Los Angeles, 1850–1930, by Robert M. Fogelson, 1967

Law and Equal Opportunity: A Study of the Massachusetts Commission Against Discrimination, by Leon H. Mayhew, 1968

Varieties of Police Behavior: The Management of Law and Order in Eight Communities, by James Q. Wilson, 1968

The Metropolitan Enigma: Inquiries into the Nature and Dimensions of America's "Urban Crisis," edited by James Q. Wilson, revised edition, 1968·

Traffic and The Police: Variations in Law-Enforcement Policy, by John A. Gardiner, 1969

The Influence of Federal Grants: Public Assistance in Massachusetts, by Martha Derthick, 1970

The Arts in Boston, by Bernard Taper, 1970

Families Against the City: Middle Class Homes of Industrial Chicago, 1872–1890, by Richard Sennett, 1970

The Political Economy of Urban Schools, by Martin T. Katzman, 1971

Origins of the Urban School: Public Education in Massachusetts, 1870–1915, by Marvin Lazerson, 1971

The Other Bostonians: Poverty and Progress in the American Metropolis, 1880–1970, by Stephan Thernstrom, 1973

Published by The MIT Press

The Image of the City, by Kevin Lynch, 1960

Housing and Economic Progress: A Study of the Housing Experiences of Boston's Middle-Income Families, by Lloyd Rodwin, 1961

The Historian and the City, edited by Oscar Handlin and John Burchard, 1963

The Federal Bulldozer: A Critical Analysis of Urban Renewal, 1949–1962, by Martin Anderson, 1964

The Future of Old Neighborhoods: Rebuilding for a Changing Population, by Bernard J. Frieden, 1964

Man's Struggle for Shelter in an Urbanizing World, by Charles Abrams, 1964

The View from the Road, by Donald Appleyard, Kevin Lynch, and John R. Myer, 1964

The Public Library and the City, edited by Ralph W. Conant, 1965

Regional Development Policy: A Case Study of Venezuela, by John Friedmann, 1966

Urban Renewal: The Record and the Controversy, edited by James Q. Wilson, 1966

Transport Technology for Developing Regions: A Study of Road Transportation in Venezuela, by Richard M. Soberman, 1966

Computer Methods in the Analysis of Large-Scale Social Systems, edited by James M. Beshers, 1968

Planning Urban Growth and Regional Development: The Experience of the Guayana Program of Venezuela, by Lloyd Rodwin and Associates, 1969

Build a Mill, Build a City, Build a School: Industrialization, Urbanization, and Education in Ciudad Guayana, by Noel F. McGinn and Russell G. Davis, 1969

Land-Use Controls in the United States, by John Delafons, second edition, 1969

Beyond the Melting Pot: The Negroes, Puerto Ricans, Jews, Italians, and Irish of New York City, by Nathan Glazer and Daniel Patrick Moynihan, revised edition, 1970

Bargaining: Monopoly Power versus Union Power, by George de Menil, 1971

Housing the Urban Poor: A Critical Evaluation of Federal Housing Policy, by Arthur P. Solomon, 1974

The Joint Center also publishes monographs and reports.